THE PEDAGOGICAL STATE

SAM KAPLAN

The Pedagogical State

Education and the Politics of National Culture in Post-1980 Turkey

STANFORD UNIVERSITY PRESS

STANFORD, CALIFORNIA 2006

Library of Congress Cataloging-in-Publication Data

Kaplan, Sam, 1958–
   The pedagogical state: education and the politics of national
culture in post-1980 Turkey / Sam Kaplan.
      p. cm.
   Includes bibliographical references and index.
   ISBN 0-8047-5432-2 (cloth: alk. paper)—
   ISBN 0-8047-5433-0 (pbk.: alk. paper)
   1. Nationalism and education—Turkey.   2. Education and
state—Turkey.   I. Title.   II. Title: Education and the politics
of national culture in post-1980 Turkey.
LC94.T9K374 2006
379.561—dc22

                                             2006004304

Typeset by G & S Book Services in 10/14 Janson

Another Brick in the Wall (Part 2)
Words and Music by George Roger Waters
© 1979 Roger Waters Music Overseas Ltd.
Warner/Chappell Artemis Music Ltd.
All Rights Reserved. Used with Permission.

To Alex and Eytan, the next generation
To Tania Forte (1959–2005), their mother

Contents

Acknowledgments

No work stands on its own. This book is no exception. The writing involved the input and encouragement of many people—teachers, colleagues, students, family, friends, and above all, those citizens of Turkey who kindly shared their knowledge and hospitality with me. I can never thank enough my Turkish hosts. They are too numerous to list here, but I would like to take this opportunity to acknowledge the late statesman Kasım Gülek, whose advice and support made all the difference.

This project has an exceedingly long history, beginning with my father and mother, who made education a top priority. It continued under the mentorship of the late Barney Cohn—teacher and friend. The importance of his work and his influence on my thinking and writing are apparent throughout this book. In my second year of graduate school at the University of Chicago, Barney introduced me to an anthropology that seriously engages with the historical mutability and flexibility of ideas and practices, critically assesses ethnographic and historical methods, and addresses the political implications of knowledge. His deceptively simple ideas, counterintuitive insights, highly accessible prose, thorough scholarship, and measure of irony are all standards to which I aspire. I hope I have met them halfway.

Studying anthropology at Chicago is anything but fun. There is no polite discussion about the weather. It's either freezing cold or hot and muggy. Conversations center sometimes on seminars or workshops but more often on the intellectual goings-on at Regenstein Library. The unabashed intellectualism and the disregard for disciplinary boundaries have left an imprint as much in my attitude to the world as in my scholarship. Due credit must be given to my teachers. John Comaroff, Jean Comaroff, Paul Friedrich,

Nancy Munn, George Stocking, George Steinmetz, and Terence Turner each challenged me to scrutinize my theoretical assumptions about society, culture, and politics. They have been invaluable guides—even, and especially, when I did not follow their lead. Much of my resistance to theory can be credited to my teachers at the Center for Middle Eastern Studies. Fred Donner and the late Fazlur Rahman provided me with insights into the diversity and complexity of Islam. Halil Inalcik spent countless hours sharing his vast erudition on Ottoman society and drawing my attention to its continued impact in republican Turkey. I cannot thank Bob Dankoff enough. He not only shared his passion for Turkey, its language and cultures, but also believed in my project. The day after my doctoral defense, he had me submit it for the Malcolm H. Kerr Dissertation Award in the Social Sciences (Middle East Studies Association in North America).

That award was both a blessing and a curse. It was a blessing since it initiated a lifetime friendship with Müge Göçek, whose steadfast support and generosity of spirit cannot be overemphasized. On the other hand, it was a curse since it inhibited me from transforming an award-winning dissertation into a thought-provoking book for area scholars in Middle East studies, politics, anthropology, and education. Since then, my years working at history departments at Israeli universities have provided me with the unique opportunity to develop interdisciplinary approaches. This book is a token of this ongoing dialogue.

Beyond that community, in correspondences ranging across the globe, I have received incisive comments on all or parts of the book at various stages of its development from Gadi Algazi, Yeşim Arat, Amílcar Barreto, Nathan Brown, Dale Eickelman, Tania Forte, Susan Gal, Müge Göçek, Jane Goodman, Haggai Ram, Natalie Rothman, Andrew Shryock, Charles Tilly, Yishai Tobin, Michel-Rolph Trouillot, and Dror Ze'evi. Their collegiality, encouragement, and insights have made a difference. I have also benefited from the toughest audience—general readers and students. They helped me reformulate ideas in a straightforward and accessible language. I would like to thank in particular Bryan Atinsky, Jordan Levine, Jared Olson, Orit Yekutieli, and my stepmother, Carolyn Potter. But my chief debt goes to Alejandro Paz. His splendid, critical readings of the manuscript are evident on every page. Gracias te lo agradezco.

Finally, I would like to thank the reviewers. Their encouraging and collegial comments helped me sharpen my arguments and situate them for a wide anthropological readership—and beyond. Kate Wahl, the acquisitions editor at Stanford University Press, and Kirsten Oster, her editorial assistant, have gone out of their way to make academic publishing, if not easy, at least feasible. To Mary Ann Short, the copyeditor, I want to express my appreciation for her meticulous final editing of the manuscript.

This project would not have happened without financial support. At various stages of its development, I was fortunate to receive funding from the American Research Institute of Turkey, the Fulbright-Hays Commission, the Wenner-Gren Foundation for Anthropological Research, the Spencer Foundation, and the Advanced Study Center at the University of Michigan. I also thank the Turkish government, which gave me permission to carry out fieldwork and library research. Grateful thanks to the publishers and copyright owners for permission to reprint lyrics from "Another Brick in the Wall (Part 2)," words and music by George Roger Waters © 1979 Roger Waters Music Overseas Ltd. Parts of this book were published in earlier versions in "Din-u Devlet All Over Again? The Politics of Military Secularism and Religious Militarism in Turkey Following the 1980 Coup," *International Journal of Middle Eastern Studies* 34 (2002), pp. 113–27; "Nuriye's Dilemma: Turkish Lessons of Democracy and the Gendered State," *American Ethnologist* 30 (2003), pp. 401–17; and "'Religious Nationalism': A Textbook Case from Turkey," *Comparative Studies of South Asia, Africa, and the Middle East* 25 (2005), pp. 665–76.

As befitting a work on childhood and children's education, I dedicate this book to my two sons, Alex and Eytan. More than anybody else, they have made this work possible. They have not read one word of it; and I am grateful that they haven't. But their presence is throughout. They have been my best teachers and critics; they have taught me humility, modesty, sensitivity, and compassion—all of which are central to my intellectual and less intellectual endeavors.

Pronunciation of Turkish

Since 1928, Turkish words are written with a version of the Latin alphabet. The letter *c* is pronounced as the hard *j* in *jazz*; *ç* (c cedilla) as the *ch* in *chair*; ı (undotted *i*) as the *u* in *run* or *er* in *water*; *i* as the *i* in *rich*; *ş* (s cedilla) as the *sh* in *ship*; *ö* (o umlaut) as the *eu* in the French *peu*; *ü* (u umlaut) as the *u* in the French *tu*; and the *ğ* (soft g) either lengthens the sound of the preceding vowel or takes on the sound of a soft *y* when it appears before front vowels.

Preface

My mentor, the late Bernard Cohn, once posed to me the innocent question, Why education? It was only some years later at an international conference on democracy at Ben-Gurion University of the Negev in Beer-Sheva, Israel, that I began to formulate an answer. There I met for the first time Yeşim Arat, a political scientist whose work on sexual citizenship and feminist religious movements in Turkey I admire. At some point in our conversation, she emphatically declared, "The problem with Turkey is education, and the solution is education." To her, schools can be either the source or the cure-all of society's ills. In other words, the success of a country hinges on the right schooling for children, future adult citizens.

Conceiving education as key to the betterment of society is not particular to Turkey. The idea of the omnipotence of education for shaping humanity has been successfully promoted all over the world, and most of all, in school systems. For a variety of reasons, I grew up in several places—New York City; suburbia in Princeton, New Jersey; the French Caribbean; Paris, France; and Israel. One outcome of my nomadic childhood was exposure to different school systems with their particular social and pedagogical norms. Yet all these societies share in the optimistic conceit the Enlightenment educator Helvetius first advanced, "L'éducation peut tout."

Despite this widespread optimism, or in fact due to it, education stirs up the greatest public controversies. It is a concept heavily charged with political connotations to which people from a wide variety of demographic and biographical conditions assign different meanings and functions. Mass education is by definition socialization within, and on behalf of, a particular political order. Through the school system, the state acts to transmit core values that promote the basic requisites of citizenship; that is to say, children must be predisposed to accept the moral and social principles underlying the polity. And because school curricula seem to play up key social issues, carry the weight of official approval, and engage a captive audience, they spur debates at all levels of society. After all, what children—the next generation of citizens—will learn about ethnic, economic, gender, and cultural differences raise fundamental political issues about identity.

In Turkey, systematic state intervention in the curricula has spurred politically motivated groups (religious nationalists, neoliberal secularists, and the military) to lobby their differences through the highly centralized educational system. Likewise, Turkish citizens from a variety of social groups place great stress on education: not only is it a source of political contention, but for many it is a means of social salvation. This is the case in Yayla, a small town of six thousand in the Taurus Mountains of southern Turkey where I conducted ethnographic fieldwork of two elementary schools and one middle school between 1989 and 1991.

This book is not intended to be an exhaustive description of the entire educational system in Turkey or a detailed ethnography of a local community. It aims rather at elucidating two interrelated issues: (1) governmentality—how politically motivated associations broker their respective cultural politics in an attempt to define both national and local experience for schoolchildren; and (2) subjectivity—how mass schooling creates contexts for individuals to insert their private selves in public discourses and thus reconceptualize their political selves in light of changing everyday realities. For this purpose, I examine the bases upon which competing interest groups build up their arguments about education, the implementation of their arguments in the curricula, and the impact of the curricula on children's political sociability in a particular locality. The very scope of these three aims has required balancing ethnographic detail and broader historical and political developments in the country. A multisited ethnography of a local school system provided an ideal field of inquiry on the tenuous relationship between curricula and life-course strategies. Through a detailed analysis of mass media (newspapers and television transmissions) and ministerial sources (textbooks, circulars, reports, and legislation), I trace how historically informed ideas, identities, and relations are converted into pedagogical practices. Parallel to these forays into textual artifacts, I probe the many ways parents and pupils direct the terms of education to their own objects. Through my many roles as foreigner, teacher of conversational English and mathematics, a jack-of-all-trades (truck driver, unskilled laborer, cotton picker, and shepherd), and spiritual kinsman, I explore how parents and pupils make sense of the curricula in their day-to-day lives. Thus, in analyzing the relation between officially prescribed representations of society and polity and different understandings of education across generations, the book lays groundwork for approaching state-endorsed identity formation from the vantage point of local facts.

The main issues that this book sets out to discuss are concerned with the political functions, sociocultural significations, and scope of school knowledge. Although these three issues overlap in many of their features, each is distinctly different.

First, the issue arises as to how to analyze the relationship between education and politics in the context of modern state formation. Because historically informed ideas are embedded and expressed in educational practices and institutions, school knowledge has political ramifications. Institutions like the school are designed to induce consent to a dominant political order. Yet consensus is never fully realized. Nor is it perduring and stable. Rather, consensus generates a gamut of contradictory and equivocal ideas among political elites and the public alike and is thus vulnerable to alternative perspectives about polity and education. Any serious examination of the politics of education requires attending to the historical mutability and flexibility of political ideals and pedagogical practices and to the power relations (i.e., accommodation, contestation, negotiation) operative in educational systems.

Second, the issue arises as to how to tackle the relationship between education and society. School knowledge is often conceived as the antithesis of popular knowledge; that is to say, educators in particular try to associate it with self-evident, disinterested facts that transcend opinion. The logic goes that when children correctly apply the curriculum in their extracurricular lives, arbitrary opinions are supposed to give way to impartial, rational pragmatism. On the other hand, it is possible to stress the common features between school knowledge and popular knowledge, rather than their apparent differences. The public at large is never entirely separate from the dominant discourses that provide the language and conceptual categories with which they articulate their political selves. To suggest otherwise is to unwittingly create an artificial (and historically skewed) divide between center and periphery, between elite forms of knowledge and indigenous ones. In turn, formulators of education do not operate in isolation from their targeted publics. Politically motivated groups will do their utmost to achieve consensus by appropriating popularly sanctioned norms and sentiments about the public good, economic activity, and community membership. The overall aim is for the citizens to internalize their value systems as part of a national outlook, as native common sense.

Finally, the issue arises as to how to fathom the relationship between education and subjectivities. The habitual routines, rituals, and discourses to which children are exposed during their years of schooling are all designed to inscribe them with a prereflective background to prescribed thought and behaviors. Accordingly, schools and the curricula within them are intended to mold subjectivities, to elicit a particular constellation of desires, fears, attitudes, and hopes around key social issues. Yet it is crucial to recognize the heterogeneity among the public, to take into consideration factors such as generation, gender, ethnicity, and class. After all, the day-to-day experiences, emotions, and political consciousness of particular individuals cannot be assumed to hold for all within a community. Thus, it is critical to explore how men and women, young and old, the educated and unlettered differentially constitute a meaningful relation between their public and private selves through school knowledge.

These three basic issues are tackled under various forms and in different contexts within the six chapters of the book.

Chapter 1, "Educational Foundations," draws out the main issues that led to the unique establishment of a modern postprimary school in Yayla, then an out-of-the-way mountain village in the 1870s' Ottoman state. The school emerged out of the confrontation between two poet-scholars—one a provincial governor and religious modernist; the other a theologian and mystic. The foundational story provides a pretext to discuss key issues in educational research: childhood, political culture and the state, citizenship and identity politics, and the politics of pedagogy.

Chapter 2, "The State of Education," takes the reader to another confrontation, this time over the role of religion in the current national educational system. It deals with the release of an educational report that unleashed a coalition crisis between neoliberal businesspeople and religious nationalists in 1990. A study of the national debate over children's schooling provides an opportunity to examine central concepts of the Turkish educational system and their political uses, the intersection of multiple global and national discourses, and the close links between education, the state, and civil society in Turkey.

Chapter 3, "Nation and Faith," explores how state policy makers, aligned with the Turkish Islamic Synthesis, have successfully promoted a rationalist, religious version of nationalism in the school system. Following a quick historical survey of this educational movement, the chapter then focuses on the interplay of religious heritage, secularity, and identity politics through school textbooks and plays. Thanks to a steadfast belief in the fixity of text, the transparency of language, and the stability of meaning, both media attempt to dissolve the disjunction between in-text/on-stage character and out-of-text/off-stage person in order that children immediately identify and emulate prescribed ideals. A detailed study of a religion textbook provides a fruitful means of examining the relation between faith and nation inside and outside the classroom. Likewise, a didactic play that young female graduates of a Qur'an course staged for a wedding dramatically draws out the multiple understandings of femininity and conjugal relations among the townspeople. Thus, school textbooks and plays provide a means for examining how curricular texts constitute political imaginaries and social relations.

Chapter 4, "Nation and Market," examines how the secular business community promoted schools as the ideal site to transform Turkish citizens into an efficient, industrious work force. Following a brief discussion on the economics of education, the chapter then explores those pedagogical values and practices that the industrialists believed were necessary for Turkey to achieve and sustain competitive advantage in the face of international competitors. To this aim, they focused on socializing pupils to a rational work ethic, inculcating progress and progressive time, and limiting urban migration and family size. These ideals informed how townspeople conceive of the historically contingent relation between *villageness* and the domestic sphere (fertility and homemaking), on the one hand, and the public sphere (public health and time discipline), on the other.

Chapter 5, "Nation and Army," explores how the military has carried its conception of political education into the school system, following the 1980 coup. To instill a spirit of law and order and inculcate obedience to state authorities, long-standing martial ideals were reformulated as part of the country's religious heritage. Central to this reformulation was linking warfare and masculinity with reverence for Atatürk, the first president of the republic, on the one hand, and piety, on the other. Moreover, the militarization of the curriculum—a syncretism of religion and militant nationalism—drew on prerepublican ethnic divisions to cast the nation as besieged from within and without the country's borders. This syncretism was far from complete, as some youth found themselves excluded from the military dream of society.

Finally, Chapter 6, "Educational Postfoundations," draws out the historical contingencies of research on schooling in a Turkish community and discusses the tensions between a school system designed to actively structure children's political behavior along collective lines and the unintended emergence of individual autonomy among schoolchildren.

Modern education and schooling have become central in constituting sovereignty and polity, not only among the Turkish townspeople of Yayla but throughout our pedagogical world. In the very act of educating children, school systems articulate a moral order that lies at the intersection of generation, gender, ethnicity, class, and consciousness. Exploring how this articulation plays itself out in a local community in Turkey provides a double lens that gazes both microscopically and telescopically into the central dynamics of modern identity formation.

THE PEDAGOGICAL STATE

CHAPTER ONE

Educational Foundations

In the land of the infidel, I have seen cities and mansions
In the dominions of Islam, ruin and devastation.

— ZIYA PASHA

Islam provides, it now appears, the fetters to all progress.
The tale is new, do not doubt its veracity, it is the fashion.
Forgetful of our nationhood in all we undertake
We bow before the thought of Frank capacity, it is the fashion.

— ZIYA PASHA

What does it mean for children to be pedagogical wards or educated citizens of a state? How are institutionalized ideas about citizenship as constituted in an educational system made credible and authoritative? In turn, how is social life organized, and reshaped, through institutions such as state-run schools? In what ways do boys and girls engage with the ideas, opinions, and sentiments offered in the curricula? Finally, how can one best retrieve the voices and critical perspectives of children and parents, whose own accounts on education have been all too often written out? All five questions lead us to reflect on the conjunction between schooling and governance, on the one hand, and subjectivity, on the other.

The founding of an advanced primary school up in the mountains of southern Turkey in 1879 offers a point of entry for reflection on this conjunction. My analysis of this case will illustrate how multiple and overlapping concepts of citizenship are deployed within state institutions, producing classificatory schemes and ultimately constituting subjects. The story instantiates the close relation between modern state formation and the cultural premises of formal schooling, between political authority and authorized representations of society, between childhood and the moral regulation of social identities—in short, the pedagogical state that today constitutes the everyday reality of Turkish citizens.

A Foundational Story

In the southern mountains of Turkey are the famous Cilician Gates, the narrow gorge from which, for thousands of years, pilgrims, merchants, shepherds and armies descended on their way from the Anatolian Plateau to the Levant. Hidden behind the narrowest part of this mountain pass in a secluded valley is Yayla, a small town of six thousand.[1] Located at an altitude of 1,100 meters above sea level, on a clear day one can make out the Mediterranean Sea and the city of Tarsus, some fifty-five kilometers to the south. In the opposite direction, at 3,524 meters above sea level, the snowcapped Medetsiz Mountain hovers over the town like an eagle with outstretched wings. It is against this pastoral background that several older men at the central coffeehouse asked, "Why would an educated person come all the way from America to study our village?" For the next two years, they continued to voice disbelief, if not downright incredulity. After all, as I repeatedly heard from townspeople, schooling is a ticket out of the community, and no urban person with a university degree would come to live in the boondocks to study the local school system. But upon my arrival, on a cold crystal-clear day in January 1989, the old men also jokingly characterized Yayla as a "university," implying that, thanks to them, I would finally complete my (doctoral) education. Irony aside, the coffeehouse patrons were in fact referring to their community's long history with formal education. With considerable pride, they referred to well-known public figures who had graduated from the local elementary school; among the graduates were a recently retired ambassador to Pakistan, a doctor who practices medicine in the United States, a judge serving on Turkey's Supreme Court, and a lawyer who owns the main electricity provider of the region. Then, taking me outside, they directed my gaze to a small square structure in the neighborhood of Peskenek, south of the coffeehouse. Currently used as an office for the Forestry Bureau, the building, they proudly asserted, had served as a *rüşdiye*, a three-year advanced primary school, over a century ago.

My curiosity aroused, I asked why government officials of the Ottoman state, the political predecessor of the current Turkish republic, had bothered to set up such a school in this out-of-the-way community of sheep and goat herders. The townsmen then referred me to Almancı Mehmet, who despite his advanced age (then over a hundred years old), narrated the foundational story of the village *rüşdiye*.

The story is about the confrontation between two poet scholars and their incommensurable worldviews. The two men were Ziya Pasha, the governor of the province of Adana, and İbrahim Rüştü, a theologian from Yayla. Each man understood differently what change was and what kinds of change were important. At the core of their differences were their respectively different interpretations of Islam. Their contemporaries, however, viewed the two with suspicion: both men unsettled the accepted social and cultural norms of the region in their actions and ideas.

Ziya Pasha was a well-known political figure, journalist, and poet. A leading member of a group of intellectuals and literary figures known as the Young Ottomans, he advocated integrating European constitutionalism and scientific positivism with state-supported orthodoxy.[2] He had spent several years in self-imposed exile in Europe before returning to government service. During his residency abroad, he used his poetic skills to advance his political views, either to lament the decline of Islamic civilization or to mock the slavish imitation of Western ("Frankish") customs.[3] Upon his return from exile, he served as governor in the provinces of Cyprus, Amasya, Konya, and Aleppo. His last appointment was governorship of Adana; it was to be brief—two years, from 1878 till his death in 1880.

In his official capacities as governor, Ziya Pasha set about combating fatalist attitudes and superstitions and exposing his officials to what he believed were the positive benefits of European civilization. He also decided to translate his strong beliefs into practice. Earlier governors, for example, had presided over rain prayers during droughts. Ziya Pasha, in contrast, refused to follow this precedent and instead insisted that the municipality build irrigation dams. He is quoted as telling a local delegation, "There is no point in performing a rain prayer on the banks of the river Seyhan. . . . If I lead the prayers for rain, then wouldn't Allah say to me: 'You were a famous governor from a big province. Rather than praying for rain, if only you would find the means to make use of the river and water the fields.'"[4] The lack of money in the provincial treasury, however, prevented the governor from initiating any irrigation works.

More irritating to his staff than his unrealized irrigation plans were the new governor's attempts to introduce Western high culture. Every morning, before they began work, officials were required to follow lessons in French. Ziya Pasha did not content himself with language instruction alone. The governor decided to introduce changes in local entertainment, including the dramatic arts. He brought from the capital city of Istanbul a theatrical troupe that played his translation of Molière's comedy *Tartuffe*. To set an example for the population, he compelled his civil servants to attend the performances.[5]

It wasn't long before local notables began to slander the governor. In his earlier posts, he had amassed many opponents who accused him of stealing from the public coffers and enriching himself at the expense of the state. These accusations followed the governor to his new duties in Adana. A local poet, who resented the governor's patronage of a rival poet, set about lampooning Ziya Pasha. Punning on the governor's name and title, he wrote on the walls of Adana, "The property has lost its light (*ziya*) when its master (*Paşa*) came."[6] Whether he embezzled or not, Ziya Pasha died penniless.

The other character in Almancı Mehmet's story about the *rüşdiye* was sitting in prison when Ziya Pasha took up his new post. The sixty-eight-year-old Ibrahim Rüştü was a theologian and mystical poet who had been convicted of corrupting orthodox practice and, as a prisoner, now became a charge of Ziya Pasha. It was customary for provincial governors to begin their tenure by pardoning prisoners, just as sultans granted amnesties upon accession to the throne. Indeed, one of the first duties Ziya Pasha undertook upon settling in his new post was to go over the list of prisoners, their crimes and sentences. At the end of the list was the entry "Ibrahim Rüştü and his accomplices." The entry mentioned neither crime nor sentence, however. Not surprisingly, this lacuna caught the governor's attention. Upon further inquiry, Ziya Pasha learned in writing from a local notable that "Ibrahim Rüştü together with his accomplices consisting of family relations has been sitting in jail for four years. Following complaints and denunciations by Muslims from the . . . subdistrict, he has been detained for the crime of leading the people astray [*dalâlet*] from the religion. He has deduced all sorts of meanings from the Qur'an and the prophet Muhammad's traditions and has created a new religious sect [*fırak-ı dalle*] within Islam, and in the process has acquired many disciples and supporters."[7] Rüştü's recidivism precluded any chance of a pardon. Even before receiving a sentence, he had already converted all two hundred inmates to his interpretation of Islam. The governor who preceded Ziya Pasha, Nusret Pasha, had insisted that Ibrahim Rüştü remain forever locked up lest he convert other Muslims outside prison to his "sect." In the meantime, the religious scholar applied his poetic skills in prison and translated the Qur'an into Turkish verses.

Who was this sixty-eight-year-old man of religion, and why was his preaching so threatening to society and polity that he was condemned to live out his days in prison? What was his heresy that seemed to attract so many followers? We know that Ibrahim Rüştü was a well-known authority on Islam in the region who was also suspicious of Western ways. Born in 1811 in Yayla, he had attended various theological seminaries (*medreses*) of the empire (Kayseri in central Anatolia, the capital city of Istanbul, and Cairo in Egypt) and taught Islamic law in the holy cities of Mecca and Medina before returning to his native community in old age. His fame, or better yet his notoriety, was not his scholarship but rather his unorthodox interpretation of Islam. In fact, his nickname, the Three Timer (*üç vakitçi*), gave away his crime. According to those villagers old enough to have heard from their grandparents about the elderly theologian, Ibrahim Rüştü had come back from his teaching duties in Arabia with a new understanding of the Muslim believer's obligations. From his reading of the Qur'an and the traditions ascribed to the prophet Muhammad, he had decided to omit the obligatory morning and night prayers; henceforth, a Muslim need pray only three times a day instead of the obligatory five. As a result, he abjured the Hanafi school of religious jurisprudence (*mezheb*), the legal school to which the Ottoman state officially adhered. More problematic to the state was that Rüştü's innovative and less demanding practices found many followers. As the local notable had written to Governor Ziya Pasha, all two hundred prisoners at Adana had become "three timers."

The new governor was intrigued by this man of religion, so strange in background, experience, and ideas, and called him into his office. At that moment, Ibrahim Rüştü was in the midst of preparing his ablutions for his afternoon prayers. The old man entered, not bothering to roll back his sleeves in honor of the governor. Worse still, he sat down without greeting the governor. To greet, or *selâm vermek*, then as now, connotes more than a mere salutation for devout Muslims; the *selâm* recognizes the addressee as a fellow believer. The government authorities had imprisoned Ibrahim Rüştü on account of his heretical interpretations of Islam. Yet it was the prisoner who refused to greet the governor, thereby symbolically removing the Ottoman official from the Islamic community.

The old man's behavior piqued the governor's curiosity, and he immediately asked the prisoner why he did not greet him. The answer was straightforward: he greeted only Muslims, and since the governor wore the fez he wasn't sure whether he was an infidel or a Muslim. In the theologian's view, the governor's dress blurred the sartorial markers that once defined clear-cut membership in a religious community. Other than the conical red fez, he dressed for all intents and purposes in the same fashion as did men hailing from London and Paris, the two cities where Ziya Pasha had spent time.[8] Ziya's costume was, in fact, common to late nineteenth-century Ottoman officials. Ibrahim Rüştü, on the other hand, kept to a wardrobe that clearly indicated his Muslim affiliation. He donned a turban on his head and wore baggy shalwar pants.

The differences between the two men were not simply over dress. Clearly, both men interpreted Islam and its role in society and polity differently. Ziya Pasha, like many self-styled reformers of the time, set about adapting Western technology and aesthetics to the dictates of state-endorsed Islam, while Ibrahim Rüştü advocated a return to those religious practices that he deemed to have once defined the pristine Muslim community. No less important were their different understandings of the relation between state and society. Religious dissent, as far as state officials were concerned (and Ziya Pasha was no exception) was understood to potentially upset the political stability of the empire. A "state of heresy and ignorance" (*bir hal-i dalalet ve cehalet*) precluded the integration and assimilation—in short, the unity—of all Ottoman Muslim subjects of the empire in one mainstream orthodoxy (the Hanafi legal school of thought) and, hence, prevented all Muslims from identifying with state and dynasty.[9] The governor, thus, had to ensure that a local man of religion, however insignificant, did not challenge the state.

First, Ziya Pasha persuaded Ibrahim Rüştü to stop propagating his innovative take on religion. The governor released him, and the old man, in turn, kept to the bargain. Ibrahim retired to Peskenek to write mystical poetry. Not quietly, however. He annexed the graveyard next to his garden. His neighbors, of course, were taken aback by this odd action. His reply was simple: "From now on there will be no need for a graveyard." For ten years, nobody died in the neighborhood.[10] He did, however, withdraw from the travails of everyday life. A few verses written during his retirement suggest as such: "We abandoned the world of earthly goods / Happy to derive virtue from poverty / To others, O you Heaven, surrender your honor and worldly possessions / We are satisfied to be one of the poor."

Ziya Pasha, on the other hand, was not the retiring kind. Nor did he forget the preacher. The governor took action. Within a year of Ibrahim Rüştü's release from prison, the governor persuaded the government to set up the advanced primary school in Peskenek whose curriculum would he hoped prevent youth from straying from state orthodoxy. At the time, there were no advanced primary schools in villages. The school, nevertheless, was modest: one headmaster and twenty pupils.[11] Nor did it survive for very long. Two years later, the government transferred funds and staff to the rapidly developing port city of Mersin.[12] The Ottoman state, however, pursued Ziya Pasha's pedagogical mission in the immediate region of Yayla. Since 1890, there has been an elementary school, and in 1934, on the initiative of the villagers, the school expanded the curriculum from three to five years and became a boarding school for the entire subdistrict. Currently, there are two coeducational elementary schools and one middle school; the total enrollment in the two elementary schools was officially 226 for the 1987–1988 school year; about half that number, mostly boys, were enrolled in the middle school.

One could ask, why bring up this lengthy anecdote when none of the townspeople, not even the venerable old Almancı Mehmet, experienced the event. The point, here, is neither about the origins of the short-lived school nor about several themes such as economic modernization, didactic plays, competing moral orders, or dress codes, which remain ever salient in the contemporary republican school system and which will be discussed at length in the book. Nor was this the first time Ottoman officials relied on state institutions to combat alternative interpretations of religion and inculcate official representations of faith. Centuries before the encounter between Ziya Pasha and Ibrahim Rüştü, deviation from state orthodoxy was equally taken to threaten the ideological foundations of the Ottoman polity. In an endeavor to curb dissident beliefs and thereby reaffirm state authority, troublesome preachers and their supporters were sometimes deported or killed, but more often the state erected Friday mosques in which state-appointed religious leaders educated the adult population in the state-approved tenets of the Islamic faith. Indeed, following religious insurrections in the sixteenth century, the Ottoman state erected such a mosque-school at Yayla.[13] Rather, the fragments of oral memory and written sources, which I have gathered to narrate the educational foundations of Yayla, call attention to a central feature of modern state formation: the state consolidating its authority by laying claims over the subjectivities of its citizens, beginning with the education of children.[14]

What was radically new at the time of Ziya Pasha was treating schools as key institutional sites at the disposal of statesmen and government officials to manage the population. Until then, formal education was the prerogative of future government officials and religious scholars, those relatively few men who were entrusted to apply their knowledge and skills to either preserve and transmit the values of their society or, conversely, to redirect and transform them. Ziya Pasha was particularly receptive to the idea of a paternalistic state, socializing children through government schools. Throughout his career he devoted great attention to state education, beginning with his translation of Jean-Jacques Rousseau's philosophical treatise on education, *Emile*, to expanding the school system in the different provinces he served in, to appointing teachers capable of instruction in secular subjects.[15] Since then, in large cities as well as small villages, state education has become *the* privileged vehicle to create citizens committed to the Turkish state and its orthodoxies. In turn, citizens from all walks of life in Turkey have come to define themselves in terms of schooling, distinguishing those "who have seen education" from those "who have not seen education."[16]

Childhood and Children's Education

From birth on, an individual is hailed as a citizen of a state—a member of a political collectivity who is everybody yet nobody in particular.[17] The task of producing citizenship has fallen on universal education, a central feature of modern state formation. Schools are more than bureaucratic institutions serving the public. They are state projects, both totalizing and individualizing, in which various forms of knowledge are deployed, imparting a sense of purpose and coherence to a population by simultaneously producing homogeneous totalizing categories (e.g., schooled or unschooled) and individuating identities (e.g., levels of education, diplomas). Moreover, schools incorporate and exemplify those state-regulated cultural forms, pedagogical practices and activities, and political representations that, taken together, are intended to have the public take for granted historically contingent identities. Or they perform what Philip Corrigan and Derek Sayer define as "moral regulation": "a project of . . . rendering natural . . . what are in fact ontological and epistemological premises of a particular and historical form of social order. . . . coextensive with state formation."[18] The habitual routines, rituals, and discourses to which children are exposed during their years of schooling are all designed to inscribe them with a prereflective background to civic action. And as the late French sociologist Pierre Bourdieu points out, "One of the main powers of the state is to produce and impose (especially through the school system) categories of thought that we spontaneously apply to all things of the social world—including the state itself."[19]

Likewise, a central tenet of the Turkish state is a commitment to produce citizens out of schoolchildren. The educational system is understood as the key institutional site from which political morality and unity are established. Through schools, children are expected to assimilate national principles relevant to their lives as adult citizens. In 1989, in his farewell address to the National Assembly, outgoing minister of Education Hasan Celal Güzel affirmed the pedagogical mission of the state: "national education is a state affair." Ever since the (short-lived) Ottoman constitution of 1876, state officials are required to supervise and control all school systems.[20] The latest constitution, promulgated three years after the military coup in 1980, reaffirms the central role of the state in educating the country's youth. Thus, article 58 asserts "the State shall take measures to ensure the training and development of youth into whose keeping our State, independence, and our Republic are entrusted, in the light of contemporary science, in line with the principles and reforms of [the first president of the Republic, Mustafa Kemal] Atatürk, and in opposition to those ideas which aim at destroying the indivisible integrity of the State." Irrespective of how the national ideals are interpreted, through the national educational system the state has custodial and tutelary responsibility to ensure that all children attain the basic requisites of citizenship. The legitimacy of the state is embodied in the claim to represent the will of the children who fall under its tutelage. Accordingly, childhood is a distinct but integral part of a society's political structure: children are forced to attend a minimum number of years of schooling as the state has not only the legal right but the moral duty to enforce "universal" education.

Raising the new generation of children as the *raison d'état* is closely linked to perceiving youth as a preparatory phase to adult citizen life, as the object of the historical destiny of a nation, and as the subject of the political vitality of the state. As the conference organizers of the tenth National Education Conference declared in 1981, Turkish society's survival hinges on passing "on the national culture to the new generations in order to attain continuity and stability in social life."[21] Education, childhood, and child development have become tropes with which a whole variety of social and political imaginaries are woven in Turkey. The national community is embodied metonymically in the classroom: all members of the polity are characterized as fraternal citizens bound with the same language, culture, and ideals. This pedagogical articulation of national identity iconically indexes not only the union of state and civil society but renders both arenas politically equivalent moral communities and thus erases any differences there may be in their respective social make-up and practices. Previously privileged categories, such as occupation, religion, social stratum, and locality, which cut across pedagogical boundaries, are demoted for the putative homogeneity that can be found in a generalized citizenship.

The preeminent role that the state takes in legally defining childhood, as a period of dependence and inculcating civic duties and rights in children, has only recently gained momentum in historical and anthropological studies. This is all the more surprising given that since the nineteenth century the progress of a country has been premised on the education of children, and accordingly, children spend many years of their lives in schools. A major stumbling block preventing scholars from seriously studying children in their historical and cultural contexts is an ongoing assumption that childhood is a temporary and impermanent period during which children passively and gradually accumulate those physical and cognitive dispositions that will turn them into full-fledged grown-ups. This assumption fits with the Aristotelian "great chain of being"—a unilinear, continuous ranking of living creatures from lower to higher forms, wherein the adult human being is at the summit of the cosmos and the child is an incomplete version of the ideal adult. With its emphasis on biology, this organic model views child development as a coherent universal process, unfolding over time along genetically programmed behavioral and cognitive functions. Indeed, much of developmental and child psychology downplays the child's different environmental and cultural conditions (e.g., Piaget's theories of universal structure). This is despite several decades of historical research that have shown that age-specific categories such as childhood and the transition between infancy and adulthood are as culturally constituted as gender, race, and status.[22]

More recently, a historical-cultural approach to the study of children has made inroads into the biological view of socialization. Inspired by the Soviet psychologist Lev Vygotsky (1896–1933), whose *Mind and Society* became widely available in the English-language world in the late 1970s, psychological anthropologists and sociocultural psychologists approach children's cognition in terms of historical, cultural, and institutional contexts. Specifically, they examine how culturally structured events and mediating institutions like schooling organize each individual child's development. The overall aim is to explore children's hermeneutic agency, that is to say, their ability to interpret self, others, and the world on their own terms.[23] Most importantly, all these scholars register the fact that children do not simply mimic adults, but actively contribute to shaping the adult culture in which they live. Children think, talk, and behave differently from adults, and only over time do they learn to adapt to the majority adult culture, to (mis)understand what grownups do and say. As Lawrence Hirschfeld observes, the fact that children "share a cultural tradition [with adults] is an achievement to be understood, not a presumption that can be ignored."[24]

Yet for the most part, sociocultural anthropologists have been reluctant to study children as social actors. Rather, they have focused on birth, child care, or adolescence, all of which directly relate to adult culture. Erika Friedl recently summarized the anthropology of childhood as one in which "children not only are underrepresented in our texts but also undertheorized and outright neglected."[25] This neglect, however, is giving way to an ethnographic literature that focuses on the impact of formal schooling on children's political sociability.[26] What set these ethnographies of education apart from psychological studies of children's culture are a concerted effort to understand how schools organize knowledge and meaning to shape people's political conscience and actions. This is understandable given that people throughout the world perceive and experience the state as a major agent in their lives, and most of all, in national educational systems.

Political Culture, Citizenship, and the State

Modern state formation has frequently been understood in terms of elite interest and competition. Indeed, the academy has institutionalized an "elitist" way of emplotting change and continuity, of inscribing traditions and memories, of narrativizing sociohistorical processes. That is, since the history of the ruling classes is realized in the state, the dominant values of the state have most often determined the criteria for what counts as historically significant.[27] In practice, this has often meant that dated and legally binding documents, written for political elites, provide the context by which scholars make sense of the past and present of a society. Any transformations of significance are credited to dominant groups (politicians, officials, journalists, and scholars) in the society, while the politically defined minorities (e.g., women, workers, children) are assumed to either acquiesce or resist the totalizing effect of domination.[28]

A more culturally attuned approach to the state is the symbolic (or interpretive) school of politics. This school focuses on those systems of signification that a regime disseminates to organize and orient political thought and action of all members of a polity. Lynn Hunt, for example, shows how images of the family in late eighteenth-century France produced a republican imaginary constituted as a self-ruling fraternal citizenry.[29] According to Corrigan and Sayer, the English bourgeoisie developed a series of positive "undefinable and inimitable qualities . . . such as reasonableness, moderation, pragmatism, hostility to ideology, eccentricity" that simultaneously defined Englishness and the English state.[30] Clifford Geertz claims that the Balinese state reproduced in the form of pageants the cosmic order to which ruler and ruled subscribed.[31] For Lisa Wedeen, repeated performance of paternal symbols and rhetoric around the cult of Hafiz al-Asad socialized the Syrian citizenry to compliance with an authoritarian regime.[32] Each of these works reveals how embedded factors of cultural significance emanating from political contexts come to define state power. Yet like their elitist counterparts, symbolic studies of politics tend to view the state as a monolithic, coherent entity having a relatively bounded political culture, distinct from and located over and above society. And as a result, they fail to consider what citizens on the political margins expect from the state or the processes by which consensus over relations of dominance and subordination is forged. This failure results to a large extent from collapsing human behavior and social structures within shared patterns of meaning.[33]

Clearly, neither the elitist nor the symbolist approach appeals to a broad range of anthropologists committed to retrieving the less tangible histories of politically marginal populations, documenting their political consciousness, and as much as possible, providing these populations with the means to represent their own views. This interest in how people of different social backgrounds define, understand, and interpret political regimes and action has occurred as scholars recognize that, one, definitions of collective identities are replete with indeterminacy and contingency among members of the same community as well as between different communities, and that, two, the power relations, in which identities are established, maintained, contested, and transformed, change over time. In other words, the notion of the state is constantly being defined within changing political and social contexts. To this effect, recent ethnographies closely follow Philip Abrams's programmatic essay in which he distinguishes between state institutions and the state as a metapolitical concept that confers legitimacy upon centralized decision making and governing institutions that often have competing agendas and interests.[34] Common to these ethnographic studies of the state are three interrelated issues, all concerned with local meanings, circulating discourses, multiple contestations, and changing forms of power: one, the state as articulating a cultural project that projects its unity onto society through institutional sites; two, the responses to state rhetoric and symbols as strategic attempts at reimagining power and its representations in everyday life; and three, alternative ideas about statecraft and the complex ensemble of social relations that mediate these ideas.

In the case of Turkey, the state commands a paramount position in the moral and political imaginaries of all citizens. Whenever one reads about national statesmen in the press, whenever one listens to townspeople and villagers comment on domestic politics, one often comes across the concept of the "father-state" (*devlet baba*). The state as father figure is a master trope of power to which many Turkish citizens appeal in making sense of their relationship to the state and government representatives. The Turkish father-state conforms in many ways to Max Weber's notion of patrimonial regimes (e.g., the *Landsvater*), which legitimate "the authoritarian relationship of father and children."[35] Yet as I will elaborate in the next chapter, as the cultural politics in Turkey has undergone radical transformations in the last sixty years, the meanings attributed to the state-idea have undergone significant changes. Civil bureaucrats who championed secular positivism no longer dominate the country's political culture. Beginning in the 1950s, religious-minded politicians and, more recently, neoliberal businesspeople have developed close relations with state institutions to promote their political and social projects on the national agenda, and most of all, in educational policies. At the same time, the military—self-styled neutral guardian of the state—casts a long shadow over Turkish politics, as it has dominated the National Security Council, the major decision organ of the country.

Consequently, the religious nationalists, the neoliberal industrialists and the military exert their views in the public sphere under the sign of a unified personified view of the state. All three groups correspond to what the Italian Marxist political theorist and activist Antonio Gramsci described as "politically motivated associations"—those intellectuals and think tanks that articulate the worldview and interests of the social group or groups they purport to represent.[36] Because of the importance granted to the state in the state-society equation, these associations invest the state with a kind of metacapital that has the power to distribute resources among the security forces, industrial enterprises, civic organizations, etc., and thereby regulate and control the power relations between the groups. The magic and danger of a highly centralized state such as Turkey stem from the ability of government institutions to structure popular perceptions of the boundaries between state and civil society and thus constitute the roles of different social agents. And because the unifying action of the state is quintessentially exercised through the schools, politically powerful associations compete with one another to gain spaces within the interstices of the national educational system. In this protracted competition over the citizenry's allegiance, each association creates alliances across social groups, at the same time trying to co-opt or eliminate their competitors' definitions of state and civil society. This is not to suggest that a particular association's political discourse is consistent. On the contrary, as Slavoj Žižek points out, the efficacy of a discourse to appeal to different audiences, each with their own particular interests, results from its internal differences and even from its inconsistencies.[37]

Closely associated with the struggle among influential associations to constitute collective boundaries and differences is a struggle over the terms of citizenship. Modern state formation is commonly associated with centralized coordination of government institutions; it is also a cultural project producing the generalized citizen and the political culture within which citizens operate. In Turkey as in many other multiparty polities, however, the relation between state and civil society has recently shifted from one in which all citizens must fuse as much as possible their private selves to the national order to one in which governments increasingly concede some autonomy and influence to subnational interest groups. The shift from a geopolitical imagination organized around the sovereign, territorially delimited state to a more heterogeneous and politically inclusive community has coincided with a scholarship that is increasingly interested in the interrelations between state institutions, citizenship, and civil society.

The move to rethink the epistemological bases of citizenship reflects a scholarly shift from a concern with "politics of people" to "politics of difference," or "identity politics." Scholars increasingly recognize that differently constituted publics demand to have their identities recognized and differences acknowledged.[38] Emphasis has, accordingly, shifted to understanding how men and women use multiple ideologies and forms of knowledge to assert a variety of claims, be they linguistic, ethnic, religious, gender, sexual, or transnational. As a result, citizenship is no longer treated as a strictly formal, legal concept. Rather, in line with Roger Brubaker's notion of "social closure," it is deemed a powerful instrument and object of exclusion—a means of discriminating not only between citizens and aliens but also among citizens of a polity—conferring certain rights and privileges, as well as certain obligations, to subnational groups.[39] Thus, the meaning of citizenship has expanded from one based on territorially defined states to one including intersocietal interactions from which people organize and shape historical consciousness and identities.

This critical addition to the study of citizenship has important implications about how we understand the state. The idea that social relations and identities within a polity are historically contingent has prompted many scholars to examine more closely the historical processes by which state institutions produce citizenship in all its facets (class, gender, biology, sexuality, language, etc.). A direct corollary of this scholarship is a rejection of overarching narratives of state formation and singular definitions of national identity—by-products of the ideological invention of the Western bourgeois nation-state. To put it another way, the concepts and categories scholars frequently deploy to organize and advance their arguments about polity and society derive from what are taken to be dispassionate epistemological premises of knowledge, premises that position an idealized West as the terminus ad quem, the final endpoint, of history.[40] More importantly, scholars are increasingly taking to task the linguistic and social impartiality of analytical concepts, that is to say, axiomatic notions about state, civil society, and citizenship that are assumed to have universal validity, irrespective of time and place, and above all, to encapsulate human agency and experience. Concepts of citizenship are thus far from straightforward or neutral. Their meaning invariably changes in conjunction with, or in response to, cultural, social, and economic resources, all of which are closely connected to historical relations of power within a society and between societies. Politically motivated constituencies, for a variety of reasons, gather together elements that they think belong, or should belong, to their notion of citizenship. In other words, the elements used to define a collective identity at any scale—be it the local, regional, national, or transnational—are reframed in terms of presentist needs.[41] Moreover, as Jacques Derrida would argue, subsequent contexts defer the final meaning of citizenship as the epistemological and discursive premises of political sociability are continually changing.[42] Thus, the premises of citizenship must be treated as objects of study and not as objective methods to study a particular society.

Foremost in rejecting the abstract class of citizens as bearers of natural and legal rights have been feminist political theorists.[43] They were particularly dissatisfied with theories that reproduced the categories and logics of a historical narrative that conflated the consolidation of capitalist society in

Europe and the emancipation of the bourgeois male individual. Anthropologists and sociologists have followed suit and attend to the ideological conditions underlying the internal cleavages that differentiate between full and partial citizens in contemporary states. Thus, Susan Gal and Gail Kligman, in their study of postsocialist east-central Europe, show how, one, unspoken assumptions about gender and sexuality are embedded and reproduced in state institutions and that, two, national unity and social relations are based on patriarchal notions of statehood and sovereignty.[44] Claudio Lomnitz argues that an ethnic citizenship has emerged as indigenous groups increasingly demand that the (Hispanicized) Mexican state recognize their cultural autonomy as well as grant them special political rights.[45] Along similar lines of thought, linguistic anthropologists Eliezer Ben-Rafael, James Collins, and Michael Silverstein, among others, have revealed how communities of interest maintain political ascendancy through language choices and uses.[46] More recent work has focused on how citizens' bodies have, in the words of Adriana Petryna, become "bureaucratized, technicized, and negotiated as part of national citizenship, as part of an entitlement system, and as part of personal identity."[47] Biological parameters such as racial characteristics, birth rate, hygiene, and public health become yardsticks with which the state diagnoses, monitors, and structures society; they also become the stakes by which citizens can claim differential rights over state resources.[48] Thus, if bodily damage (as in Petryna's case study of the Chernobyl nuclear disaster) has paradoxically become a resourceful means to accrue power over other citizens in post-Soviet Ukraine, people with AIDS are lumped into the category of those whose bodies preclude them from full citizenship in the United States.[49] All of these works reflect a move away from a consensual equilibrium model of political society and primordial identities toward approaches that emphasize more fragmented and contested readings of national societies.[50] Other studies on citizenship, on the contrary, exemplify what Arjun Appadurai calls "deterritorialization of persons, images, and ideas"; namely, the processes by which social groupings increasingly transcend politically instituted territorial boundaries and identities.[51] The recent domination of neoliberal policies (privatization, deregulation, and free trade), which foster notions of individual choice and personal independence, has prompted scholars—for example, Yasemin Nuhoglu Soysal, Stephen Gill, Saskia Sassen, Matthew Sparke, to mention just a very disparate few among others—to examine how economic citizenship has changed from one in which the state supplies the educational resources and provides for material welfare of citizens to one in which a multitiered labor force has widely different abilities to practice labor flexibility and mobility in an increasingly globalized market.[52] Thus, Aihwa Ong, for example, has studied the many ways Chinese commercial families acquire multiple citizenships and passports in the context of rapid international transfers of capital and labor.[53]

However different their topics and approaches, all these studies point to a major paradigmatic shift in scholarship: the view of the state as a power-neutral institution delegating rights and duties to generalized citizens to one that seriously deals with the multiple ways citizenship is taken up as people respond to state institutions and the discourses therewith.

Likewise, my ethnographic research of a local school system in southern Turkey suggests that young and old articulate an ensemble of contingent subject positions as they come to understand and describe citizenship not only in ethnocultural terms, for example, but also in biological, sexual, moral, economic, and linguistic ones—all of which are closely interconnected. Much of this awareness and perception of multiple subject positions is, in large part, a result of their schooling. In a country such as Turkey where there is a strong state tradition, schools play a central role in forging a consensual understanding of state and society, in educating the general population in citizenship, and thus in imposing specific interpretations on key social issues and relationships that are widely perceived to define national experience for children. Through the school system, the Turkish state makes claims over the citizens' bodies and minds, whether in terms of economic productivity and military service or in reference to the more personal and intimate spheres of everyday life such as procreation and consumption. Citizens are expected to sacrifice parts of their private selves to the state. Many part with some of their income in the form of taxes; others, their bodies in time of war; and still others give birth to and nurture these bodies. Citizens also demand rights and encode their interests in the political language of rights and obligations they learned most often at school.

What emerges from my study on education in the town of Yayla is that the meanings of citizenship oscillate between local ideas about the contract between rulers and ruled and a more global concept of the universal rights-bearing subjects. This oscillation occurs as men and women, young and old, the schooled and the unlettered, formulate within local, context-specific semantic and pragmatic frames their understanding of political participation as they try to make sense of their day-to-day lives. The very modes of representation, which state-run schools disseminate to consolidate a citizenry, have become forms of knowledge that individuals use to assert a variety of claims over the state. Such a composite view of the relationship between state schools and their elaboration in social interaction requires attending to the juxtaposition of different notions of citizenship in the curricula and the complex ways these notions work back upon local systems of signification, generating multiple ideas about action and thought. Thus, this study sets out to examine the relation between political movements and modern state formation, on the one hand, and different understandings of school knowledge, on the other.

With all this in mind, I have structured the book in the following manner: first, Chapter 2 is a case study of the effects of an educational report released in 1990, which precipitated a government crisis involving its neoliberal industrialist sponsors and national religious public figures; next, three chapters covering the different ways each politically motivated association (religious nationalists, secular industrialists, and the military, respectively) has inserted their worldviews into the educational system; and finally, how the multiple and conflicting ideas in the authoritarian curriculum have spurred children to imagine a more emancipatory pedagogical state.

Toward a Politics of Pedagogy

The main issue I have set out to address in this book is the pedagogical processes that constitute the relations between citizens and the state, as well as among citizens of that state. To best explain and interpret these relations, my study raises two crucial questions: How does mass education configure an ideal citizenry out of ostensibly a priori but in fact fluctuating social divisions and relations (e.g., gender, age, class) to legitimate a particular social and political order? And what aspects of citizenship emerge from the nexus between school knowledge and particular social contexts?

One prominent approach, which draws on the ideas of Antonio Gramsci, conceives the state as an ideologically motivated educator rather than as a power-neutral political institution that exists somehow outside of society. Focus is on hegemony—the systematic pedagogical practices by which the ruling classes induce consent to the dominant political order through the school system. Along these lines first developed by Gramsci, scholars have challenged a meritocratic ideology that legitimates class differences and ensures the coexistence of different socioeconomic life courses and political unity. Specifically, their studies reveal how class, gender, or ethnicity structure children's experience of schooling. Pierre Bourdieu and Shirley Brice Heath, working respectively in France and the Piedmont Carolinas of the United States, have shown how class-based linguistic and social skills, which children acquire in informal social settings like the family, strongly determine the students' academic achievements.[54] Still in the Gramscian mode, Paul Willis focused on the relation between mainstream middle-class school values and political consciousness among working-class youth: the aggressive masculinity cultivated among high school lads in an English factory town cemented a class conscience that, in turn, ensured their subordinate status in capitalist society.[55] The emphasis on the reproduction of social inequality through school systems is undeniably important given that, too often, scholars envision education as insulated from the actual economic and political organization of society, as if schooling were a special sphere of knowledge exempt from ideological considerations, as long as it complies with mainstream pedagogical thought and methods. All the same, emphasis on the hegemony of upper-middle-class values in the school system suffers from a decidedly teleological cast; namely, that structural and class positions of individual subjects ultimately determine schoolchildren's present political consciousness as well as their future livelihood. And as a result, the central role of the state has all but disappeared from the analysis of national education.

An equally important approach focuses on the pedagogical mechanisms by which institutional sites shape how people imagine, experience, and understand political and socioeconomic processes. As Corrigan and Sayers point out, "a central dimension—we are tempted to say, the secret—of state power is the way it works within us."[56] Seminal have been the ideas of French historian Michel Foucault, who explored how the state renders populations governable through an array of rationalities of governance that centers on autonomy, self-control, and responsibility of the citizenry.[57] Central to Foucault's ideas is his concept of *discourse*—a culturally and historically contingent domain of knowledge and practice that establishes truth claims about self, other, and world, which in turn mediate an internal sense of belonging, an outward sense of otherness. In exploring how a dominant discourse is organized, legitimated, and stabilized in such a manner that certain kinds of behavior and ways of reasoning become nondeliberative, he showed how state institutions marginalize alternative ways of acting and thinking. Applying Foucault's insights on modern forms of power, Timothy Mitchell attended to the historical conditions within which the Western division of reality into a metaphysical order and a material world of representations was handmaiden to British economic imperialism in late nineteenth-century Egypt. Specifically, Mitchell showed how imported educational practices (e.g., the Lancaster system) relied on the body-mind duality such that "power . . . not only [worked] upon the exterior of the body but also 'from the inside out' by shaping the individual mind."[58] Although Foucault and Mitchell provide productive ways of looking at power that overcome the divide between the instrumental and the symbolic operative in conventional political thought, they presume that a normative ideal of the bourgeois public sphere is integrated into the behaviors and discourses of citizens. Even though state institutions like schools recruit subjects as productive citizens, this does not explain how individuals from a wide variety of social backgrounds either experience or assess their education, that is, in what particular ways people come to inhabit the roles offered by institutional sites.

As a counter to these top-down perspectives on power in the Foucauldian tradition, more recent research on education has drawn on cultural studies associated with Stuart Hall and others at Birmingham, and in parallel with Michel de Certeau's notion of "tactics"—the nonsystematic combination of disparate and inchoate elements within society, which politically disenfranchised groups use to assert their own interests and thus gain (partial) autonomy.[59] At its best, this scholarship reveals the specific lived experiences of individual pupils, their social values and political consciousness as they accommodate to, contest, and subvert stereotypes and forms of knowledge they are subjected to at school. For example, Ann Ferguson explores how a group of eleven- and twelve-year-old boys in an urban West Coast U.S. school, whose behavior the personnel have identified as incipient adult criminal behavior, cope with the stigma of being troublemakers inevitably bound for jail; Abdullah Sahin demonstrates how Muslim youth in Birmingham, U.K., schools forge their cultural heritage anew as they navigate between school and home cultures; Ann Solberg shows how Norwegian schoolchildren actively negotiate their "social age" in their quest for greater autonomy from adults; and Barrie Thorne, in her study of two elementary schools in the United States, argues that boys and girls simultaneously enforce gender boundaries and undermine the sense of gender as division and opposition.[60] Common to all these studies is showing that the organization and meaning of education are influenced by race, ethnicity, age, gender, and social class and that they shift with social context. Ideally, this bottom-up view attributes "power to subjects and subcultural groups to intervene in signifying and political systems and produce change."[61] A major drawback of this "critical" approach to education, however, is limiting the concept of resistance to what is confrontational. That is, it highlights only the political, social, and economic order children (and, very often, the researchers) are struggling against. Paradoxically, these scholars assume hegemony to be monolithic, and thus the struggle against it easily defined, when, in fact, identification of consensus and its characteristic internal tensions are far from obvious, and the key question becomes one of how a counterculture can recognize this consensus and operate in opposition. Thus, to fully address the many ways people engage with power, it is crucial to specify what political and social imaginaries schoolchildren and youth are struggling for.[62]

Whatever their respective shortcomings, all three approaches make a powerful appeal to think critically about education as configuring personal and collective identities. In my study of the interaction between children and state-run schools, I have found Michael Bakhtin's ideas about speech to offer a useful way to integrate the insights of these approaches. Bakhtin emphasizes how social relations are maintained through "heteroglossia" in a community—that is to say, the constant process of contradistinguishing and differentiating forms of speech characteristic of social groups and actors. Each form of speech is oriented toward a particular group of speakers, taking into account their social position, ideological commitments, and constellation of values, assumptions, and experiences. In this respect, the social world is composed of overlapping languages.[63] As will be evident in the book, the townspeople of Yayla, young and old, are exposed to a wide variety of (socioideological) languages: the language of secular positivism, the language of Islamic eschatology, the language of the market, the language of the army, the language of newspapers, the language of adults, the language of children, and so forth. The townspeople are also involved in disseminating or transmitting these different languages in such a way as to make them relevant for themselves.[64] Each social formation, thus, comes to define its own language to some extent, by which its members become recognizable. However, against this centripetal tendency, Bakhtin points out that there is also a centrifugal tendency in each utterance, thanks in large measure to its context of usage.[65] Thus, although two politically motivated associations may both use the term *citizen*, each may inflect it differently according to their particular positions in the public sphere.

As is the case in other countries, Turkish political elites believe they can project their ideas to schoolchildren via the language that gets congealed (or "entextualized") in pedagogic manuals, school curricula, educational directives, dictionaries, and so on.[66] Their organizations, working in conjunction with the national school system, attempt to determine the parameters of collective identity for the entire citizenry. The various attempts to establish coherence to the terms of Turkish citizenship—and thus to "entextualize authoritatively, and hence, in one relevant move, to fix certain metadiscursive perspectives on texts and discourse practices"—is disrupted by the varying interests of differently positioned social actors.[67]

But the differences between political elites are not the only significant nexus of the centripetal and centrifugal forces at play in constituting a national citizenry through education. Another level of sophistication is required to comprehend how new understandings of social and cultural differences are generated. To Bakhtin, people experience the meaning of a word or discourse precisely because they constitute their social and political identities in and through language. Meaning, therefore, emerges through interaction as participants try to achieve their own ends, to consciously establish a social position with respect to other persons.[68] So at the level of social action as well, an educational discourse or a key term like *citizen* cannot be reduced to a singular, stable meaning; on the contrary, it evokes multiple and overlapping meanings as individuals within a society position themselves differently in terms of life history, gender, age, socioeconomics, locality, and consciousness.[69] It is thus necessary to pay close attention to the social context in which local actors use terms to understand how they "re-entextualize" the language of political elites.

Applied to this study of a local school system in Turkey, a broadly con-strued Bakhtinian ("heteroglossic") approach provides a productive frame-work to capture the indeterminate and contingent links between multiple discourses on state and citizenship, pedagogical practices, and relations of power, especially how these links are refracted in everyday consciousness. In other words, schoolchildren's experience of education is replete with inde-terminacy and contingency, given the uneasy relation between official can-ons of representation, performances of hierarchy, and different understand-ings of polity and society across generations.[70] Thus, this study moves beyond formalistic approaches to education, politics, and society and instead seeks out the variety of cultural and political processes by which the mean-ings of education are configured around interests, understandings, hopes, and dreams for different sectors of contemporary Turkish society. The var-ious forms of school knowledge that individuals draw upon inform present experiences and condition future social actions.

Methods of Research

To make salient the interplay between school-mediated forms of knowledge and the social and political imaginaries among townspeople and children, I have based my study on extensive fieldwork and open-ended interviews in Yayla and surrounding communities, covering a period of twenty-five months (January 1989–February 1991), as well as archival research in the capital city of Ankara. The primary written sources for analyzing the rela-tionship between education and politics were the biweekly *Tebliğler Dergisi* (*Communications Journal*), which has reported all decisions of the Ministry of Education since 1939. These reports along with pedagogical training manu-als reveal the range and type of discourses existing at different sociohistori-cal moments: ministers' speeches, national education conferences, organiza-tion of different school programs, criteria for selection of curricula, staff, and primers. I also examined the textbooks then in use in the local schools and a selection of earlier textbooks that parents found meaningful for their own socialization. All of these sources provide useful prompts to compare the ideological shifts in the school system as well as changes in school knowledge.

As the national school system is a concern for many politically motivated associations, some of whom operate within state institutions, others not, I make extensive use of all the major newspapers (*Cumhuriyet, Güneş, Sabah, Tercüman, Zaman*; the satirical press; and several tabloids), which I read consistently throughout my stay. Magazines, semiautobiographical novels, memoirs, leaflets, sermons, legislation, mass media transmissions, political campaigns, and public advertisements constitute a significant portion of the textual corpus I assembled and analyzed. In many ways, it was through the prism of these nonpedagogical sources (such as television news and sermons in the mosque) that townspeople engaged with the multiplicity of political and social visions disseminated in the state-run schools.

The analysis of education is not limited to only formulation, dissemination, or criticism of the curricula. To fathom the relationship between education and society, on the one hand, and subjectivity, on the other, I observed in-class performance of the curricula and their impact, or lack thereof, outside the schools. This was considerably facilitated by my role, first, as a substitute math teacher in the middle school and, later, instructor of conversational English during the summer recesses. My classes brought together children from different school systems (secular and religious, public and private, academic-, magnet-, and vocational school–track) and different family histories (local residents, migrants living in either shantytowns or city centers proper). To prepare for in-class dialogues, I assigned essays in Turkish on various topics, ranging from the family to modernity. Through these essays and follow-up conversations with pupils, I was able to probe how young people make sense of their formal education and in what ways they engaged with the curricula in their daily lives. The children's oral and written expressions, however fragmented in terms of coherence and consistency, constitute synecdoches for political and social consciousness.[71]

The ethnographic study of the educational system would not be complete without mentioning the face-to-face encounters with particular persons, the many hours I spent hanging out in coffeehouses, homes, and gardens when not herding sheep up the mountains at night, picking cotton in the sweltering heat of the lowlands, delivering produce to the major cities of the country, or teaching rudimentary English. Such are the travails of participant observation, a trademark of the anthropological discipline. My active partici-pation in community life notwithstanding, I was always taken as an outsider. This said, within a few months, the townspeople not only tolerated my in-trusive presence but went out of their way to include me in their daily lives, including observation of all-women activities.[72] No doubt my status as a rel-ative by marriage to a highly respected statesman of the country, a protégé of one of the leading businessmen in the region, a teacher of their children, a spiritual kinsman (*kirve*) to one of the leading families that automatically conferred on me fraternal status with the women of the household, and a writer of amulets in Qur'anic Arabic considerably helped my integration. In sum, the frustrations at acquiring fluency in Turkish as well as gaining the trust of most townspeople provided occasions for understanding the many ways social practices and values within the community work themselves back into the classroom and, no less importantly, have an impact on the formula-tion of the curricula and the debates over education at the national corridors of power.

Finally, before and even more so following fieldwork, this study has been considerably informed by further library and archival research in Turkey, France, and Chicago. The primary sources, secondhand ethnographic and historical studies that bear directly on the town and the region, and the ex-tensive literature on the transformation of the different ideologies operative in the country provide (albeit retrospective) insights to current political, economic, and cultural developments at all levels of society.

For conceptual orientation, the analysis of the (oral and written) sources used in the book draws on a scholarship interested in exploring the nexus be-tween political consciousness, language, action and power relations. The overall aim is to give testimony to modes of experiencing sociohistorical transformations, which are not based on an unreflective realism. To this end, I have used the strategies of deconstructionism, given its emphasis on the cultural and linguistic processes by which the meanings of concepts are both fragmented and reconfigured around different political and social imaginar-ies. Deconstruction, as Gyan Prakash states, "is emphatically not about showing the arbitrariness of our categories; rather, its purpose has been to show that structures of signification effect their closures through a strategy of opposition and hierarchization that edit, suppress, and marginalize every-thing that upsets founding values."[73] This textual approach radically departs from conventional (positivist) approaches to text and language. Too often, the sources from which many historians and ethnographers cull facts are treated as noise, out of which a systematic, coherent voice can be constituted only by the skills of the scholar.[74] That is, somehow the "hard facts" a scholar ferrets out inherently organize themselves into a logical scheme, a coherent narrative. Yet as Prakash notes, sources "come to us already with some stories to tell."[75] Accordingly, the challenge is to be attuned to those "noises," those social and political imaginaries that surreptitiously creep into written and oral communication and partially disrupt authorized discourses.[76] Thus, a central feature of this book is to maintain as much as possible the complex everyday realities that policy makers, government officials, teachers, parents, and the children experience, to provide a more sensitive account of the multiple and conflicting responses to power, knowledge, and social change.

Envoi

I began this chapter by describing the confrontation between two poet-scholars, a confrontation that led to the educational foundations of Yayla. The description not only illustrated the pedagogical mission of the modern state but also provided the pretext to reflect upon the scholarship on childhood, citizenship, and education. Very often, in a pursuit of logical consistency and completeness, studies on education have viewed the state as a stable self-sufficient whole, whose elements constitute an integrated culture and bounded system of social relations. This Kantian emphasis on coherence and stability winds up imposing one-to-one correspondence between state institutions, primordial identities, and political socialization. As a result, the multiplicity of subject positions and the interpretative variability in a collectivity is forsaken for essences that defy contingent power relations in society. This tendency to suppress unstable and inconsistent representations and identities elides the ambiguous connections between educational processes and the fluid social situations that comprise the day-to-day understandings of citizens. Yet it is the instability and incompleteness of hegemonic orders that allow alternative perspectives to constantly crop up and disrupt any initial coherence in the school system.

In Turkey, the national educational system is continually shot through with tensions reflective of ongoing debates over the multiple meanings of citizenship, which structure the boundaries between state and society. The state is very much part of the stakes as competing politically motivated associations stake claims to the citizens' future. This is the gist of the next chapter—another confrontation over the state of education. This time, in 1990 in the capital city of Ankara, between religious-minded public figures and neoliberal industrialists, coalition partners of the government party.

Notes

1. On the permanent and seasonal fluctuations of the local population, see Chapter 4.

2. Serif Mardin, *The Genesis of Young Ottoman Thought: A Study in the Modernization of Turkish Political Ideas* (Princeton, NJ: Princeton University Press, 1962), pp. 115–20.

3. Examples of Ziya Pasha's poetry in English translation can be found in Nermin Menemencioğlu, *The Penguin Book of Turkish Verse*, collab. Fahir Iz (Harmondsworth, Middlesex, UK: Penguin, 1978), pp. 164–65.

4. Taha Toros, *Şair Ziya Paşa'nın Adana valiliği* (Adana: Yeni Adana Basımevi, 1940), p. 24. Toros's book corroborated and elaborated upon the information I received in the interview I had conducted with Almancı Mehmet, the elderly informant. To note, all translations from Turkish sources are mine.

5. Toros, *Şair Ziya Paşa'nın Adana valiliği*, 31. Ziya Pasha was not the only government official dabbling in theatre. Ahmed Vefik Pasha (1823–1891), the governor of the province of Bursa, also translated Molière's plays into Ottoman Turkish and obliged the provincial elite to attend the performance of these plays. See Selim Deringil, "The Ottoman Origins of Kemalist Nationalism: Namik Kemal to Mustafa Kemal," *European History Quarterly* 23 (1993), p. 167.

6. Toros, *Şair Ziya Paşa'nın Adana valiliği*, p. 19. The Turkish is *ziyâsı kalmadı mülkün gelince Paşası!*

7. Toros, *Şair Ziya Paşa'nın Adana valiliği*, 19. The word *dâlalet* literally means "leading astray" the Muslim community and contrasts with the straight and narrow road leading to the canonical law. Ottoman officials claimed in the name of the state to uphold religious canons.

8. Since 1829 Ottoman civil officials had to wear the fez. Many Muslim men of religion, however, associated the new headgear with the Ottoman state's adoption of Western infidel ways.

9. Selim Deringil, *The Well-Protected Domains: Ideology and the Legitimation of Power in the Ottoman Empire, 1876–1909* (London: I. B. Tauris, 1998), pp. 19, 71, 77.

On the then reigning Sultan Abdul Hamit II's policy to convert dissident religious sects to state orthodoxy, see XX, "L'Islam et son avenir," *Revue des Deux Mondes* 64 (1 August 1921), 674. Government policy included constructing schools and mosques, appointing spiritual leaders, and enlisting all eligible Muslim youth in the army.

10. Women from all over the immediate vicinity continue to visit Ibrahim Rüştü's grave, where they pray for the health of their loved ones.

11. *Salnâme-i Vilâyet-i* (Adana: Vilayeti Matbaası, [1312] 1894), p. 180.

12. Zeki Teoman, "Tarih boyunca Mersin," *Tarih ve edebiyat mecmuası* 14 (1978), p. 85.

13. Suraiya Faroqhi, "Rural Society in Anatolia and the Balkans in the Sixteenth Century, I," *Turcica* 9 (1977), pp. 166–67. On inculcating orthodoxy in the masses in the sixteenth century, see Halil Inalcik, "State, Sovereignty and Law during the Reign of Süleyman," in *Süleymân the Second and His Time*, ed. Halil Inalcik and Cemal Kafadar (Istanbul: Isis Press, 1993), p. 70.

14. It goes without saying that the consolidation of government authority in southern Anatolia was accomplished as much through coercive military means as through schooling. In 1866, the government sent an expeditionary force, the Fırka-Islâhiye (Division of Reformation), to crush the local valley lords. A year later, the Ottoman state implemented a French-derived administrative division of the empire to better manage the country's populations. See Andrew Gordon Gould, "Lords or Bandits? The Derebeys of Cilicia," *International Journal of Middle Eastern Studies* 7 (1976), 485–506.

15. M. Kaya Bilgegil, *Ziyâ Paşa üzerinde bir araştırma* (Erzurum: Atatürk Üniversitesi Basımevi, 1970), pp. 284, 475, 477.

16. In Turkish, *eğitim görmüş* and *eğitim görmemiş*, respectively.

17. In theory, birth grants automatic citizenship. This has not always been the case in practice, however. In Israel, for example, children of undocumented foreign workers are threatened with expulsion from the state as are Palestinian citizens who are deemed to be a threat to the country.

18. Philip Corrigan and Derek Sayer, *The Great Arch: English State Formation as Cultural Revolution* (Oxford: Basil Blackwell, 1985), p. 4.

19. Pierre Bourdieu, "Rethinking the State: Genesis and Structure of the Bureaucratic Field," in *State/Culture: The Study of State Formation after the Cultural Turn*, ed. George Steinmetz (Ithaca, NY: Cornell University Press, 1999), p. 53.

20. Known as the *Teşkilât Esasiye Kanunu*, the 1876 constitution was based on the Belgian monarchial constitution of 1831 and, with slight modifications, remained in use until the military coup of 1960. See M. Rauf İnan, "Anayasalarımızda ve anayasalarda eğitim," in *VIII. Türk tarih kongresi: kongreye sunulan bildiriler: Ankara, 12–15 ekim 1976* (Ankara: Türk Tarih Kurumu Basımevi, 1983), 3:2117–85.

21. Onuncu Millî Eğitim Şûrâsı, *Onuncu Millî Eğitim Şûrâsı: 23–26 Haziran 1981* (Ankara: Milli Eğitim Basımevi, 1981), p. 17.

22. E.g., Philippe Aries, *Centuries of Childhood: A Social History of Family Life* (New York: Vintage, 1962); N. Ray Hiner and Joseph M. Hawes, ed., *Growing up in America: Children in Historical Perspective* (Urbana: University of Illinois Press, 1985); Avner Gil'adi, *Children of Islam: Concepts of Childhood in Medieval Muslim Society* (New York: St. Martin's, 1992); Hughes Cunningham, "Histories of Childhood," *American Historical Review* 103 (1998), pp. 1195–1208; and Colin Heywood, *A History of Childhood: Children and Childhood in the West from Medieval to Modern Times* (Malden, MA: Blackwell, 2001).

23. For exemplary studies, see Gustav Jahoda and I. M. Lewis, *Acquiring Culture: Cross Cultural Studies in Child Development* (London: Routledge, 1988); Jean Lave and Etienne Wenger, *Situated Learning: Legitimate Peripheral Participation* (Cambridge, UK: Cambridge University Press, 1991); James V. Wertsch, *Voices of the Mind: A Sociocultural Approach to Mediated Action* (Cambridge, MA: Harvard University Press, 1991); Lucien T. Winegar and Jaan Valsiner, ed., *Children's Development within Social Context: Metatheory and Theory* (Hillsdale: Erlbaum, 1992); and Lawrence Hirschfeld, *Race in the Making: Cognition, Culture, and the Child's Construction of Human Kinds* (Cambridge, MA: MIT Press, 1996).

24. Lawrence Hirschfeld, "The Inside Story," *American Anthropologist* 102 (2000), p. 622.

25. Erika Friedl, "Why Are Children Missing from Textbooks," *Anthropology News* 43 (2002), p. 19.

26. E.g., Charles F. Keyes, "The Proposed World of the School: Thai Villagers' Entry into a Bureaucratic State System," in *Reshaping Local Worlds: Rural Education and Cultural Change in Southeast Asia*, ed. Charles F. Keyes (New Haven, CT: Yale Center for International and Area Studies, 1991), pp. 87–138; Judith Marshall, *Literacy, Power, and Democracy in Mozambique: The Governance of Learning from Colonization to the Present* (Boulder, CO: Westview, 1993); Manuela Carneiro da Cunha, "Children, Politics and Culture: The Case of Brazilian Indians," in *Children and the Politics of Culture*, ed. Sharon Stephens (Princeton, NJ: Princeton University Press, 1995), pp. 282–91; Bradley Levinson, Douglas Foley, and Dorothy Holland, eds. *The Cultural Production of the Educated Person: Critical Ethnographies of Schooling and Local Practice* (Albany: State University of New York Press, 1996); Deborah Reed-Danahay, *Education and Identity in Rural France: The Politics of Schooling* (Cambridge, UK: Cambridge University Press, 1996); Gregory Starrett, *Putting Islam to Work: Education, Politics and Religious Transformation in Egypt* (Berkeley: University of California Press, 1998); Amy Stambach, *Lessons from Mount Kilimanjaro: Schooling, Community, and Gender in East Africa* (New York: Routledge, 2000); and Fiona Wilson, "In the Name of the State: Schools and Teachers in an Andean Province," in *States of Imagination*, ed. Thomas Blom Hansen and Finn Stepputat. (Durham, NC: Duke University Press, 2001), pp. 313–44.

27. See Ranajit Guha, "The Small Voice of History," in *Subaltern Studies IX*, ed. Shahid Amin and Dipesh Chakrabarty (New Delhi: Oxford University Press, 1996), p. 12.

28. See note 55.

29. Lynn Avery Hunt, *The Family Romance of the French Revolution* (Berkeley: University of California Press, 1992).

30. Corrigan and Sayer, *The Great Arch*, p. 103.

31. Clifford Geertz, *Negara: The Theatre State in 19th Century Bali* (Princeton, NJ: Princeton University Press, 1981).

32. Lisa Wedeen, *Ambiguities of Domination: Politics, Rhetoric, and Symbols in Contemporary Syria* (Chicago: University of Chicago Press, 1999).

33. The homology between a particular mind-set and a specific society or state derives from Clifford Geertz's problematic, mentalistic definition of culture "as a system of symbols by which man confers significance on his own experience." See his "Concepts of Culture," in *The Interpretation of Cultures: Selected Essays* (New York: Basic Books, 1973), p. 250. At issue is a lingering methodological individualism, which reduces social complexity to already constituted interests and identities, to fixed compartmentalized identity groups, and to a singular state-idea. What I am addressing is a tendency among scholars to elide distinctions between analytical vocabulary and hegemonic representations of politics, between social entities and social actors, between discrete observations of political behavior and interpretation of society and culture—that is to say, distinctions between contextual specificity and generalization. For an excellent overview of the philosophical foundations and ambiguities of methodological individualism, see Rajeev Bhargava, *Individualism in Social Science: Forms and Limits of a Methodology* (Oxford: Clarendon, 1992); and David Nettle, "On the Status of Methodological Individualism," *Current Anthropology* 38 (1997), pp. 283–86.

34. See Philip Abrams, "Notes on the Difficulty of Studying the State," *Journal of Historical Sociology* 1 (1988), p. 71. Ethnographies that draw out the multiple meanings of the state include among others Richard Handler, *Nationalism and the Politics of Culture in Quebec* (Madison: University of Wisconsin Press, 1988); Michel-Rolph Trouillot, *Haiti, State against Nation: The Origins and Legacy of Duvalierism* (New York: Monthly Review Press, 1990); Michael Herzfeld, *The Social Production of Indifference: Exploring the Symbolic Roots of Western Bureaucracy* (Chicago: University of Chicago Press, 1992); Ann Anagnost, *National Pastimes: Narrative, Representation, and Power in Modern China (Body, Commodity, Text)* (Durham, NC: Duke University Press, 1997); Thomas Blom Hansen and Finn Stepputat, eds., *States of Imagination: Ethnographic Explorations of the Postcolonial State* (Durham, NC: Duke University Press, 2001); and Veena Das and Deborah Poole, eds., *Anthropology in the Margins of the State* (Santa Fe, NM: School of American Research Press, 2004).

35. Max Weber, *Economy and Society, II* (Berkeley: University of California Press, 1968), p. 1107.

36. Antonio Gramsci, *Selections from the Prison Notebooks*, trans. Quintin Hoare and Geoffrey N. Smith (New York: International Publishers, 1971), p. 5. For the purposes of this study, I eschew the term *interest group* since in U.S. political usage this

term conflates the intellectuals or organizations with the social groups they claim to represent.

37. Slavoj Žižek, *The Sublime Object of Ideology* (London: Verso, 1989), p. 75.

38. Clearly, there is congruence between the dominant theoretical paradigm and the political preoccupation of the time.

39. Roger Brubaker, *Citizenship and Nationhood in France and Germany* (Cambridge, MA: Harvard University Press, 1992), p. 23.

40. My point resonates with Dipesh Chakrabarty's argument that the categories and strategies (including the strategy of historicizing) that Western scholars adapt from European thought are both indispensable and inadequate in describing and theorizing the social and political transformations of a non-Western community such as Yayla. See his "Postcoloniality and the Artifice of History: Who Speaks for 'Indian' Pasts," *Representations* 37 (1992), pp. 1–26.

41. As Friedrich Nietzsche states, "All concepts in which an entire process is semiotically concentrated elude definitions; only that which has no history is definable"; see his *On the Genealogy of Morals* (New York: Vintage, 1967), p. 80.

42. See Jacques Derrida, "Structure, Sign and Play in the Discourse of the Human Sciences," in *Writing and Difference*, trans. Alan Bass (London: Routledge, 1978), p. 280.

43. E.g., Judith Butler, "Contingent Foundations: Feminism and the Question of 'Postmodernism,'" in *Feminists Theorize the Political*, ed. Judith Butler and Joan Scott (New York: Routledge, 1992), pp. 3–22; Iris Marion Young, *Intersecting Voices: Dilemmas of Gender, Political Philosophy and Policy* (Princeton, NJ: Princeton University Press, 1997); and Elizabeth Frazer and Nicola Lacey, "Public-Private Distinctions," in *Contemporary Political Thought*, ed. Alan Finlayson (Edinburgh: Edinburgh University Press, 2003), pp. 328–32.

44. Susan Gal and Gail Kligman, *The Politics of Gender after Socialism: A Comparative-Historical Essay* (Princeton, NJ: Princeton University Press, 2000). For recent discussions on the role of gender in reshaping citizenship and social relations, three thought-provoking essays have come from Ursula Vogel, "Is Citizenship Gender-Specific?" in *The Frontiers of Citizenship*, ed. Ursula Vogel and Michael Moran (London: Macmillan, 1991), pp. 58–85; Suad Joseph, "The Public/Private: The Imagined Boundary in the Imagined Nation/State/Community—The Lebanese Case," *Feminist Review* 57 (1997), pp. 73–92; and Deniz Kandiyoti, "The Politics of Gender and the Conundrums of Citizenship," in *Women and Power in the Middle East*, ed. Suad Joseph and Susan Slyomovics (Philadelphia: University of Pennsylvania Press, 2001), pp. 52–58.

45. Claudio Lomnitz, *Deep Mexico, Silent Mexico: An Anthropology of Nationalism* (Minneapolis: University of Minnesota Press, 2001). Other exemplary studies on group-differentiated citizenship include Deborah Yashar, "Indigenous Movements and Democracy: Contesting Citizenship in Latin America," *Comparative Politics* 31 (1998), pp. 23–42; Alsion Brysk, *From Tribal Village to Global Village: Indian Rights*

and International Relations in Latin America (Stanford, CA: Stanford University Press, 2000); and Renato Rosaldo, ed., *Cultural Citizenship in Island Southeast Asia: Nation and Belonging in the Hinterlands* (Berkeley: University of California Press, 2003).

46. Eliezer Ben-Rafael, *Language, Identity and Social Division* (Oxford: Clarendon, 1994); James Collins, "Our Ideologies and Theirs," in *Language Ideologies: Practice and Theory*, ed. Bambi Schieffelin, Kathryn Woolard, and Paul Kroskrity (Oxford: Oxford University Press, 1998), pp. 256–70; and Michael Silverstein, "The Whens and Wheres—As well as Hows—of Ethnolinguistic Recognition," *Public Culture* 15 (2003), pp. 531–57.

47. Adriana Petryna, *Life Exposed: Biological Citizenship After Chernobyl* (Princeton, NJ: Princeton University Press, 2002), p. 3.

48. E.g., Robert Proctor, *Racial Hygiene: Medicine under the Nazis* (Cambridge, MA: Harvard University Press, 1988); Kalpana Ram and Margaret Jolly, *Borders of Being: Citizenship, Sexuality and Reproduction in Asia and the Pacific.* (Ann Arbor: University of Michigan Press, 2001); Kamran Asdar Ali, *Planning the Family in Egypt: New Bodies, New Selves* (Austin: University of Texas Press, 2002); and Alison Bashford, *Imperial Hygiene: A Critical History of Colonialism, Nationalism and Public Health* (Basingstoke, UK: Palgrave Macmillan, 2004).

49. Thomas Yingling, *AIDS and the National Body* (Durham, NC: Duke University Press, 1997), p. 29.

50. Homi K. Bhabha, "DissemiNation: Time, Narrative, and the Margins of the Modern Nation," in *Nation and Narration* (London: Routledge, 1990), pp. 291–322.

51. Arjun Appadurai, "Global Ethnoscapes: Notes and Queries for a Transnational Anthropology," in *Recapturing Anthropology: Working in the Present*, ed. Richard Fox (Santa Fe, NM: School of American Research Press, 1991), p. 192.

52. Yasemin Nuhoglu Soysal, *Limits of Citizenship: Migrants and Postnational Membership in Europe* (Chicago: University of Chicago Press, 1994); Stephen Gill, "Globalisation, Market Civilisation and Disciplinary Neoliberalism," *Millennium* 24 (1995), pp. 399–423; Saskia Sassen, "Economic Globalization and the Redrawing of Citizenship," in *Moral Imperialism: A Critical Anthology*, ed. Berta Esperanza Hernanez-Truyol (New York: New York University Press, 2002), pp. 135–50; and Matthew Sparke, "Passports into Credit Cards: On the Borders and Spaces of Neoliberal Citizenship," in *Boundaries and Belonging: States and Societies in the Struggle to Shape Identities and Local Practices*, ed. Joel S. Migdal (Cambridge, UK: Cambridge University Press, 2004), pp. 251–83.

53. Aihwa Ong, *Flexible Citizenship: The Cultural Logics of Transnationality* (Durham, NC: Duke University Press, 1999). It is important to note that the flexible citizenship that Ong describes reinforces the boundedness of political entities (witness the legal troubles of undocumented foreign workers).

54. Pierre Bourdieu, "The School as a Conservative Force: Scholastic and Cultural Inequalities," in *Contemporary Research in the Sociology of Education*, ed. John Eggleston (London: Methuen, 1974), pp. 32–46; Shirley Brice Heath, *Ways with*

Words: Language, Life, and Work in Communities and Classrooms (Cambridge, UK: Cambridge University Press, 1983).

55. Paul Willis, *Learning to Labour: How Working Class Kids Get Working Class Jobs* (New York: Columbia University Press, 1977). Willis belongs to a collective of scholars (E. P. Thompson, Raymond Williams, and Stuart Hall, among others), associated with the British New Left. A major goal of this collective was to debunk the notion of the "trickle-down effect"—the idea that middle-class values simply trickle down to workers. These British scholars investigated society from below and set out to recover the struggles and lived experiences of politically and economically weak groups, their social values and political culture; see E. P. Thompson, "History from Below," in *The Essential E. P. Thompson*, ed. Dorothy Thompson (New York: New Press, 2001), pp. 481–89. The aim was to show, one, how plebeian populations come to experience themselves as a class with different interests and expectations than the middle classes, and, two, how the values people take up as "real" result from historically contingent class interests that mask themselves as cultural values, which in turn mask themselves as natural instincts. This concerted effort at producing narratives that centered on the politically and economically underprivileged populations fit well with the radical politics of the 1960s and 1970s in Western industrialized societies, what was then known as "politics of the people." Not surprisingly, the overall argument of Willis's book is captured in the subtitle: "How Working Class Kids Get Working Class Jobs." Yet in limiting his case study to twelve rebellious "lads," he overlooks the experiences of "ear'oles," those students who identified with middle-class education, and thus he downplays the heterogeneity among working-class youth.

56. Corrigan and Sayer, *The Great Arch*, p. 200.

57. Michel Foucault, *Language, Counter-Memory, Practice*, trans. Donald Bouchard (Ithaca, NY: Cornell University Press, 1977), p. 200.

58. Timothy Mitchell, *Colonising Egypt* (Cambridge, UK: Cambridge University Press 1988), p. 94.

59. See Jean Lave, Paul Duguid, Nancy Fernandez, and Eric Axel, "Coming of Age in Birmingham: Cultural Studies and Conceptions of Subjectivity," *Annual Review of Anthropology* 21 (1992), pp. 257–82; and Michel de Certeau, *The Practice of Everyday Life*, trans. Steven F. Rendall (Berkeley: University of California Press, 1984), pp. 36–37.

60. Barrie Thorne, *Gender Play: Girls and Boys in School* (New Brunswick, NJ: Rutgers University Press, 1993); Ann Solberg, "Negotiating Childhood: Changing Constructions of Age for Norwegian Children," in *Constructing and Reconstructing Childhood: Contemporary Issues in the Sociological Study of Childhood*, ed. Allison James and Alan Prout (London: Falmer, 1997), pp. 126–44; Ann Arnett Ferguson, *Bad Boys: Public Schools in the Making of Black Masculinity* (Ann Arbor: University of Michigan, 2000); Abdullah Sahin, "Critical/dialogic Islamic Education: Modes of Religious Subjectivity towards Islam among British Muslim Youth" (PhD diss., Department of Education, University of Birmingham), 2003.

61. Graeme Turner, *British Cultural Studies: An Introduction* (Boston, MA: Unwin Hyman, 1990), p. 215.

62. As Saba Mahmood suggests, we ought to "think of agency not as a synonym for resistance to relations of domination, but as a capacity for action that historically specific relations of subordination enable and create." See her "Feminist Theory, Embodiment, and the Docile Agent: Some Reflections on the Egyptian Islamic Revival," *Cultural Anthropology* 16 (2001), p. 203.

63. M. M. Bakhtin, "Discourse in the Novel," in *The Dialogic Imagination: Four Essays by M. M. Bakhtin*, ed. Michael Holquist, trans. Caryl Emerson and Michael Holquist (Austin: University of Texas Press, 1981), p. 276. The Soviet linguist purposely distanced himself from a methodological empiricism that privileges the individual as unit of language since a system of signification is not the property of individuals. Thus, he writes that

> All words have the "taste" of a profession, a genre, a tendency, a party, a particular work, a particular person, a generation, an age group, the day and hour. Each word tastes of the context and contexts in which it has lived its socially charged life. (p. 289)

64. See Asif Agha, "Register," *Journal of Linguistic Anthropology* 9 (2000), pp. 216–19.

65. Bakhtin, *The Dialogic Imagination*, p. 272.

66. Richard Bauman and Charles L. Briggs define *entextualization* as the process through which a text is lifted out of a previous and surrounding discourse and inserted into another discourse associated to a new context. See their "Poetics and Performance as Critical Perspectives on Language and Social Life," *Annual Review of Anthropology* 19 (1990), p. 73.

67. Michael Silverstein and Greg Urban, "The Natural History of Discourse," in *Natural Histories of Discourse*, ed. Michael Silverstein and Greg Urban (Chicago: University of Chicago Press, 1996), p. 11. In his discussion on the constraints about text and textual representation, V. N. Vološinov points out that "the stronger the feeling of hierarchical eminence in another's utterance, the more sharply defined will its boundaries be, and the less accessible will it be to penetration by reporting and documenting tendencies from outside." See his *Marxism and the Philosophy of Language* (Cambridge, MA: Harvard University Press, 1973), p. 123.

68. Bakhtin, *The Dialogic Imagination*, pp. 291–96, 337–42.

69. Ludwig Wittgenstein, *Philosophical Investigations* (New York: Macmillan, 1953), par. 66. For an application of Wittgenstein's concept of language games, see Sam Kaplan, "Nuriye's Dilemma: Turkish Lessons of Democracy and the Gendered State," *American Ethnologist* 30 (2003), pp. 401–17.

70. It is with these interrelated issues in mind that the book illustrates Michael Silverstein's point about the "special position of certain institutional sites of social practice, as both *object* and *modality* of ideological expression." See his "The Uses and

Utility of Ideology: A Commentary," in *Language Ideologies: Practice and Theory*, ed. Bambi Schieffelin, Kathryn Woolard, and Paul Kroskrity (New York: Oxford University Press, 1998), p. 136; emphases his.

71. Any analysis of verbal interaction must consider the social context of the speech acts. Clearly, the children's written statements and oral comments were geared toward me; I was both their English teacher and a representative of Western modernity, however vaguely defined. Yet their ability to interpret and act on a school-mediated, state-supervised language presupposes contexts that precede and supersede my presence. As French philosopher Maurice Merleau-Ponty points out, all knowledge inherits meanings already constituted in the past and anticipates meaning still to be constituted in the future; see his *Phenomenology of Perception*, trans. Colin Smith (New York: Humanities Press, 1962), p. 190.

72. Lale Yalçin-Heckmann rightfully criticizes those non-Turkish anthropologists who carry out their research only within the same-sex group; see her "Anthropological Studies on Turks in Turkey and in European Migration: Recent Works in German Language," *New Perspectives on Turkey* 16 (1987), p. 113.

73. Gyan Prakash, "Can the 'Subaltern' Ride? A Reply to O'Hanlon and Washbrook," *Comparative Studies in Society and History* 34 (1992), p. 172. Founding values are those irreducible essences that resist further breakdown of meaning.

74. Historians and anthropologists working on text are not merely copyists. In producing a narrative, they evaluate evidence and select themes and, most importantly, follow a set of rules and procedures in writing about a society. All the same, many scholars fall prey to a naïve epistemology that treats text as a neutral repository of facts. For a fuller discussion of the relation between sources, canons of representation, scholarship, and relations of power, see Sam Kaplan, "Documenting History, Historicizing Documentation: French Military Officials' Ethnological Reports on Cilicia," *Comparative Studies in Society and History* 42 (2002), pp. 344–69; and "Territorializing Armenians: Geo-texts, and Political Imaginaries in French-occupied Cilicia, 1919–1922," *History and Anthropology* 15 (2004), pp. 399–423.

75. Prakash, "Can the 'Subaltern' Ride?" p. 176.

76. The challenge often appears to be indomitable. As feminist and postcolonial critic Gayatri Chakravorty Spivak notes, it is not clear how scholars cannot but distort the voices of politically subordinate people, that is, "hear (out)" those individuals who "speak" outside dominant linguistic and cultural registers; see her provocative essay "Can the Subaltern Speak?" in *Marxism and the Interpretation of Culture*, ed. Cary Nelson and Lawrence Grossberg (Urbana: University of Illinois Press, 1988), pp. 271–313.

CHAPTER TWO

The State of Education

Recalling the past (remembering) occurs only with the intention of making it possible to foresee the future; we look about us from the standpoint of the present in order to determine something, or to be prepared for something.

— IMMANUEL KANT   *Anthropology from a Pragmatic Point of View*

All attempts to naturalize a contingent claim (for example, the legitimacy of a new government) therefore claim to be statements, or representations of fact. By treating them as performatives, and by focusing on the constructedness of their factuality, one can challenge their legitimacy.

— MICHAEL HERTZFELD   *Discourse and the Social Life of Meaning*

Educational reform ranks high on the agenda of governments. Policy makers deliberate on the problems in school systems and articulate policies to meet the current and future needs of society. The plans of action are all intended to build consensus among different political and social groups. To this effect, documentation of education has become central in constituting sovereignty and polity.

This was evident 18 September 1990 with the release of a report on the state of education in Turkey. The report unleashed a coalition crisis between neoliberal industrialists and religious nationalists in the government Motherland (*Anavatan*) Party, commonly known by its acronym ANAP. Over three thousand copies of the report were printed. The press, president, prime minister, and minister of Education each received a copy. Titled *Education in Turkey: Proposals for Structural Adaptations to Problems and Changes* (*Türkiye'de Eğitim, Sorunlar ve Değişime Yapısal Uyum Önerileri*), the 248-page report generated acrimonious debates over how best to prepare Turkish children for faith, market, and nation. Its sponsor was the highly influential Turkish Industrialists' and Businessmen's Association (Türk Sanayici ve İş Adamları Derneği, henceforth TÜSİAD), committed to neoliberal economic policies.[1]

The findings were hardly encouraging for a country aspiring to join the European Community (EC).[2] At the time, Turkey was one of twelve countries in the world that required only five years of schooling. The report mentioned how minimal investment in national education perpetuated long-standing problems typical of underdeveloped nations: double-shift lessons, overcrowded classrooms, poorly trained and underpaid teachers, insufficient vocational training, and disparity in the rates of literacy and school attendance between the sexes and among different income groups. None of these findings were surprising. Rapid population growth, widening disparities in income, regional imbalances, and long-standing prejudices about coeducation had considerably hampered the educational system.

However, the controversy centered on the few pages devoted to state-supported religious-track schools, the İmam-Hatip middle and high schools originally set up for the training of prayer leaders and preachers, and the state-supervised postelementary Qur'an courses intended to teach children to read and memorize the Qur'an.[3] The report implied that the coexistence of religious-track schools and secular ones threatened to implode national unity.

> The gap between the two tracks is increasingly growing. Two separate tracks are producing two different cultural identities, national personalities, dress codes, values, and worldviews, in short, educating two separate youth generations with very different educational profiles. This development contradicts the principle of a single, unified educational system. It also has a negative impact on structurally harmonizing the educational system with democracy. Thus, in accordance with the Law of Unification of Instruction and the Law of Basic Education, it is necessary that the İmam-Hatip schools correspond to the Law of Basic Education and be treated as vocational schools. It is also necessary to limit enrollment in these schools.[4]

In singling out religious-track schools as the major problem in the national educational system, the TÜSİAD report drew attention to the substantial differences between secular and religious policy makers over the social and political purpose of education in Turkey in 1990. The report is what anthropologist Sally Falk Moore defines as a "diagnostic event"—a historical moment revelatory of "ongoing contests and conflicts and competitions" that "display multiple meanings in combination."[5] To put it another way, it is a critical text to explore the historical mutability and flexibility of political concepts and collective experience. From the multiple readings of this report, one can meaningfully identify and explain the political conditions and implications of schooling. Thus, a historical survey of the national debate over children's schooling provides an opportunity to examine central concepts of the national educational system and their political uses, the intersection of multiple global and national discourses, and the close links between education, state, and civil society in Turkey.

Secular Foundations of Education

The Law of Unification of Instruction was one of the first legislative acts of the new Turkish Republic, following the demise of the multiethnic Ottoman Empire in 1922. It placed all educational institutions in the country, other than the military academies, under the sole control of the Ministry of Education. Henceforth, the state alone would supervise all personnel, policies, and curricula. Underlying the legal measure was the belief that the Ottoman Empire had suffered from several educational systems, whose conflicting ideological and pedagogical goals prevented the Turkish people from realizing themselves as a nation. According to this reasoning, only a single educational system could articulate those cultural and moral characteristics that distinguish one people from others.

This solidarist view of education was first formulated by the sociologist Ziya Gökalp (1876–1924), whose ideas about society remain seminal in Turkish pedagogical thought. A leading spokesman of Turkish nationalism in the first two decades of the twentieth century, Gökalp drew on corporate solidarism and collective conscience, as elaborated by the French sociologist Emile Durkheim, to argue that nurture (e.g., schooling and culture) alone determined an individual's level of civilization.[6] This understanding of the relation between education and society stood in contrast to the "nature equals culture" thesis, which indexed moral and intellectual capacities of a people with biological heredity (a common physical and cognitive racial stock).[7] During the late nineteenth century, many Western political leaders and intellectuals resorted to bioracial categories as organizing principles for representing different populations in the world.[8] These categories were commonly used to justify imperial domination over non-Western polities like the late Ottoman Empire.

Thus, crucial to the sociologist's pedagogical mission was showing that the political and economic decline of the Ottoman state did not result from any innate defects in the Turkish people but rather from the multiplicity of incommensurable and incongruent forms of knowledge. To prove his argument, Gökalp typecast citizens to a historical period according to the education they received. Specifically, he chronologically ordered different societal groups into levels of civilization, with Western modernity at the apex. In 1920, he wrote, for example,

> In this country there are three layers of people differing from each other in civilization and education: the common people, the men educated in *medreses*, the men educated in (modern) secular schools. The first still are not freed from the effects of Far Eastern civilization; the second are still living in Eastern civilization; it is only the third group which has had some benefits from Western civilization. That means that one portion of our nation is living in an ancient, another in a medieval, and a third in a modern age. How can the life of a nation be normal with such a threefold life? How can we be a real nation without unifying this threefold education?[9]

The same evolutionary reasoning underlay the sociologist's ideas about political organization. The history of the Turks unfolded, as it were, in secular stages: from primitive tribal origins in Central Asia to medieval Islamic sultanate and, ultimately, a modern nation-state.[10] According to him, the problem was that much of the country's population remained out of sync with global developments in politics and knowledge.

To eradicate the temporal differences among citizens, Gökalp proposed a national curriculum that would combine the best from each civilization while rejecting what he deemed to be their respective shortcomings.

All schoolchildren would identify themselves with Turkish folklore and rational Islam, on the one hand, and with Western technology, on the other. In implementing these pedagogical goals, Gökalp resignified two widely shared concepts of knowledge, *terbiye* and *talim*: until then, they had respectively connoted moral behavior and mastery of Qur'an-centered knowledge; henceforth, they would mean national culture and positive sciences, respectively.[11]

The resignification of Islamic concepts provided the semantic field for associating Turkey with a more Western (read, more modern and secular) conceptualization of polity. Today, the use of the terms together, *terbiye* and *talim*, means formal education: to wit, the name for the powerful Council for Educational Policy, the Talim ve Terbiye Kurulu. This council has sole responsibility in determining the organization of the national educational system, the curricula, textbooks, timetables, appointments, budget, and other pedagogical agendas of the country. Its decisions are binding on all schools—private schools, minority schools, technical schools, as well as public schools.

Many of Gökalp's ideas about education became state credo under the country's first president, Mustafa Kemal Atatürk (1881–1938). Two days before the Law of Unification of Instruction was passed, the statesman took up the argument of one nation, one education. "Two types of education in one country raises two types of persons. If this be the case, it is totally injurious for the aims of uniting sentiment, thought and solidarity. . . . As long as there isn't a single system of education, it is futile to find a way to fashion a nation in which the people share the same thoughts and mentality."[12]

There were substantial differences between the sociologist's ideas about national education and their subsequent implementation in the new Turkish Republic, however. During the single-party regimes of Atatürk and his successor, İsmet İnönü (1924–1946), religion was no longer perceived as an integral component of national identity. Republican statesmen and policy makers, collectively known as Kemalists, or followers of Mustafa Kemal (Atatürk), the president, did their utmost to disassociate themselves from the duality of state and faith (*din-u devlet*), which had served as a viscerally powerful mechanism for political consensus in the Ottoman Empire.[13] And to realize a social memory completely divorced from the religiously sanctioned dynasty, prerepublican Islamic references were excised from the educational system. Secularization entailed the dissolution of otherworldly political goals and the rejection of the absoluteness of authority in religion.

Indicative of the secular turn in the country's political culture was how the new regime applied the Law of Unification of Instruction.[14] First, the Ministry of Education took over all 454 theological seminaries, which until then were the prerogative of the Sharia and Pious Foundations Ministry; none of the seminaries continued operation.[15] Then, a year after the use of Latin characters and Western (i.e., Arabic) numerals was officially mandated in 1928, the study of Arabic and Persian was eliminated in government schools. Finally, the study of Islam was gradually eliminated from the national curricula; by 1938, neither urban nor rural schools offered religious instruction.[16] The curriculum reflected the secular shift in the country's political culture. Given that most rural inhabitants (especially women) did not attend even elementary school, textbooks were often designed with the unschooled family members in mind. School primers, as an anonymous author writing in *Ülkü*, the official journal of the government-run People's Houses argued,

> must address new social and national knowledge to grown-up members
> of the child's household (mother, father, and siblings) who don't attend
> school. . . . The texts and drawings of primers have been composed in a
> manner that children will be able to grasp the differences between the for-
> mer regime and the republican one, and appreciate the good and beautiful
> things the republic has brought. The texts have been reinforced with com-
> parative drawings and graphs. . . . All the texts and drawings have been cho-
> sen for the impact they will leave on village children and adults when read
> and shown.[17]

This desacralization of school knowledge was based on secular positivism, which maintains that reality is experienced only through rational observations, not through a preset, otherworldly cosmology.[18] Universal scientific and causal laws were upheld as the only credible source of truth and, thus, the only reliable means for national salvation.[19] In their attempts at desacralizing cosmos and knowledge, the Kemalists mounted a campaign against Muslim clerics, who had run most of the schools in the Ottoman Empire.

Branded as enemies of science (*ilim düşmanı*) and scholastic obscurantists, clerics were contemptuously dismissed as incapable and unwilling to prepare the youth to deal with the complexity of the contemporary world.[20] Thus, they were blamed for purposely perpetuating illiteracy, material backwardness, and superstitions among the common people. In this sense the critique of the scholastic deceit was part of an ongoing struggle to create a society in line with scientific rationality. It was understood that religion would inevitably give way to science, as a scientific mentality in all its cognitive and intellectual functions would take hold of the masses and liberate them from poverty and ignorance. And in this vein, the Kemalists wrested all educational and cultural institutions from Muslim men of religion, conferring them instead upon the secular state.

The Kemalist dream of a Turkish nation where all thought and actions would conform to secular positivism never came about. The introduction of multiparty elections in 1946 halted the antireligious bias in the national school system. The newly formed Democrat Party (DP), a loose coalition of the national bourgeoisie and rural notables, claimed to represent the national will (*millî irade*) and actively appealed to the electorate's religious sentiments.[21] As a result, the government party, the Republican People's Party, found itself on the defensive and introduced religious classes for fourth and fifth grades in 1949. The following year, following the landslide victory of the DP, the new government began to actively integrate Islam into the political culture of the country, including the opening of Qur'an courses and the religious-track İmam-Hatip junior and senior high schools.[22]

Before this religious shift in the national educational system gained momentum, the military overthrew the government in 1960. The junta accused the DP politicians of undermining the secular legacy of Atatürk and thus of turning the republic into a theocracy.[23] Before returning power to civilians, they had enacted a radically liberal constitution that promoted a democratic social-welfare state. However, the new civil freedoms went in tandem with radicalization of the youth and labor force and, in particular, Marxist organizations and parties that openly opposed their country's membership in Western military alliances, NATO and the Central Treaty Organization (CENTO).[24] Military leaders began to reverse their attitude to religion. As civil violence and labor unrest erupted all over the country during the next two decades, military leaders mobilized the Islamic heritage to foster unity against what they labeled godless communists.[25]

Coincidental to this shift in the military's attitude to religion was the resurgence of religious views in national politics and in the educational system. In this new political climate, two small parties emerged: Colonel Alpaslan Türkeş's irredentist Nationalist Action Party, which advocated the political union of all Turkic peoples within and outside Turkey, and Necmettin Erbakan's overtly religious National Salvation Party, which championed Islamic values for the moral and material rejuvenation of Turkey. Both parties entered into coalitions with the more mainstream parties. They held the swing votes in the deadlock politics between the left-of-center Republican People's Party and the right-of-center Justice Party. In 1977, Erbakan and Türkeş joined the Nationalist Front (*Milliyetçi Cephe*), a coalition led by the Justice Party. Together, the two marginal parties successfully manned the Ministry of Education with their supporters, all the while promoting a more positive assessment of Ottoman Islamic heritage in the curricula. No less important was the political ascendance of the Turkish Islamic Synthesis (Türk İslam Sentezi), a group of intellectuals who advocated greater integration of Islamic values in the nation's political culture. According to their cultural program, more of which will be discussed in the next chapter, Islam provides the nation with a powerful element of historical legitimacy and continuity.

An opportune moment to reinvent a more religious Turkish polity came in 1980. Following a decade-long period of political instability and civil violence, on 12 September 1980, the commander in chief of the Turkish Armed Forces, Kenan Evren, and his colleagues imposed martial law on the whole country.[26] The army had intervened twice before, in 1960 and 1971, but this time the generals considerably tightened the institutional links between the armed forces and the national educational system. Thus, before returning power to civilian politicians three years later, the military instituted a series of educational reforms that sought to prevent at all costs the consolidation of distinct identities that threatened to fragment the nation into a polity riddled with divisions. The religious orientation the military adopted for education manifested itself in the months following the coup. The National Security Council, which they dominated, approved the opening of 92 new İmam-Hatip high schools in addition to the existing 249; at the same time, another 35 İmam-Hatip middle schools were planned. Article 24 of the 1982 military-endorsed constitution provided an even more radical concession to the religious public: "Education and instruction in religion and ethics shall be conducted under State supervision and control. Instruction in religious culture and moral education shall be compulsory in the curricula of primary and secondary schools." The article obligates all school children, from fourth grade till graduation from high school, to take Religion and Morals (*Din kültürü ve ahlâk bilgisi*). The new course combined two previously separated subjects: the obligatory civics and the optional religion lessons. Morals lessons (*Ahlâk dersi*) were made mandatory in 1974, following a coalition agreement between the left-of-center Republican People's Party and the religious National Salvation Party. Until 1983, religious lessons were offered only from fourth to seventh grades. The military's goal was to prevent the growing polarization between youth educated in secular and religious schools by retaining children from traditional backgrounds in the secular-track school system. Furthermore, obliging citizens to accept the new curriculum was intended to foster greater social cohesion. As stated in a confidential report circulated among the members of the junta, "the optional [religious] lessons negatively affected the relations among the students. . . . Fashioning a national culture was not achieved with the [previously optional] religion lessons."[27] Finally, no less important, the military approved graduates of İmam-Hatip high schools enrolling in secular university programs.

It was against this political background that militant secularists, self-designated guardians of secularism (*laikliğin bekçisiyiz*), took issue with the religious orientation in the national educational system. Prominent among the supporters of a single, secular school system was Zekâi Baloğlu, the author of the aforementioned TÜSİAD report.

Baloğlu was well-known for his opposition to religious education. As head of the influential Council of Educational Policy in 1970, he succeeded in having the military close down the junior high sections (grades six to eight) of the İmam-Hatip schools.[28] His success was short-lived, however. Two years later, on account of coalition politics, they were reopened. Since then, the schools grew exponentially in numbers and evolved into preparatory schools admitting girls and boys, most of whom opt to pursue advanced university degrees in secular subjects.[29] In 1952, their first year of operation, there were only 7 İmam-Hatip schools in the entire country. By 1990 there were 389 with a total enrollment of 300,000 students, of which 70,000 were girls, and 10 and 12 percent of all middle school and high school students, respectively, attended an İmam-Hatip school.[30] Parallel to the phenomenal growth of these schools has been that of the Qur'an courses. At the time of the report, there were 4,715 legal (*izinli*) programs that annually enrolled about 150,000 children, in addition to the estimated 20,000 illegal (*kaçak*) ones, which operated independently of state supervision and catered to over 500,000 children.[31]

The TÜSİAD report was only the latest articulation of the veteran educator's anxiety over the growth of İmam-Hatip schools and Qur'an courses.[32] The many pages of text, the battery of references, the pie charts, and the statistics were all used to elicit a visceral reaction against religious-track education.

> Thousands of Qur'an courses . . . are opened and managed by organizations and people, the majority of whom belong to illegal religious brotherhoods. They do not shy from making known the tolerant support they receive from political parties and statesmen. Likewise, İmam-Hatip junior and senior high schools whose enrollment has rapidly increased are providing a separate education for Turkish youth. . . . Graduates of these schools who complete higher education are recruited in general educational and government institutions. Also, with the support of political circles, they enter universities wearing symbolic clothes like the large headscarf and long coat. Finally, the number of prayer rooms in many public organizations and ministries, including National Education, continues to grow.[33]

Understood is that these institutions were breeding grounds for Islamic fundamentalism.

Committed to many of the themes first articulated in the 1920s and 1930s, Baloğlu linked the nation's political destiny with inexorable progress and a commitment to dynamic change. In the report, he blamed Islamic educational institutions and forms of knowledge for arresting Turkey's economic and political liberalization. For him, like his Kemalist predecessors, Islam is an otherworldly, historically backward (*gerileme*) system of thought and action, thereby countering the evolutionary movement toward rational-ism begun in the Enlightenment. Not surprisingly, he frequently associated supporters of a religious worldview with *irtica*, a term of opprobrium that earlier had meant "returning to the past or carrying the past to the present" and now most often refers to religious fanaticism or fundamentalism. Con-versely, he repeatedly characterizes the secular West as imbued with "pro-gressive historical time" (*ilerleme*) and "freedom of thought" (*özgür düşünce*). Thus, he assumed an isomorphism between Turkey and the West to argue that Islamic societies are fundamentally incapable of adopting novel forms of governance, including democracy and individual liberty. Or as he asked rhetorically, "In the entire Islamic world is there freedom, is there democ-racy?"[34] In imputing the radical alterity of Islam, Baloğlu merely tapped into a widely held idea that Islam and Western secularity are two incommensu-rable cultural entities at loggerheads.[35]

Far more condemning was the educator coming close to accusing leading statesmen and government officials of flouting the Law of Unification of In-struction and thereby surreptitiously chiseling away at the secular founda-tions of the country.[36] Any Turkish public figure who disagreed in one form or another with the educator's brand of secularism was assumed to hide ul-terior and suspect motives. As the preceding TÜSİAD report quote sug-gests, the educator implied that the Qur'an courses and İmam-Hatip schools were producing an Islamist electoral base and political leadership intent on transforming Turkey into a theocratic state. To corroborate his claim, he showed that more than two thirds of religious-track graduates applied to law school and public administration and that only one tenth of those enrolled in higher education studied at a divinity school.[37] But what most riled Ba-loğlu were the hiring practices of the Ministry of Education: not only were İmam-Hatip graduates hired to teach the mandatory Religious Culture and Morals lessons but also to man directorates and other senior administrative posts in the ministry.[38]

To stem the growth of religious-track schools and the political influence of their graduates, Baloğlu vigorously campaigned for the application of the 1973 Law of Basic Education. The law raised the mandatory period of pri-mary school education from five to eight years as well as demoted middle schools (grades six to eight) to the second part of primary education. This would have effectively eliminated the religious-track junior high sections and adversely affected enrollment in senior high sections as students would need extra preparatory years of Arabic and Qur'anic sciences to succeed in their studies. Furthermore, the educator would have İmam-Hatip high schools revert to their former status of vocational schools, training preachers and prayer leaders only. Were Baloğlu's recommendations implemented, they would have had far-reaching implications. One, all female students would be removed since, on account of their sex, they cannot be hired as religious functionaries. Two, graduates would be prevented from enrolling in secular university programs. Three, the number of schools would be considerably reduced as the Directorate of Religious Affairs hires less than seventy thousand new personnel a year. As to attendance at full-time Qur'an courses, Baloğlu would restrict it to graduates of middle schools and limit attendance to the briefer summer courses to only pupils who completed fifth grade. The overall idea was that by slashing enrollment in religious-track schools and Qur'an courses, their political impact on society would be considerably curbed.

Prominent public figures who supported a strict separation of state and religion in the national educational system welcomed the report. It was cause for some hope that it would help prevent (what they perceived to be) the makings of a fundamentalist theocracy and a reactionary society. Not surprisingly, the Social Democratic Populist Party (SDPP), the main opposition party at the time, hailed the report as "scientific and objective."[39] Two weeks later, claiming that "a merciless cultural warfare and moral collapse is increasingly prevailing with a backward, medieval understanding of education," the opposition submitted a no-confidence motion against the government.[40] The motion did not pass.

Even more vocal in their outrage over the political implications of religious-track schools was the secular press. For decades, this press ran stories on the upsurge of religious activities in public schools and other state institutions. It often directed readers' attention to the ratio between primary schools and mosques. The liberal daily *Güneş* claimed that there was one mosque for every 857 citizens, one primary school for every 1,000.[41] In a similar vein, the left-of-center newspaper *Cumhuriyet*, then considered the preeminent newspaper in Turkey, gave wide coverage to the organization Call for Secularism, which demonstrated against the Directorate of Religious Affairs in the capital city of Ankara.[42] The demonstrators protested the use of endowed land for a projected mosque. Marching under the banner "A secular, democratic, and modern Turkey" (*Laik, demokratik, çağdaş Türkiye*), the protestors demanded that the land be used for an elementary school and green park space. Although the poorly attended protest failed to accomplish its goals, the newspaper article provided a forum to disseminate the secularist demonstrators' grievances. Prisons have not been spared from the intense scrutiny of the secular press. *Güneş*, for example, reported that the majority of journals available to prisoners were religious in nature. Prisoners may seem an ideal captive audience, but as the article admitted, the most widely read book in Turkish prisons remained Henri Charrière's *Papillon*, a novel based on its author's escape from a penal colony in French Guyana.[43]

Secular journalists have not limited their criticism to institutional forms of religious knowledge. They have regularly accused devout politicians of practicing *takiye*, that is to say, dissimulating their true intentions (e.g., instituting a theocracy through education). As anthropologist Talal Asad notes in the context of Turkey, secularists find "deprivatized religion . . . intolerable . . . primarily because of the motives imputed to their opponents rather than anything the latter have actually done. The motives signal the potential entry of religion into space already occupied by the secular."[44] It is this unspecified threat that motivated journalist Güngör Mengi to assert in an editorial for the mass daily *Sabah* that "İmam–Hatip schools are protected as innocent appearing institutions . . . when, in fact, they are aimed at dismantling the secular state."[45] To make his point, Mengi claimed that, over the past six years, two thirds of the district administrators (*kaymakam*) that the Ministry of Interior appointed had received their education in İmam-Hatip schools. The following day, *Güneş* informed its readers that one fifth of the directors presiding over district education committees hailed from divinity schools.[46]

The campaign against a perceived religiosity in national education equally enlisted caricaturists. In reaction to the growing militancy of religious students, the popular weekly satirical journal *Gırgır* published a cartoon showing boys and girls dressed in visibly non-Western clothes exiting from two adjacent İmam-Hatip schools.[47] In the background are the police who assume that the student body is demonstrating for a theocratic state. As the policemen are on the verge of dispersing the students with their clubs, a portly bearded man, wearing a skullcap and fiddling with his prayer beads, puts out his hand, saying: "Stop! Nobody is demonstrating. It's time for the high school students to leave school. Everybody is going home." The caricature of the students' dress—the girls' all-enveloping garments and the boys' skullcaps and baggy shalwar pants—were all designed to invoke a threatening throwback to a prerepublican society when religious norms prevailed. Several secular newspapers reproduced this cartoon, along with one that first appeared on the front page of *Cumhuriyet*. The latter cartoon drew upon a well-known photograph of Atatürk demonstrating Latin characters of the new Turkish alphabet, one of the major reforms he instituted so that the country would be in line with Western forms of knowledge; until 1928, Turkish was written in Arabic script. The cartoonist showed Atatürk teaching a child the characters *A, B, C, D, S, V, K* and *M*; the boy, in turn, answers back pronouncing the letters as if they were Arabic letters ("Elif, Be, Djim, Dal, Sin, Vav, Kaf, Mim"). To the average Turkish citizen, the caricaturist's message was clear: the dead statesman's reforms had backfired.[48]

It is this sense of betrayal of Kemalist ideals that motivated the author of the TÜSİAD report and his secularist allies in politics and media to insist that religious forms of knowledge be removed from the public sphere, that graduates of Qur'an courses and İmam-Hatip schools confine themselves to the mosque. Otherwise, they feared an imminent political cataclysm, namely, the end of the secular republican regime, the beginning of an illiberal theocracy.

Unity in Diversity

Not all shared in Baloğlu's apocalyptic scenario. Nor did he have the last word on the state of education in Turkey. It was not long before Avni Akyol, then the minister of Education, took the counteroffensive and defended the government's educational policies. In the ministry's flagship journal, *Millî Eğitim* (*National Education*), the minister dedicated nine pages to bring forth counterclaims discrediting the reliability of the report. While Akyol did concede that, "in a rapidly changing, developing, and growing society," the educational system had suffered from "some unexpected and unwanted results," he was not of the opinion that these difficulties warranted a public outcry.[49] Writing this article invariably brought to bear ideas about his reading public (ministry officials and teachers). He anticipated producing negative reactions to the report, on the one hand, and forging a unity of outlook, on the other.

Whenever the minister critically parsed the report, he took recourse to a highly formalized academic prose, replete with social scientific concepts.[50] In mobilizing the language of scientific research and framing the discussion in dispassionate, nonjudgmental terms, he set about dismissing the report's research methods as unreliable and its findings as invalid. Moreover, his mastery of academic categories and discourses indexed his expertise on education. Unlike his immediate predecessors at the ministry, Akyol was a professional educator who had earned a doctorate in the United States. Aware of his status as research scholar, the minister used his authority to question the academic credibility and credentials of Baloğlu. According to Akyol, the report suffered from "serious deficiencies as a result of a single person preparing it, the lack of systematic analysis, and incomplete collection of information."[51] Throughout the article, the minister repeatedly invoked the need for proper scientific methods in order to judge the government's educational aims and means. This is evident in how Akyol subtly belittled the research strategies Baloğlu used to produce the report. To wit, "In this report, social demand and manpower-needs planning was used. In our times, however . . . the most widely used method to evaluate productivity is cost-efficiency analysis."[52] Further into the article, the minister couched a far stronger criticism of the model and techniques used in the report in a highly abstract language chock full of social scientific neologisms and passive constructions, many of which his readers would have not fully fathomed. "In preparing this report, a survey research and evaluation approach was used, and accordingly, the interpretations and assessments are based on this approach. In other words, it is clear that the report was prepared from gathering information from available sources. Thus, it is unclear whether the report findings are related to either a theoretical or applied experimental method. For this reason it is impossible to make a scientific evaluation."[53] The overall effect was to impart impersonal, objective information that transcended the minister's personal views. Rather, his mastery of pedagogical sciences gave his criticism of the report the stamp of referential credibility. Lest his readers misunderstood his academic language, the minister elsewhere explicitly accused the report of "sensationalism and misleading information," of "wrong interpretations and gross mistakes."[54]

While Akyol certainly voiced strong disapproval about the report, he avoided attacking directly its sponsors, the TÜSİAD industrialists. Rather, he commended them for their charitable involvement in the country's schools and even described their chairman Cem Boyner as a "valuable realist and idealist."[55] In this context, the minister switched from an impersonal academic language to a more intimate, all-inclusive one that expressed and confirmed national solidarity. In his capacity as a public official and spokesman of the Turkish nation, he invoked political unity, exemplified by his repeated use of personal suffixes and personal pronouns (the collective *we*), whether discussing "the employment of our youth" or conveying "our thanks to our invaluable industrialists and businessmen."[56]

The minister's subordinates were not the only recipients of his remarks, even if he needed their moral support. Far more decisive were the opinions of his political colleagues and the entire citizenry. In fact, the minister did not limit his remarks to writing. Nor did he always express himself in a conciliatory tone. In an interview he gave to the widely distributed daily *Türkiye*, which adopts an ultra nationalistic conservative outlook, he questioned the scientific credentials of the author and sponsors of the report.[57] "Members of TÜSİAD are known to criticize National Education. I had once told them that you are not a scientific institution. You could have asked specialists to do scientific research. If some might consider Zekâi Baloğlu to be a specialist, I do not. For a person to be a researcher he must be a professional academic [*akademisyen*]. He doesn't even have a bachelor's degree. Would I hand over an academic topic to such a person? The report is not an academic one. Nor is it objective."[58] The face-to-face conversation with the journalist, which mimicked a personal dialogue between the minister and the industrialists, strongly contrasted with both the authoritative language of science and the warm language of solidarity he adopted in the article he wrote in the ministry's journal. The upshot was that no outside body could call on any expert to verify the state's ability to educate the country's youth.

The Ministry of Education was in no hurry to apply the 1973 Law of Basic Education, which would have required all pupils from first to eighth grades to attend the secular-track school system. As Abdurrahman Dilipak, one of the most vocal religious critics of the country's secular policies, pointed out in his controversial book *This Is Not My Religion: A Critical Approach to the Teaching of "Official Religion,"* "were a child to study for eight years at an elementary school, he would lose three years of Arabic or Persian; nor does he learn there the Qur'an, the hadiths, jurisprudence, and religious commentaries."[59] In any case, several months before the release of the report, the minister of Education had made it clear that he had no intention of either closing down the junior high section of İmam-Hatip schools or denying its graduates entrance into secular university programs. To a question about the government's position on religious-track education, Akyol responded, "This society is not irreligious. The state has no religion; the state can't be religious. But people have beliefs. . . . We teach Islam. Go and see for yourself. All over the world, religious instruction is mandatory. In Europe and America, there are churches in school backyards. Of course, Christians teach Christianity; Muslims, Islam. . . . Religion means morals."[60] In his criticism of Baloğlu's report, he granted a religiously tolerant West hierarchical eminence in defining the acceptable parameters of school knowledge in Turkey. Ubiquitous Western ideas about schooling and democracy served to advance an educational agenda that gave priority to religion.

Conservative public figures, many of whom were members of the government and known in political circles as the "Holy Alliance" (*Kutsal İttifak*), rallied around the minister. To them, religion is as central to national collective identity as history and language. Thus argued former minister of Education Ali Naili Erdem. During his tenure at the ministry (1975–1977), he had played an instrumental role in expanding religious-track education. As he stated in an interview he gave to the daily *Türkiye*, ten days after the public release of the TÜSİAD report, "All nations educate their people in conformity with their culture. A French person cannot educate a Turkish person. Nor can an American school educate a Japanese person. Are children who graduate from these [religious-track] schools growing up outside Turkish culture? No. Are they enemies of our history? No. Are they enemies of our language and religion? No."[61] It was not coincidental that the former minister appealed to culture; the concept as first formulated by Gökalp is taken to be an impartial determinant of a national society in Turkish political discourse. It also provided the basis and rationale for establishing truth claims that uphold religion as the crucial link between education, population, and governance in Turkey and, thus, for systematically indexing distinctions between Turkey and Western polities. Nor was his emphasis on enemies accidental. Devout policy and opinion makers have long deemed an inviolable religious education (which they associate with cultural authenticity) as best able to prevent civil strife as well as to ensure social and political stability within the country.[62] For example, Fehmi Koru, the chief columnist of the Islamic newspaper *Zaman*, attacked the TÜSİAD industrialists and their sponsored educational report for implying that religious-track schools breed a youth intent on sabotaging the nation. "Businessmen are trying to clip the wings of these institutions which supposedly breed 'terrorists.' But has it been proven that many who graduated from İmam-Hatip schools are involved in terrorist activities and robberies in the country? . . . Are there many venal officials, immoral and dishonorable doctors, and plagiarist faculty among İmam-Hatip graduates?"[63] According to this logic, those citizens who purposely distanced themselves from their religious heritage experienced profound alienation from the national society and were liable to betray their country. Thus, Hikmet Tanyu, a professor of comparative religion and a major figure in the pan-Turkist movement, wrote in his *Enemies of Islam and Believers in Allah*, a work then widely circulated among educated religious readers, "People who do not know their history, their national values, . . . the system of belief in their society, . . . in other words, themselves, will become foreign and will easily become tools of foreign ideologies and interests."[64] This was equally the gist of a cartoon that appeared in the same issue as Fehmi Koru's editorial. The cartoonist suggested that the secular press consistently dishonors the country with slander about religious fundamentalism: he drew two journalists frantically searching files, and one says to the other, "If you cannot come up with a report on fundamentalism to send abroad, then give them the TÜSİAD educational report."[65] Associating (potential or real) treason with enemies of religion (*din düşmanı*) is a highly effective means of arousing popular animosity toward secularists' worldviews and thereby questioning their right to Turkish citizenship. Thus, Oğuzhan Asıltürk, the general secretary of the overtly religious Welfare Party, characterized the report as another aspect of the "ongoing enmity to religion."[66]

It is along this line of reasoning that religious public figures have linked the loss of spiritual values in the country with a retreat (*gerileme*) in progressive, historical time. Much of the blame they have pinned on a political culture and educational system that, since the nineteenth-century Tanzimat (Westernizing) reforms, first attenuated, later eliminated, public access to the Islamic heritage. To them, the ensuing mimicry of Western ideas and lifestyles put an end to the age of science (*ilim çağı*) that began with the prophet Muhammad's revelation of the Qur'an. Rather, Ottoman reformers and their secular republican successors had, as it were, reinstituted the pre-Islamic Age of Ignorance (*Cahiliye*) and attendant moral and social problems (such as white-collar crime, prostitution, and civil unrest). In other words, unconscious imitation (*şuûrsuz taklitçilik*) of the West had reinstated ignorance (*cehalet*) among the people.[67] The religious intelligentsia did not satisfy themselves with inverting the secular reading of national history. They also associated Islamic forms of knowledge and education with the spirit of progress and the possibility of human improvement. Thus, Mehmet Kutlular, the owner of *Yeni Asya*, a major religious daily, marshaled philology to recast the long-maligned term *irtica* to its original meaning—recovery of Islamic ideals—to positively assess the resurgence of religious education in the country. "If Islam becomes its master once more, going back [*rücu*] will rise again. The İmam-Hatip schools and the Qur'anic courses have opened up. All of this is part of *rücu*."[68]

But the person who most ranged against Baloğlu's report was none other than President Turgut Özal, founder of the then ruling ANAP and prime minister from 1983 to 1989. A devout Muslim, Özal made a point of reconciling personal piety with neoliberal economics and a democratic political culture. During his prime ministership, he had outraged secularists, first, for making the hajj, or pilgrimage to Mecca, and then for publicly stating, "The state is secular, I'm not. I'm a Muslim." Not surprisingly, the president found Baloğlu's conceits about religious-track education to be fundamentally undemocratic. For the president, democracy begins with democratization of knowledge, that is to say, with a multiplicity of school programs for different sectors of Turkish society. In other words, the state was held accountable to meet the educational needs and desires of society—a volte-face to the long-standing top-down approach to education in Turkey. Moreover, as he noted in an interview to the daily *Sabah*, İmam-Hatip schools, which are for the most part built using private citizens' funds, catered to rural children, who otherwise would not attend middle school.[69] Thus, Özal was of the opinion that two tracks of education (secular and religious) fostered democracy in the country.[70] Similarly, Hasan Celal Güzel, who had served as minister of Education in Turgut Özal's government between 1987 and 1989, declared that "the most important defining characteristic of a democracy is to act according to social demands, . . . to the desires of the community."[71] The Islamist journalist Ahmet Selim went further. In an op-ed piece for *Zaman*, he claimed that Baloğlu was a despot, exploiting the concept of "unification of education" (*tevhid-i tedrisat*) to institute de facto "separate educational systems" (*tecrid-i tedrisat*) for different sectors of the population.[72] In short, he accused the secular educator of purposely sowing divisiveness, the ultimate crime against the Turkish state. As far as Selim and his religious-minded readers were concerned, genuine democracy would be realized only if the state provided equal opportunities for all children, irrespective of their social and educational backgrounds.

The religious nationalists' interpretation of the report accomplished an amazing reversal of the Turkish state's pedagogical mission. Whereas Baloğlu and the secular business community were eager to impose secular positivist ideals as the means for national unity, his religious opponents took up the idea of national unity to unravel the secular foundations of the school system. The latter selectively retrieved certain themes from the secular republican regime, in anticipation of a future in which Islamic values once more prevailed. The particular meanings they ascribed to religion and secularity anticipated a re-semantization of the country's political culture. To this effect, they directed a series of oppositions—"enemies of science" / "enemies of religion," "unification of education" / "separation of education," "reactionary fundamentalism" / "recourse to the past," and "progress" / "backwardness"—to their own social objectives, thereby reconstituting the semantic field of state, nation, and civil society. It is along these lines of thought that one can make sense of the statement of Hannah Arendt, political philosopher and scholar of totalitarianism: "The quest for meaning, which relentlessly dissolves and examines anew all accepted doctrines and rules, can at any moment turn against itself, produce a reversal of the old values, and declare these contraries to be new values."[73]

Documenting Education

For all the uproar, the divisive issues the TÜSİAD report raised and the growing differences between secular and religious public figures were common knowledge. Polarized discussion about national education is a standard feature of contemporary politics in Turkey. The politicization of education has arisen in the contexts of heightened national self-consciousness in which crises of republican identity are articulated as crises of youth and moral-political orders. After all, which worldviews, social practices, and cultural norms will dominate the school system, arguably the most accessible and influential of all state institutions, has a considerable impact on the country's future. In this regard, newspapers have played a central role in whipping up controversy over education. They regularly cover debates over educational curricula and programs, and the featured articles and editorial pieces are as much geared to news value as a concern for the nation's children. In turn, influential public figures turn to the media to publicize their opinions. For three weeks after the publication of the TÜSİAD report, the press reported on the reactions of statesmen and opinion makers. They varied considerably: some favored eliminating the Qur'an courses and religious-track secondary schools; others, increasing their numbers and expanding the religious curriculum; still others, maintaining the uneasy status quo.

Despite their differences over national education, the intellectual maneuvers that the author of the report and his ideological opponents used to sway policy makers and public opinion reveal the processual nature of producing education in text. The debates the report generated raised fundamental issues about the nexus between documentation, state, and civil society, on the one hand, and between crisis, youth, and the future, on the other.

Policy documents in the form of reports are more than position papers. By definition, they inscribe as well as produce policy; that is to say, they organize knowledge and prescribe what designated readers are charged to know and act upon. Through documenting facts on the ground, the author of a policy document establishes and confirms a political imaginary with which he identifies. The evidence and evidentiary practices are all designed to naturalize contingent claims and thus produce a sense of reliability and credibility for its readers. Of course, neither the author of the TÜSİAD report nor its sponsors had control over how the findings would be assessed. A sense of hazard always attends the reception of a text.[74] Well before the public release of the report, entrenched factors such as the different political entities and their respective allies in the media served to diffuse its political aims. The terms and ideas Baloğlu used to impose an authoritative view of the state of education in the country were particularly vulnerable to divergent interpretations as individuals mobilized well-established cultural schemas and political visions at variance with one another.

Yet however much the veteran educator failed to elicit cooperation from all parties, both his supporters and detractors assumed that a direct correlation between education, people, and state was normative and that any disruption of this correlation was an aberration. All regarded the highly centralized educational system as a power-neutral means to social and political ends; they equated national unity with cultural uniformity and, furthermore, believed that this equation can be achieved only through education. Key to this reasoning is treating Turkishness as an inviolable fact that reflects an a priori reality. Here, neoliberal secularism and Islamism emerge as different guises for a culture of statism where different politically motivated associations compete to claim a singular Turkish culture for society at large. All parties tapped into the idea that the educational curricula should reflect, express, and generate systematic cognitive, behavioral, affective, and moral ideas that collectively distinguish the Turkish nation from other nations. This steadfast belief in the fixity and uniqueness of national identity elides internal differences among citizens precisely because both secular and religious public figures anticipated surpassing the present experience of disunity.

Vesting themselves with a pedagogical mission of general interest, the secular business community could claim a moral prerogative to produce educational propositions on behalf of and reflecting national interests. This claim to be solely motivated for the public good granted the TÜSİAD report a prescriptive force in the debates over state education. The text they supported was a particularly effective means to produce an authoritative version of the public sphere all the while de-legitimating alternative interpretations of polity and society. Nevertheless, the reactions that it elicited made evident the inner complexity and political volatility of the state (machinery) as much as they revealed how the boundaries separating the political and the educational spheres are seldom clear-cut. The report, which reflected the views of business organizations operating independently of state institutions, became perceived as a critical and threatening artifact of statecraft. Its legitimacy and authority derived in no small measure from the author's past experiences as a major policy maker in the Ministry of Education. Through such a text, industrialists and businesspeople sought moral and pedagogical leadership of the country as they took it upon themselves to shape, guide, manage, and regulate the national educational system and foremost its organizational structure and ways of reasoning. In this endeavor, they simultaneously appealed to state and society: on the one hand, they tried to sway policy makers to adopt their educational goals; on the other, they sought public consent of these goals through the media. All the same, the public release of the report posed a threat to state officials—less because of its controversial (but well-known) contents than the fact that a nongovernmental body usurped the right of state officials to define national agendas.

Blurring the distinction between state and civil society is not particular to the neoliberal industrialists and businessmen. Religious nationalists have rhetorically figured themselves as representatives of society struggling against an antagonistic secular state to reclaim a national culture for themselves and their life practices.[75] This rhetorical conceit has not prevented religious political figures from actively lobbying their views about polity and society in state institutions. A month after the report was released, conservative members of parliament belonging to ANAP drafted a motion to open prayer rooms (*mescit*) in elementary and middle schools and require children to learn how to pray.[76] Although the parliament's Education Commission rejected the motion, their devout constituencies expected them to persist in meeting what they considered to be their children's spiritual needs.

Thus, despite the wide spectrum of views among journalists, politicians, public intellectuals, and their respective publics, all have reinforced the centralization of the educational system, while differentially redefining the meaning of Turkish state and society. Fueling the divisive debates over the relation between education, state, and civil society has been a state-of-emergency discourse. The TÜSİAD report was one of many responses to a perceived crisis in national life all the while substantiating the reality of a crisis-ridden nation. Bewildered by the radical changes in the educational system that no longer sustained his secular worldview, Baloğlu discursively transformed the collision of two worldviews into an explosive catastrophe waiting to happen and immersed the public in the panic of his discourse. Or as de Certeau would argue, the veteran educator transmuted the misfortune of his theory into a theory of misfortune.[77] Here, crisis becomes a fundamental moral concept to indict current educational policies as well as to raise fears about the future life course of the country. To believe the report, state policies had failed to make a positive correlation between educational input and social output. This failure was framed in relation to incremental progress, a teleology that saturates pedagogical discourses in the country. Progress, here, refers not simply to technological developments but, above all, to a historical form of agency, leading to a better and radically different future.[78]

Central to this teleological reasoning is the belief that how the educational system treats children will determine the future political, economic, and moral roles that young men and women will assume as adults. All sides positioned the youth as a risk group; youth either posed a threat to the nation's future or inspired hope. Schoolchildren come to epitomize the future. But for many opinion makers, they seemed to embody a future full of uncertainties and anxieties—ranging from unemployment, political intolerance, and immorality to crime—all of which could wreak social and political havoc.

This fear of an imminent national apocalypse draws on widely held ideas about the critical role that schools play in socializing children. In Turkey, the schoolchild is treated as an impressionable, raw material malleable enough to be turned into a rationally responsible citizen. Childhood is treated as a period of control and passivity, during which the educational system transforms children from innocent natural beings to civilized individuals, ready to be admitted into adult society.[79] Thus, for example, two weeks after the 1980 military coup, the military-appointed counselor for the Ministry of Education, Abdullah Nişancı, inaugurated the new school year with a statement that, during the first five years of schooling, "the desired model of person can be easily shaped" precisely because teachers can "fill the still empty and untarnished heads and hearts of our dear small ones."[80] In this vein, the pupil is often characterized as putty that the teacher kneads into shape.

This image finds expression, for example, in the poem "My Dear

Teacher," which appeared in the fifth-grade reader: "I am a child. . . . I am very soft dough / Never been kneaded before / Ready to be put into any shape."[81] Instructors, in turn, take on the role of surrogate parents, who provide the necessary nurture for the children's eventual integration into adult society. In fact, the entire pedagogical apparatus constantly deploys a language normally associated with family and patriotism—both domains of disinterested love and solidarity. The state-run school becomes simultaneously a national extension of the home and a domestic version of the nation. In effecting this move from home to school to nation and back, the curriculum is replete with a vocabulary usually reserved for family members. Pupils are "siblings" to one another, and the teachers and principals are "parents" who manage well, supervise, and support this familial order. Thus, the second-grade regional life science textbook introduces the school as the pupils' "second home," except that it has many more "brothers and sisters" and more sets of "parents."[82]

In contrast to the nurturing environment of the state-run school, the extrascholastic environment is characterized as having a potentially deleterious influence on children. The standard instructional manual, *The Elementary School Program*, explicitly states as much: "The teacher must draw the pupils' attention to the wrong and harmful traditions which they encounter in their families and persuade them to get rid of these traditions."[83] In the hope of immunizing children from the wrong knowledge, educators and policy makers enlist an arsenal of medical tropes—the language of germ (*mikrob*) warfare, contagion (*bulaşma*), and inoculation and inculcation (*aşılama*).[84] Thus, incumbent on the state is to supply the vaccinations, to continue with the clinical metaphor. The trick is to administer the correct dose (*doz*) of knowledge; an overdose, as it were, would debilitate the children's immune system. Thus, a ministerial directive warns eighth-grade civics instructors "that an extreme 'dose' of examples taken from other subjects must be avoided," lest the pedagogic means overtake the national ends.[85] Depending on the type of instruction, school knowledge can either sap or boost the health of the nation and its citizens.

Education, here, is an exogenous entity that can either strengthen or undermine the student body and, thus, determine the country's future viability. In the very efforts to define and consolidate national education, adherents and opponents of religious-track schools have taken recourse to

psychological tropes to determine the collective psyches and political pro-
files of schoolchildren. To neoliberal industrialists and their secular supporters, the ever-expanding enrollment in Qur'an courses and İmam-Hatip
schools was producing a student body indisposed to a capitalist and democratic mind-set. According to them, Turkey ideally should be brought within
the orbit of the industrial and financial West rather than the Islamic Middle
East, and for that purpose, Western secular forms of knowledge were pre-
sumed to be the only viable instrument for change. Religious nationalists, on
the other hand, were of the opinion that cultural survival of Turkey de-
pended on inculcating greater religiousness in the youth: reimmersion in Islamic values provided the ultimate moral anchor for the Turkish people.

In this Gramscian war of positions, both sides repeatedly circulated what
anthropologist Begoña Aretxaga called "mirroring phantoms"—Islamist
and Western phantoms.[86] The secularists were haunted by the phantom of
Islam impeding the country's ability to integrate in an increasingly globalized economy; the religious, by that of a West, destroying the moral fiber of
the country. Both of these phantoms have a long history in Turkish political
thought. I recall here my discussion in the previous chapter about the confrontation between a provincial governor and a local preacher over the
meanings of Islam, the West, and education in the 1870s. All the same, definitions of subversive and desired collective phantoms are replete with inde-
terminacy and contingency because the political and social contexts, in
which these phantoms were established, maintained, contested, and transformed, have changed over time. In the context of post-1980-coup Turkey,
as long-established (Kemalist) state orthodoxies no longer held sway in the
political culture, the distinctions between the West and Islam were once
again up for grabs. Then as now, ambivalent and vacillating representations
in the political sphere precluded any semblance of national consensus over
the future course of education, state, and civil society.

Envoi

To many readers, this particular case study—the struggle between secular
and religious public figures over the future direction of national education in

1990 Turkey—is no longer relevant. Or they take for granted that representations of education in text are forms of objectification. Yet the ethical and political issues underlying this struggle and its representations perdure. Baloğlu and his allies felt themselves on the defensive not only because they believed that they were losing the cultural war over the nation's children but, more importantly, because they had failed to reconcile national unity and democracy with educational diversity. Their ideological opponents were no more satisfied. As far as the latter were concerned, they had so far failed to implement religious values at all levels of national education. Keeping religion out of the public school system, they argued, precluded full inclusion of all citizens. What fueled and continues to fuel the sometimes acrimonious debate is the systematic state intervention in children's political socialization. This has spurred policy and opinion makers to continue to lobby their claims and repudiate the opposing case, in short, to act as moral agents in education. After all, what children—the next generation of adult citizens—will acquire during their school years is believed to have an enormous impact on the future viability of polity and society.

As much as the TÜSİAD report galvanized the attention of politicians, journalists, businesspeople, and public intellectuals, the townspeople of Yayla were indifferent to the educational debates among secular and religious public figures. While there was no popular demand for a religious-track school, parents intended to continue sending their elementary school-age children to the local preacher to learn the prayers during the summer recess. At the time of the release of the report, what captured the immediate attention of the local community was Iraq's invasion of Kuwait and its impact on the local economy. As soon as Iraq closed its borders with Turkey, many truck drivers found themselves without a livelihood. To make matters worse, in this relatively poor town, almost all the households were struggling with price hikes for fuel and electricity as well as the increase in value-added taxes, all of which they blamed on the government's neoliberal policies. Given the immediate economic concerns of the townspeople, their indifference to the educational report was to be expected.

Yet the townspeople were far from indifferent to many of the issues raised in the report: issues such as unequal access to economic resources, unemployment, politics of biological reproduction, gender relations and identities, and ethnic and religious differences were widely discussed and debated in coffeehouses and homes. Of central importance was the debate over cultural authenticity and collective national identity. This particularly divisive issue articulates a moral universe that lies at the intersection of education, faith, and nation. I will therefore discuss in the next chapter how this articulation plays itself out among schoolchildren and their families in the local community.

Notes

1. Founded in 1971, TÜSİAD in 1990 consisted of the largest holding companies and the most prominent industrial entrepreneurs.

2. In November 1993, the European Community became known as the European Union (EU).

3. Official Qur'an courses take four to five years of study to complete.

4. Zekâi Baloğlu, *Türkiye'de eğitim, sorunlar ve değişime yapısal uyum önerileri* (İstanbul: TÜSİAD Yayınları, 1990), p. 133.

5. Sally Falk Moore, "Explaining the Present: Theoretical Dilemmas in Processual Ethnography," *American Ethnologist* 14 (1987), pp. 730, 735.

6. Gökalp shared much in common with Durkheim, his intellectual mentor. Both men applied the new discipline of sociology to education to bring about the political consolidation and moral regeneration of their respective societies. No doubt their outsider status colored their nationalist version of educational sociology. Durkheim, who came from a long-established line of rabbis in Alsace-Lorraine, broke with Judaism altogether and set about creating a secular morality for Third Republic France. Gökalp, having failed to persuade the Kurds in his native province of Diyarbakir (eastern Anatolia) to adopt nationalism, set out to reorganize the Turkic world into a morally homogeneous and politically exclusive nation. See Ahmed Emin, *Turkey in the War* (New Haven, CT: Yale University Press, 1930), p. 190.

7. To those detractors who, on account of his Kurdish ancestry, called into question his allegiance to the new Turkish nation, Gökalp responded, "I learned through my sociological studies that nationality is based solely on upbringing" (quoted in Taha Parla, *The Social and Political Thought of Ziya Gökalp 1876–1924* [Leiden, Netherlands: E. J. Brill, 1985], p. 11).

8. See George W. Stocking, "Bones, Bodies, Behavior," in *Bones, Bodies, Behavior: Essays on Biological Anthropology*, ed. George W. Stocking (Madison: University of Wisconsin Press, 1988), pp. 3–17.

9. Ziya Gökalp, *Turkish Nationalism and Western Civilization* (London: Allen & Unwin, 1959), p. 278.

10. Gökalp, *Turkish Nationalism*, p. 271.

11. Apt equivalences to the concepts of *talim* and *terbiye* are the German notions of character formation (*Bildung*) and education (*Erziehung*), respectively the emotional and cognitive development of children. Already during the final decade of the Ottoman Empire, Gökalp's ideas found expression in the 1911 Universal Primary Education Regulations. According to the regulations, the curriculum would inculcate "the new generation of school children with religious and national traditions, on the one hand, and prepare it for the present-day conditions and necessities." Maarif-i Umumiye Nezareti, "Mekâtib-i İptidâiyye-i Umumiye Talimatnamesi," 23 September 1329, p. 1.

12. Mustafa Kemal Atatürk, *Atatürk'ün Söylev ve Demeçleri II* (Ankara: Maarif Matbaası, 1952), p. 160.

13. The Ottoman sultan went by the titles Caliph of all Muslims on Earth and Protector of the Two Holy Cities (Mecca and Medina). In turn, the sultanate was imbued with sacredness, as befit its official name—the Well-Protected (by God) Domains (*memalik-i mahrusa*). As all state apparatuses garnered their legitimacy through close association with Islam, Ottoman officials harnessed the curriculum to those civic and moral values that shored up the religious-political foundation of the empire; see Deringil, *Well-Protected Domains*; and Benjamin C. Fortna, *Imperial Classroom: Islam, the State and Education in the Late Ottoman Empire* (Oxford, UK: Oxford University Press, 2002).

14. The republican regime recognized that religion was too powerful a force to be left in the hands of potential opponents. Islam would either be eliminated or subordinated to the republican regime. Kemalist policy makers chose to do both. The abolition of the caliphate on 3 March 1924 portended the secular character of the nascent republic. The sultan no longer reigned as caliph or spiritual head of Islam. That same year, the government eliminated religious courts, which in turn prepared for the introduction of the secular Civil Code and the Criminal Code two years later; the two codes were respectively based on Swiss and Italian ones. These policies were aimed at removing religion from all public institutions not directly concerned with worship. Republican statesmen did not tolerate any autonomous religious organizations or activities, however. The state remained responsible for all appointments and salaries of Muslim preachers and clerics. And to stem any religious opposition to the government, the Parliament promulgated the Law for the Maintenance of Order in 1925; Article 1 made "exploitation of religion toward political ends" a capital punishment. Immediately following this law, the government outlawed all religious brotherhoods and closed down religious shrines and sectarian convents, which were often the centers of religious protest. Finally, in 1928, the Parliament repealed from the constitution article 2, which had stated that the "religion of the Turkish state is Islam." Henceforth, Turkey would officially be a secular republic. The secularization of the political culture reached its peak from 1933 to 1935: the government trans-

formed the Theological Faculty at the University of Istanbul into the newly formed Islamic Research Institute, banned the wearing of ecclesiastical garments outside places of worship, abolished traditional religious titles, turned the mosque of Aya Sofya into a museum, made Sunday the official day of rest, and proscribed books connected in any way with religion from the libraries of thousands of cultural centers being set up around the country. Nevertheless, the citizens' religious affiliation was listed on their national identity cards.

15. P. Xavier Jacob, *L'enseignement religieux dans la Turquie moderne* (Berlin: Klaus Schwarz Verlag, 1982), p. 57. On the same day as the Law of Unification of Instruction was adopted, the Sharia and Pious Foundations Ministry was demoted to a government agency, the Directorate of Religious Affairs.

16. Howard Reed, "Secularism and Islam in Turkish Politics," *Current History* 32 (1957), pp. 333–38.

17. "Köy öğretmen ve eğitmeni yetiştirme işi," *Ülkü* 8 (1936), pp. 264–65. Through the nationwide network of People's Houses (*Halkevleri*), the Kemalists disseminated their notions of cultural modernization; see Kemal H. Karpat, "The People's House in Turkey," *Middle East Journal* (1963), pp. 55–67.

18. Removal of religion from the curriculum in Turkey was based on the educational reforms implemented in France in the 1880s. Jules Ferry as prime minister (1880–1881, 1883–1885) established free compulsory secular education and forbade clerics from teaching in government schools.

19. Serif Mardin, "The Just and the Unjust," *Daedalus* 120 (1991), p. 124.

20. Typical of this attack on men of religion was a series of articles in 1933 on village education that ran in *Ülkü*. Mehmet Saffet, a prominent Kemalist who championed "scientific mentality," described villagers "as ninety percent illiterate and the sad truth is that they are under the corrupt influence of superstitious religious traditions." See his "Köycülük nedir?" *Ülkü* 6 (1933), p. 424.

21. The first open signs of a greater laxity toward religion came to the fore during World War II when a neutral Turkey underwent full mobilization. First, the army reinstituted Muslim chaplains. Then, with the partial lifting of censorship in 1943, there was a resurgence of publications with a decidedly Muslim perspective. Of particular importance was the monthly *The Great East* (*Büyük Doğu*); the periodical exhorted its readers to abandon the immoral materialist lifestyles of the secular West and return to traditional Islamic values. See Ahmet Yalman, "The Struggle for Multiparty Government in Turkey," *Middle East Journal* 1 (1947), p. 54; and Bernard Lewis, "Islamic Revival in Turkey," *International Affairs* 28 (1952), p. 40.

22. Howard Reed, "Turkey's New Imam-Hatip Schools," *Welt des Islam* 4 (1956), p. 152.

23. Binnaz Toprak, "The State, Politics and Religion in Turkey," in *State, Democracy and the Military: Turkey in the 1980s*, ed. Metin Heper and Ahmet Evin (Berlin: Walter de Gruyter, 1988), p. 123.

24. Feroz Ahmad, *The Turkish Experiment in Democracy, 1950–1975* (Boulder, CO: Westview, 1977), pp. 294–95.

25. Feroz Ahmad, "Politics and Islam in Modern Turkey," *Middle Eastern Studies* 27 (1991), p. 12.

26. To justify the coup, the junta charged that the civilian politicians were unable to govern the country and deal with the increasing breakdown of law and order. Between 1971 and 1980, there had been no less than nine coalition governments. Violence, first in the cities and on university campuses and later in villages and high schools, had claimed thousands of lives. For fuller coverage of the political turmoil before the military coup, see Joseph S. Szyliowicz, *A Political Analysis of Student Activism: The Turkish Case* (London: Sage, 1972); Arnold Leder, *Catalysts of Change: Marxist versus Muslim in a Turkish Community* (Austin: University of Texas Press, 1976); Serif Mardin, "Youth and Violence in Turkey," *Archives européennes de sociologie* 19 (1978), pp. 229–54; and Paul Magnarella, "Civil Violence in Turkey: Its Infrastructural, Social and Cultural Foundations," in *Sex Roles, Family and Community in Turkey*, ed. Çiğdem Kâğıtçıbaşı (Bloomington: Indiana University Turkish Studies, 1982), pp. 383–401.

27. Quoted in Yelda Arslan, Sefa Kaplan, and Erdal Kılıçoğlu, "Din eğitimi, laiklik ve ötesi," *Nokta* (26 March 1989), p. 16.

28. Nahid Dinçer, *1913'ten günümüze imam-hatip okulları meselesi* (İstanbul: Şule Yayınları, 1998), p. 111. Besides serving in the Council of Educational Policy, Baloğlu was cultural attaché in Bern and Paris, inspector of Turkish education in Europe, and minister of Youth and Sports under the government of Sadi Irmak (1974–1975). The educator was one of the founders of the Nationalist Democratic Party (*Milliyetçi Demokrasi Partisi*), which the military junta approved and supported in 1983.

29. Since 1974, graduates from religious-track high schools are allowed to enter any university program. According to the daily *Güneş* (16 February 1990), out of one hundred graduates who won admission to a university, only 14 percent opted for religious studies; most preferred to study public administration or international affairs.

30. During the 1989–1990 school year, 189,447 students (of which 49,904 were girls) attended 383 İmam-Hatip junior high schools and 93,077 (of which 19,267 were girls) were in 366 senior sections. Female graduates do not pursue careers in religion. About 40 percent of the curriculum is devoted to religious studies (e.g., classical Arabic, Qur'an); the rest follow approximately the literature track of secular high schools.

31. *Milliyet* (26 October 1986). The law of associations allows organizations that claim to be nonpolitical to organize informal study sessions. Religious brotherhoods, which are legally banned but receive active support from many conservative politicians, have been able to organize informal Qur'an courses. The Süleymancı brotherhood, for example, instructs as many students in the Qur'an as do the state-supervised programs.

32. Already in 1975, Baloğlu presented his views on religious-track schools in a report to the president, Fahri Korutürk. Titled "Our Religious Education and İmam-Hatip Schools—General Situation, Problems and Preventive Measures," the report created an uproar. Twelve years later, over three consecutive days, a major liberal daily published installments of his article "Reactionary Frontiers in Our National Education" (*Güneş*, 19–21 January 1987). He has equally appealed to foreign readers to share in his secular vision of national education. Thus, in an article he wrote for a collection of essays that the French Association of Turkish Studies published in 1981 on the occasion of the hundredth anniversary of the birth of Mustafa Kemal Atatürk, Baloğlu emphatically declared, "that it is in the vital interest of Turkey that . . . all necessary steps be taken to prevent duality [in the educational system] and eradicate it in such a manner that it will not reappear in the future." See his "Atatürk et l'enseignement religieux en Turquie," in *La Turquie et la France à l'époque d'Atatürk*, ed. Paul Dumont and Jean Louis Braqué-Grammont (Paris: Association pour le développement des études turques, 1981), pp. 227–28.

33. Baloğlu, "Atatürk et l'enseignement religieux en Turquie," p. 8.

34. Baloğlu, "Atatürk et l'enseignement religieux en Turquie," p. 7.

35. Baloğlu draws upon the French notion of *laïcité*—the noninterference of the state in matters of personal conscience and faith—to question the compatibility of democratic forms of governance with Islam. A similar argument has most recently been popularized in the United States as the "clash of civilizations." Thus, Samuel P. Huntington asserts, "Islamic culture explains in large part the failure of democracy to emerge in much of the Muslim world." See his *The Clash of Civilizations and the Remaking of World Order* (New York: Simon & Schuster, 1996), p. 29.

36. The rationale behind these allegations is the close ties between conservative statesmen and religious brotherhoods, which are prohibited in Turkey. President Turgut Özal and former minister of Education Vehbi Dinçerler (1983–1985), for example, were closely allied with the İskenderpaşa branch of the Nakshibendi brotherhood.

37. Baloğlu, *Türkiye'de eğitim*, p. 133.

38. Baloğlu, *Türkiye'de eğitim*, p. 10.

39. "TÜSİAD eğitim raporu Meclis'te," *Güneş* (26 September 1990), p. 5.

40. "İrticaya gensoru önergesi," *Güneş* (12 October 1990), p. 1.

41. "Kur'an kursuna kolaylık," *Güneş* (19 November 1990), p. 2. The Turkish secular-religious Kulturkampf has often been expressed as a contest between mosque and school. This became evident during the 1950s when the ruling DP catered to the religious sensibilities of the electorate. In the course of eleven years, from 1950 to 1960, the government built an equal number of mosques and schools; five thousand each. See Walter F. Weiker, *The Turkish Revolution, 1960–1961: Aspects of Military Politics* (Washington, DC: Brookings Institution, 1963), p. 9.

42. "Cami protestosuna polis engeli," *Cumhuriyet* (12 July 1990), p. 11.

43. "Mahkûmun elkitabı: Kelebek," *Güneş* (11 October 1990), p. 10.

44. Talal Asad, *Formations of the Secular: Christianity, Islam, Modernity* (Stanford, CA: Stanford University Press, 2003), p. 199.

45. Güngör Mengi, "Eğitim hasta!" *Sabah* (20 September 1990), p. 3.

46. "İmam hatipliler kamu yönetimine soyunuyor," *Güneş* (21 September 1990), p. 1.

47. *Gırgır* (19 March 1989), p. 3.

48. *Cumhuriyet* (3 August 1990), p. 1. To demonstrate the alphabet reform and explain how the letters were to be pronounced, President Atatürk traveled all over the country with a portable blackboard. Arabic script, it was argued, was unsuitable to Turkic languages because it lacked vowel symbols. The switch to Latin characters was also a powerful means of breaking cultural and religious ties with the Islamic heritage. At the time of the reform, many photographs were taken showing the president teaching the public the new alphabet (e.g., the cover of the 13 October 1928 issue of the widely circulated French magazine *L'Illustration*). The symbolism of the blackboard is self-evident: the entire nation is a classroom, its citizens are pupils.

49. Avni Akyol, "TÜSİAD'ın hazırlattığı 'Türkiye'de eğitim' raporu üzerine," *Millî Eğitim* 102 (1990), p. 5.

50. On the conscious application of a restricted syntax and vocabulary typical of scientific journals, see Basil Bernstein, "A Sociolinguistic Approach to Socialization, with Some Reference to Educability," in *Directions in Social Linguistics: The Ethnography of Communication*, ed. J. G. Gumpertz and D. Hymes (New York: Holt, Rinehart, & Winston, 1972), p. 474.

51. Akyol, "TÜSİAD'ın hazırlattığı 'Türkiye'de eğitim' raporu üzerine," p. 4.

52. Akyol, "TÜSİAD'ın hazırlattığı 'Türkiye'de eğitim' raporu üzerine," p. 4.

53. Akyol, "TÜSİAD'ın hazırlattığı 'Türkiye'de eğitim' raporu üzerine," p. 6.

54. The minister's remarks aptly exemplify what Foucault calls a society's "régime of truth": those discourses and discursive procedures that sanction one's social views as true. See his "Truth and Power," in *Power/Knowledge: Selected Writings 1972–1977* (New York: Pantheon, 1980), p. 131.

55. Akyol, "TÜSİAD'ın hazırlattığı 'Türkiye'de eğitim' raporu üzerine," p. 12.

56. Akyol, "TÜSİAD'ın hazırlattığı 'Türkiye'de eğitim' raporu üzerine," p. 12.

57. The newspaper *Türkiye* belongs to Enver Ören, owner of the important enterprise İhlas Holding, and leader of the Işıkçılar brotherhood, an offshoot of the larger Nakshibendi brotherhood.

58. "TÜSİAD'a imtiyaz vermem," *Türkiye* (9 October 1990), p. 11. In the article he penned for the ministry's journal, Akyol was more generous in his appraisal of Baloğlu; there, the minister qualified him as "an educator who has spent his entire professional life in National Education, and in recent years has taken top positions for important services." Akyol, "TÜSİAD'ın hazırlattığı 'Türkiye'de eğitim' raporu üzerine," p. 4.

59. Abdurrahman Dilipak, *Bu din benim dinim değil: "resmi din" öğretisine eleştirel bir yaklaşım* (İstanbul: İşaret-Ferşat Ortak Yayınları, 1990), p. 45.

60. "Öğretmenin tadı yok," *Güneş* (30 June 1990), p. 11.

61. "İmam Hatip liselerini millet istedi," *Türkiye* (28 September 1990), p. 3.

62. On the fusion of military secularism and religious militarism, see Chapter 5.

63. Fehmi Koru, "Raporun ardındaki zihniyet," *Zaman* (22 September 1990), p. 10.

64. Hikmet Tanyu, *İslâm dininin düşmanları ve Allah'a inananlar* (İstanbul: Burak Yayınevi, 1989), p. 198.

65. *Zaman* (22 September 1990), p. 8.

66. "İmam hatipliler kamu yönetimine soyunuyor," *Güneş* (21 September 1990), p. 12.

67. Since the late nineteenth century, religious-minded public figures have charged that imitation of the West will inevitably sap the strength of the people. Thus, Mehmet Akif, the author of the Turkish national anthem and an outspoken opponent of the Kemalist reforms, wrote, "People of a nation whose religion is imitation, whose world is imitation, whose customs are imitation, whose dress is imitation, whose greetings and language are imitation, in short, whose everything is imitation, are clearly themselves mere imitation human beings, and can on no account make up a community and, hence, cannot survive." (Quoted in Nur Yalman, "Islamic Reform and the Mystic Tradition in Eastern Anatolia," *Archives européennes de sociologie* 10 (1969), p. 45.)

68. "Müslümanım, laik değilim," *Güneş* (14 December 1990), p. 8.

69. "Cumhurbaşkanı Rapor'a kızdı!" *Sabah* (20 September 1990), p. 13.

70. "Din eğitimi ürkütücü boyutlarda," *Güneş* (20 September 1990), p. 1.

71. "İmam Hatip liselerini millet istedi," *Türkiye* (28 September 1990), p. 3.

72. Ahmet Selim, "TÜSİAD'ın raporu," *Zaman* (22 September 1990), p. 2.

73. Hannah Arendt, *The Life of the Mind*, vol. 1 (London: Secker & Warburg, 1978), p. 176.

74. Webb Keane, *Signs of Recognition: Powers and Hazards of Representation in an Indonesian Society* (Berkeley: University of California Press, 1997), p. 9; see Erving Goffman, *The Presentation of Self in Everyday Life* (New York: Doubleday, 1959), pp. 27, 80–83.

75. See Yael Navaro-Yashin, *Faces of the State: Secularism and Public Life in Turkey* (Princeton, NJ: Princeton University Press, 2002).

76. "Okulda secdeye tepki," *Güneş* (6 November 1990), p. 1.

77. de Certeau, *Practice of Everyday Life*, p. 96.

78. Reinhart Koselleck, "'Progress' and 'Decline': An Appendix to the History of Two Concepts," in *The Practice of Conceptual History: Timing History, Spacing Concepts*, trans. Todd Samuel Presner et al. (Stanford, CA: Stanford University Press, 2002),

p. 225. The Western idea of a future, which cannot be entirely derived from previous experience, stands in contrast to premodern observations of society. Then, Ottoman observers explained political impasses with reference to the cyclical nature of dynastic polities (birth, rise, maturity, stasis, and decline and ultimate disintegration). This organic model of society relied on precedent and imitation to resolve presentist problems; see Cornell Fleischer, "Royal Authority, Dynastic Cyclism, and 'Ibn Khaldūnism' in Sixteenth-Century Ottoman Letters," *Journal of Asian and African Studies* 18 (1983), p. 203.

79. Childhood is popularly associated with innocence, more specifically, with the lack of *temayüz*, the ability to discriminate between permissible and proscribed behavior with regard to the Islamic faith. See Gil'adi, *Children of Islam*, p. 83. During the late Ottoman regime, local parish schools were referred as *sıbyan mektebi* ("children's school"); *sıbyan* being the plural of *sabi*, a term that denotes a male child and evokes inexperience. Since the establishment of the republic, schools are designated as *okul* (ostensibly from *okumak*, the Turkish word meaning "to study" but more likely a calque from the French *école*).

80. "Millî eğitim bakanlığı müsteşarı Abdullah Nişancı'nın 1980–1981 öğretim yılı ilköğretim haftasını açış konuşması," *Tebliğler Dergisi* [henceforth *TD*] 43 (29 September 1980), pp. 201–2.

81. *İlkokul Türkçe ders kitabı 5* (İstanbul: Hürriyet Ofset, 1990), p. 59. The poem was first published in the ministry's official journal *Millî Eğitim* 80 (November-December 1988), p. 26.

82. Mehmet Karayiğit and Birgül Karayiğit, *Çukurova için hayat bilgisi—Türkçe kaynak kitabı sınıf 2* (Adana: Güney Matbaası, 1986), p. 18.

83. Millî Eğitim Bakanlığı, *İlkokul Programı* (İstanbul: Millî Eğitim Basımevi, 1968), p. 87. Even before the republican regime, the educationalist İsmail Hakkı Baltacıoğlu wrote in *Terbiye-i Avam* (1914), a journal devoted to adult education, that "public instruction and education are being adversely affected by their environment—the home, the streets, the mosques and the coffeehouses." (Quoted in Ilhan Başgöz, and Howard E. Wilson, *Educational Problems in Turkey 1920–1940* [Bloomington: Indiana University Publications, 1968], p. 121.)

84. Describing society and polity in terms of health and disease goes back to nineteenth-century European criticism of the politically weak Ottoman state, then known as the "Sick Man of Europe." This stigma has continued to populate political consciousness in republican Turkey and even finds expression in textbooks. Thus, a third-grade reader states, "We hear about the discoveries of Turkish scientists. These great developments show how far Turkey has come from its deathbed." (Quoted in İsmail Aydoğdu, *Türkçe ilkokul 3* [Ankara: Öğün Yayınları, 1986], p. 147.)

85. "Ortaokul vatandaşlık bilgileri programı," *TD* 48 (29 July 1985), p. 289.

86. Begoña Aretxaga, "Terror as Thrill: First Thoughts on the 'War on Terror-

ism,'" *Anthropological Quarterly* 75 (2002), pp. 39–150. For a fascinating study on the circulation of phantom representations of Islamic fundamentalism and Western rational thought, see Roxanne L. Euben, *Enemy in the Mirror: Islamic Fundamentalism and the Limits of Modern Rationalism, a Work of Comparative Political Theory* (Princeton, NJ: Princeton University Press, 1999).

CHAPTER THREE

Nation and Faith

It is interesting that the front covers of all religion textbooks are adorned with a portrait of a thirty-five year old Mustafa Kemal Atatürk, wearing a bow tie and a tuxedo, whom the artists have depicted in the manner of a Sheikh ül-Islam. . . . Although you expect to see the *bismillah* [article of faith] on the first page of the religion textbook, you encounter a saying of Atatürk, followed by his "Speech to the Youth" and the words of the National Anthem.

— A B D U R R A H M A N   D I L I P A K   *Bu din benim dinim değil*

Forging a morally homogeneous and politically exclusive community of citizens is central to modern state formation. In this geopolitical imaginary, the moral qualities of citizenship, that is to say, ideas about groupness and identity provide rationales for systematically indexing distinctions within and between territorially delimited sovereign states. In recent decades, all over the world, policy and opinion makers increasingly mobilize social scientific paradigms to organize fractured experiences of a country's population into a homogeneous nation. Specifically, they appeal to the concept of *culture* to craft group solidarity and define territorial sovereignty. This cultural fundamentalism, as Verena Stolcke argues, "emphasizes the distinctiveness of cultural identity, traditions, and heritage among groups and assumes the closure of culture by territory."[1] At the core of this assumption lies a notion that politics and society are self-evident separate entities and that culture provides the causal relation between the two. Sustaining this reasoning is a strong commitment to educational policies that establish and maintain immutable differences between national societies.

Indeed, the contentious debate over the Turkish educational system that the TÜSİAD report generated can be understood as a struggle to publicly define the cultural and, thus, moral parameters of Turkish citizenship. Its author, Zekâi Baloğlu, had despaired that previously un(der)represented religious publics increasingly participated in defining national culture in the public sphere and, most importantly, on his turf—the national education system.

The debate over the secular and religious character of Turkish society is neither recent nor limited to opinion and policy makers. Already forty years ago, in his monumental work *The Development of Secularism in Turkey*, the sociologist Niyazi Berkes argued that "the basic conflict in secularism . . . is often between the forces of tradition, which . . . promote the domination of religion and sacred law, and the forces of change."[2] To Berkes, Islam is an unwieldy and unreflective religion that had brought about the stasis and final disintegration of the prerepublican Ottoman state. His description of religious tradition was as much a prescription for secular modernity. The conceit is that, as societies modernize, societies secularize. In other words, only when religion is eliminated from the public sphere can Turkey transform itself into a prosperous, worldly, and democratic country. Otherwise, according to the logic, Turkish citizens will remain behind the times and, thus, out of place in the secular West.

Berkes's views still hold sway among many contemporary scholars who assume secularism to be a (desirable) universal phenomenon independent of time and place, all the while treating religion as cultural relic of the past. According to this overarching narrative of innovation and decline, pre- or nonmodern religious publics are bound to a timeless, unreflective, and unchanging tradition while secularists can be fully associated with reflexively organized knowledge, self-conscious improvement, and empirical observations—idealized features of Western modernity. Thus, for example, in his magisterial study of educational ideologies in the Turkish educational system, the political scientist İsmail Kaplan facetiously uses the term *Islamic laicism* to describe the incongruity of religious values and a secular educational system.[3] To him, secularity should mean the rejection of any religious system of ethics in governance, while the principle of laicism should subsume the total separation of religion from politics, the relegation of religious beliefs and practices to the private sphere, and the elimination of religious studies in state schools. Fundamental to this secularist understanding of polity and society is taking the usage of *religious/traditional* and *secular/modern* to be normative and thereby remaining oblivious to the historical and cultural specificity of secularism and religion, tradition and modernity.[4]

In lieu of this referential use of political language, I understand the particular usages of religious and secular discourses and terms as strategic means by which individuals define self, other, and world. My overall aim is to highlight the complex and changing relationships that different publics with their respective religiousnesses entertain with regard to tradition and modernity. This chapter thus explores how religious nationalists have engaged with secular, rational values and practices and set in motion novel reconfigurations of sanctity and profanity in Turkey.

In what follows, I briefly discuss how state intellectuals who belong to a highly influential think tank, the Türk İslam Sentezi (Turkish Islamic Synthesis), have inserted their moral imaginary and political vision into the national educational system.[5] Then I explore how, through a religion textbook, these nationalists juxtapose hallowed traditions with secular progress to anchor the sense of anteriority and homogeneity in the Turkish nation, all the while asserting that their national community rightfully belongs to the contemporary, scientific, and rational civilization. In the process, they insert the universal Islamic community into the geopolitical borders of the Turkish nation-state. Islam provides the nation a powerful element of historical legitimacy and continuity. The final product is an Islamic secularity. In the second part of the chapter, I examine how religious nationalists have taken recourse to social scientific laws about society and evolution of societies as well as to culture-and-personality studies to reorganize family, gender relations, and identities along specific patriarchal ideals. Underlying this appeal to social sciences is a widely shared belief in the inherent links between social customs and national essences; namely, a cultural conceptualization of social beliefs and practices permits moral readings of an ethnos and its history. Finally, I show how they have unwittingly laid the groundwork for an Islamic feminism that challenges this patriarchal order. A village wedding provided the opportunity for women graduates of a Qur'an course to advance a feminist reading of the Islamic corpus and proffer alternative gender relations that neither the Turkish Islamists nor the townspeople of Yayla had ever imagined.

The Turkish Islamists, Cultural Brokers of Post-1980 Turkey

The 1960 military coup leaders, who had ousted the Democrat Party (DP) from power, enacted the most liberal constitution the Turkish Republic had up to then known: freedom of speech and association, redistribution of state lands, more equitable taxation, social security, workers' representation in unions, and Marxist-inspired political parties. Not all influential members of the public sphere welcomed the new political orientation of the country. Among the critics were a group of scholars in the Faculty of Humanities at the University of Istanbul. In 1962, they formed a think tank, the Intellectuals' Club (*Aydınlar Klübü*), later rebaptized as Intellectuals' Hearth (*Aydınlar Ocağı*). In their workshops and publications, they were determined to convert the Ottoman Turkish heritage into political reality. To them, only a synthesis of Islam and Turkish nationalism—what they branded the Turkish Islamic synthesis—could bring about political stability and national unity. The 1980 military coup provided the opportunity to apply their social agenda as the junta made them major cultural brokers of the state. Their major sounding board has been the State Planning Office (SPO), the official organ responsible for formulating the country's five-year plans. Turkish Islamists were equally well represented in the postcoup civilian governments; two members of the Intellectuals' Club, Tahsin Banguoğlu and Hasan Celal Güzel, became ministers of Education; and Prime Minister Turgut Özal belonged to the İlim Yayma Vakfı (Dissemination of Science Foundation), which is closely associated with the religious nationalists.[6]

A central tenet of the Turkish Islamists is associating Western, secular humanism with antinomianism, the absence of any moral values. According to them, an international cosmopolitan outlook and an overemphasis on the individual has had a nefarious influence on polity and society. In 1986, at an SPO session attended by the military president Kenan Evren, the chief of staff, the ministers of Education and Culture, and the prime minister Turgut Özal, the Turkish Islamists linked civil disobedience to individualism. "In the twentieth century, a new type of person—an extraordinarily different personality type was born . . . : pragmatic, inconsiderate of life, aggressive, anti-authoritarian, inconsiderate of the state, not thinking of the nation, customarily believing in his errors. . . . These kinds of persons are cut off from our national cultural unity. . . . As long as their numbers increase, our national culture will implode into a worthless state."[7]

The Turkish Islamists, here, do away with the Turkish sociologist Ziya Gökalp's distinction between national culture and international (read, Western) civilization and his evolutionary schema of world civilizations. Dispensing with the concept of *civilization*, religious nationalists view Turkish society as one ever-evolving culture (*kültür*) grounded on an unchanging ethos (*öz*). As a professor of sociology, sympathetic to the movement, explained to me, "Culture changes; its essence does not" (*kültür değişir, özü değişmez*). The same SPO report on national culture elaborates on the professor's statement.

> Culture is not static; it is dynamic. It is in a state of change and development. These factors impart form and content to a culture. . . . Yet change and development can only be viable if new and old cultural elements mesh with existing social values, behavior, and institutions. One of the main reasons that the majority of cultural elements brought in from Western culture could not be applied to the Ottoman Empire's administrative, technical, and educational fields was that these elements did not mesh well with the old values and behaviors. The sources of our national culture—Turkish culture and later Islamic culture—attained a complete synthesis in Anatolia with the [medieval] Seljuks and especially with the Ottomans. A mature synthesis came about as Islamic and Turkish components of the people's culture complemented and strengthened one another. This synthesis gave strength, form, and spirit to the Ottoman Empire, one of the largest and most perduring empires in the civilized world.[8]

At the core of this historical narrative, which nostalgically looks back at the prerepublican Ottoman society, is positing that only religion can effectively link an ever-changing material culture with an invariant native essence. This theory of society and history is best summed up by two statements that the religious state intellectuals gave at the SPO in 1983: "Science without religion is the source of all disaster," and "Religion is the essence of culture while culture is the form of religion" (*Din kültürü özü, kültür ise dinin formudur*).[9] To corroborate this cultural approach to religion, Turkish Islamists argue that Japanese economic and technological successes resulted from retaining native Shintoist values.[10] The logic goes the following: cutting the Turkish people from the Islamic faith results in acculturation, which in turn condemns the people to perpetual underdevelopment; religion, not secular humanism, is the means for national salvation. And since the military coup in 1980, they have succeeded in inserting this view in the educational system. The curriculum presents the Turkish people's Islamic heritage as the major source of national unity, at the same time associating an inviolable Turkishness as integral to an essential and transhistorical religious truth.[11]

The Turkish Islamists' argument persuaded the military-interim government to institute mandatory lessons on religion and ethics for all pupils from fourth grade on. As a 1982 ministerial directive stated, "Just as we cherish our national values, customs, and traditions, we acknowledge that one of the important components of a nation is religion."[12] More than any other subject, religious lessons were touted as the subject matter with which Turkish citizens can positively identify with modernity, nationalism, and above all, secularism.

Textbook Islam

A productive way for gauging how the Turkish Islamists have immersed their social and political ideals into the country's political culture is a study of school textbooks. Through a detailed examination of the seventh-grade textbook *Din Kültürü ve Ahlâk Bilgisi 2* (literally, *Religious Culture and Knowledge of Morality 2*), first published in 1987, I will show how religious nationalists selectively draw on sacred and profane ideas to articulate a syncretism of religion and nationalism. The author, Professor Cihad Tunç, who formerly taught in the Faculty of Divinity in Ankara, was one of the original members of the Intellectuals' Club.

Of all printed media, textbooks play an inordinate role in fashioning a national identity. Because such texts are widely distributed, seem to play up key social issues, carry the weight of official approval, and engage a captive audience, they serve as a source of instruction or a frame of reference for the more general understanding of society and polity. Moreover, they are perceived as defining national experience for schoolchildren: those in positions of authority mandate and canonize a selective reading of society that transcends indeterminacy and contingency, just as alternative perspectives are silenced. State officials and policy makers, in fact, aim at molding the collective consciousness of children by linking didactic methods to a monologic voice in the text. The texts so produced appear to embody truth values, to provide (in the words of Gregory Starrett) "the liturgy for ritual dramatizations of the moral authority of the state."[13] As a result, a particular worldview rigidly delimits what is taught at school and how. And what makes textbooks so effective is that there is little semantic space to question privileged representations. The simple and straightforward language, clear-cut definitions, and unambiguous narratives constrain interpretations to a predetermined field of associations. Moreover, the curriculum and pedagogy focus on reproducing the right answers for national exams. In the classroom, pupils (and, for that matter, instructors) rarely challenge the framing and wording of ideas, that is to say, rarely scrutinize the linguistic and ideological knowledge constituted in the curriculum. Thus, textbooks are critical sources for examining the cultural politics of a society as the texts within them are deeply entrenched in the political culture of that society. Intended or not, such authoritative texts not only represent politics in their contents but also set up the terms of citizenship in the nation.

The seventh-grade religious studies textbook elaborates four central points. First, that the Turkish people have an innate spiritual affinity to Islam; second, that the Turks contributed a great deal to both Islamic and world civilizations; third, that Atatürk successfully mediated and exemplified the relation between state, citizen, and religion; and fourth, that only the state-endorsed version of Islam is compatible with both nationalism and modernity. As I will show, all four points provide legitimacy and credibility to a rationalist, religious version of nationalism.

Ever since the formation of the republic in 1923, the curriculum has been continually developed to stress a historical narrative that distinguishes the Turkish nation-state from other nations. Without exception, textbooks pattern the nation's history according to a single model: migration of pastoral nomads and their settlement in their adopted homeland (Anatolia), the golden age of cultural and political ascendancy followed by a decline (the "Dark Ages") some time under the Ottoman sultanate, and a regeneration under the current republican political regime. Underlying this articulation of the past is defining the *öz*, the eternal cultural and moral characteristics of the Turkish people. Here, history consists of temporal variations on an invariant, historicized essence.

For much of the twentieth century, the curricula emphasized how European civilization racially and intellectually originated with the Turkish people. In this secular, materialist conception of the nation, Turkish history rightfully belonged to the European past. At first, in the 1930s, Kemalist policy makers and educators advanced the argument (the Turkish History Thesis) that all major civilizations ultimately derived from a common proto-Turkish culture in central Asia. Taking recourse to historical linguistics and physical anthropology, they stretched the lineage of the Turkish people back to a racially pristine unspecified past, to a past that predated Islam by thousands of years. Intent on disproving those Europeans who assigned the Turks to an inferior yellow race, the Kemalist leadership had the curriculum represent the Turkish people as Turano-Aryans—blond, blue-eyed ancestors of the current Aryan race in northern Europe.[14] Underlying this appeal to biology was a widely shared belief in the inherent links between bioracial characteristics and ethnonational identity; namely, morphological conceptualization of the body's overt forms permitted moral readings of an ethnos and its history.[15] The upshot was promoting a definition of Turkishness that did away with the religious affiliation that had underpinned the collective identity in the prerepublican Ottoman polity. Only secular criteria—language and somatic traits—constituted irrefutably objective evidence for nationhood. In this historical narrative, an unchanging body type constituted the authentic origins of the people and thus became the moral source of political unity.[16]

In conjunction with this corporeal reading of the Turkish people, textbooks cast the Islamic faith as a foreign (Arab) nationalist movement that impeded the realization of the Turkish *öz*. Thus, in an attempt to reclaim a racially pristine pre-Islamic past, the Kemalists portrayed Islam as an Arab, not a universal, religion that corrupted and stifled the secular genius of the Turkish people. A high school sociology textbook from the 1930s would have the readers understand that "[b]efore the Turks accepted the religion of the Arabs, they were a big nation. The [Islamic] religion . . . slackened the Turkish nation's national bonds, numbed their national feelings and enthusiasm, since the aim of the religion, which Muhammad had founded, was the political domination of the Arab nation over all other nations."[17]

Not surprisingly, with the shift in the country's political culture since the 1980 coup, this secular historical narrative is absent in the current seventh-grade religion textbook. Rather, emphasis is on the natural fit between the Turkish people and Islam. Specifically, the Turkish people's *öz*, or primordial ethos, was only realized in Islam. That is, there is a clear shift from a representation based on historical commonalities between pre-Muslim Turkic peoples and citizens of the current Turkish Republic to one that stresses a historically deeper spiritual identity. Thus, the seventh-grade textbook states that earlier religious beliefs in shamanism, Manichaeism, and Buddhism, "never suited the Turk's *öz*." Rather, as the author Cihad Tunç elaborates,

> It was as if the Turks had been aware for centuries [before their conversion] of Islam's moral laws. . . . The Turks are from birth a nation of soldiers. Islam commands one to fight for the fatherland. The Turks are a nation which doesn't know the meaning of lies and hypocrisy; Islam forbids all this bad behavior. . . . The Turks are a nation of realists who dislike pursuing imaginary things and who love to work. Islam commands one to work and forbids laziness. Thus, the first and most important reason that the Turks became Muslims was that Islam was a religion appropriate to their origins. In entering Islam, the Turks chose the religion most appropriate for them.[18]

It is with this reasoning that the textbook author explains why the Turkish people, unlike the Arabs and Persians, did not immediately convert to Islam. Conversion, accordingly, followed only after Abu Muslim, "a Muslim Turk from Khorasan" defeated the Ummayads who "went against Islam's principles."[19] The discussion of precedence is significant. One, the author is suggesting that Islam finds its most fitting adherents in the Turkish people. Two, he stretches the Turks' confessional lineage back to a racially pristine unspecified past, that is to say, to a past that predated Islam. If the Kemalists treated the Turks as proto-Aryans, the Turkish Islamists have rendered the same people into proto-Muslims.

While the author makes explicit the links between Islam and the present Turkish nation-state, he nevertheless downplays its extraterritorial origins in

Arabia. This is most evident in the chapter "Belief in Books"—a chapter devoted to the revelation of the Qur'an and the early history of Islam. The names of the Prophet and the first four caliphs as well as the cities of Mecca and Medina are printed in boldface. They all allude to Arabia, not to the Turkish people. Yet the author succeeds in capping the chapter by inserting the early roots of Islam inside Turkey. This is evident in the statement "today we possess hand-written copies of the Holy Qur'an by [the caliphs] Uthman and Ali at the Topkapı Palace in Istanbul and other museums."[20] The words "Topkapı Palace" are in boldface, marking its importance. In the textbook, the cities of Mecca and Medina are described as the places of residence of the Prophet; not once does the author mention their holy status. Furthermore, the pictographic representation of Islam in the textbook sustains this nationalist vision of religion. Pictures are limited to mosques and historical sites in Turkey. The Kaaba, in the court of the Great Mosque at Mecca and the most hallowed shrine in Islam, is conspicuously absent as are other holy sites outside the country and the Arabic script, language, and calendar.[21] What I am suggesting is that nationalist interpretation of religion attempts to strengthen the sense of Turkish identity at the expense of one based on the universal Muslim community, the *ümmet*. This community, however, has not been totally eliminated. It provides a powerful element of historical continuity for the Turkish people and, accordingly, has been reinscribed within the geopolitical boundaries of present-day Turkey.

If the textbook glosses over the foreign (Arabic) origins of Islam, it makes clear the crucial role "Turkish" men played in developing and propagating positive sciences throughout the world—an argument that resonates with the earlier Turkish History Thesis. In this endeavor, the religion textbook assigns Turkish ancestry not only to the Muslim legalists Abu Hanifa and Maturidi but also to the philosophers Ibn Sina and Farabi, the geographer Biruni, and the algebraist Harezmi whose "fame spread as far as Europe."[22] Nowhere in the religion textbook are there any references to ideas or inventions borrowed from another society or to non-"Turkish" Muslim scholars. Rather, the textbook explicitly mentions Westerners' approval of Islam, be it Thomas Carlyle's praise of Muhammad or Maxim Robinson's admiration for Muslim armies.[23] It is irrelevant whether pupils or their instructors have heard of either of these two nineteenth-century Englishmen; what matters is that the West admires the genius of Islam, that is, the Turkish schoolchildren's faith.

Clearly, the text sets out to forge powerful emotional bonds between Turkey's Islamic heritage and the modern sciences, to inculcate school children to see themselves following a scientific tradition their ancestors began with conversion to Islam. As I showed in the previous chapter, secularists had long held Islamic men of faith, theologian seminaries, and scholastic forms of knowledge responsible for the economic and political gap between the industrialized West and the late Ottoman Empire. To counter the claim that Islam arrested the secular genius of the Turkish people, and thus prevented the Turks from evolving into a modern, industrial nation, supporters of the Turkish Islamic Synthesis invoke the positivism in Islamic sciences all the while disassociating scientific reasoning from secularism and the West. Crucial to this endeavor is making evident the links between the Qur'anic scriptures, past Muslim Turkish scholars, and the modern sciences. In an article that appeared in the ministry's flagship journal, Veysel Gani, who was then responsible for all Turkish education outside Turkey, insisted that the curricula make clear that "Islam, the last and most perfect religion, gives great importance to science and experimentation and, thus, has been the reason for the development of modern sciences."[24] Accordingly, Turkish Islamists expect the curricula to propagate the idea that faith and science are compatible. Thus, Amiran Kurtkan Bilgisen, a social psychologist and one of the prominent women figures of the Turkish Islamic Synthesis, argued that writers of textbooks should "translate Qur'anic verses that fit with modern biology, sociology, and the other sciences."[25]

Nevertheless, the tension between modernizing Islam in light of irrefutable scientific discoveries and Islamizing a modernity often at variance with central tenets of the faith remained an ongoing issue for Turkish Islamists. Some have tried to render Islamic beliefs scientific, be it belief in angels, jinns (supernatural spirits inhabiting the world), or the Holy Scriptures.[26] Others have designated as scholastic (*skolastik*) thought whatever Western forms of knowledge that contradict the Qur'anic message. In 1985, the then minister of Education Vehbi Dinçerler, who was rumored to be a member of the influential Nakshibendi religious order, had Darwin's evolution theory removed from primary and secondary curriculum.[27]

In this religiously sanctioned scientific discourse, Mustafa Kemal Atatürk plays a central role in linking religion with science, on the one hand, and modernity with nationhood, on the other. This is a radical shift from earlier portraits of the founding father of the Turkish Republic and his relation to Islam. I recall here that among his last reforms was defining the Turkish state as a secular one and that, during his presidency, religious education was phased out of the curriculum. In that period, religion textbooks avoided associating Atatürk with religion; rather, they stressed how Islam was compatible with a secular worldview. The prophet Muhammad was often cast as promoting the secularization of Turkish society. The following passage typifies the secular turn in religious instruction in the late 1920s: "If [the Prophet] had lived in our day there is no doubt that he would have commended Boy Scouting and modern games like football, volleyball, tennis, and hiking, and he even would have played himself. He would have made his people wear hats, which is a civilized and healthful covering. . . . The Prophet ate and drank with good manners and behaved absolutely like a civilized man."[28]

The Atatürk presented in the current religion textbook differs radically from an earlier generation of textbooks. Not only does Atatürk share the same charismatic features that the universal Islamic community attributed to the prophet Muhammad, but his personhood also mediates between Turkey's Islamic heritage and Muslim citizenry. Citizens, that is, the schoolchildren, are exhorted to model themselves after Atatürk's exemplary behavior. Thus, according to the textbook, "The Great Atatürk who pondered every subject . . . lived from birth to death a philosophy of love, unique to him. . . . Throughout his life, Atatürk never separated himself from truth, justice, and goodness."[29] In addition to this disinterested love for his nation, the leader stands out for his deeds and civic virtues, his "diligence, self-sacrifice, heroism, gratitude, goodness and honesty."[30] Here, Atatürk epitomizes the temporal culmination of a national, religious narrative; the nation's future, an inevitable repetition of the statesman's past religiousness.

Thus, the author Cihad Tunç repeatedly draws out the parallels between the lives of the Turkish statesman and the Prophet. Both men, for example, are portrayed as overcoming obstacles for the greater welfare of their respective communities; Muhammad resisted and defeated the Meccans, while Atatürk led the struggle for national independence.[31] Yet it would be wrong to assume that the statesman is the secular version of the Prophet. The overall aim is to show how Atatürk successfully embodies the relation between dedication to the state and good citizenship on account of his strong adherence to Islam. Thus, the textbook explicitly asserts that Atatürk "accepted the Islamic religion with all Allah's decrees and prohibitions and saw it necessary to apply them."[32]

Needless to say, the curriculum presents both Atatürk and Muhammad as beyond reproach; they are objects of faith. Total identification with these authoritative figures complements the overall aim of the religion textbook: children must completely identify with the state-endorsed version of Islam, including accepting its compatibility with modernity and nationalism. By law, all religion textbooks must end with the chapter "Laicism and Islamism" (*Laiklik ve İslâmlık*)—a chapter that distinguishes a priestless, personal Islam from a clerical, hierarchical Christianity all the while arguing for the Turkish state's right to regulate and administer religious practices and institutions. Only those affiliated with the state-endorsed religion are competent to interpret faith; all other alternative interpretations are proscribed as divisive or fanatical or both and, as a result, harming national interests.

This discourse is not directed to republican secularists, however. It is mainly geared to those religious movements that exclude the Turkish state from the realm of Islam (*darüsselâm*) (since the Shariah is not legally binding), repudiate nationalism as tribal sectarianism inimical with the idea of a universal Muslim community, or reject technological advances as deriving from a materialist conception of the universe.[33] What is evident is that the religious nationalists have taken up the earlier, republican discourse attacking "false teachers of religion" and "superstitions."[34] To them, incremental progress and positive sciences are the quintessential sign of a modern state and, by implication, that of its Muslim laity.

Of central importance is defining a rational Islam attuned to the activities of the world and affirming the laws of nature, however vaguely related to divine origins. Emphasis is on the worldly present and future, not with eschatology and the ultimate destiny of mankind. This instrumentalist orientation to the world is evident in how the textbook condemns those religious publics who hold onto a fatalist interpretation of the material world, that is, find confirmations of a truth known in advance. Not surprisingly, nonrational, mystical approaches to religious observance are considered to impede the country's progress. According to the 1982 ministerial directive on the Religion and Morals program, one of the main aims of the program is to replace popular superstitions with scientific reasoning.

> Without insulting the pupils, the erroneous knowledge and influences that they bring from outside the school will be corrected with a scientific [*bilimsel*] approach. It will be grasped with several examples that Islam is a rational [*akılcı*] and modern religion, with no connections to superstitions . . . , that it is an active [*aktif*] religion with continuous vigor and desiring progress [*ilerleme*].[35]

Many passages of the seventh-grade religion textbook are, accordingly, devoted to admonishing the faithful to abandon fatalism and to adopt a more rational, vigorous Islam in their lives.[36] Much emphasis is thus placed on the role of Islam for cleanliness, work, and social order, and clearly the focus is on villagers who, at least according to the religion textbooks, are most likely to fall prey to fatalism. For example, in their lessons on religion, seventh graders will have read that "a farmer first plows his field, sows seeds, and takes all the necessary precautions and then only afterwards does he resign his fate to God" or "to not take necessary precautions to protect our forests and to feign patience by saying that 'a flood happened' is not true patience; it is only indolence and laziness."[37] This attitude against fatalism holds for the pupils; the textbook reminds them that "a student who never studies his lessons shouldn't leave it up to Allah, saying, 'whatever is my fate, whatever Allah grants, I'll pass.' Such a behavior goes against Allah. . . . First one must study as best as one can and learn all the topics of the lesson, then afterwards resign one's fate to Allah."[38]

Such rhetorical strategies are clearly meant to foster a better work ethic and study habits for schoolchildren. They are also intended to mold the political ideals of boys and girls. The religious lessons to which Turkish children are exposed during their years of schooling are all designed to align their support for three long-standing government ideals: identification with the Turkish nation and its glorious history, economic and technological modernization, and obedience to state authorities. Indeed, the religion textbook repeatedly situates all three of these ideals within the Turkish people's Islamic heritage. This is why Atatürk, the twentieth-century statesman, is presented as having succeeded in forging a national community out of a seventh-century prophet's universal, religious message. Atatürk died in 1938 but his statements continue to serve state policies and, in the context of post-1980 Turkey, state policies have come to mean rallying the youth around scientific modernity, national unity, and no less importantly, a rational faith. Thus, the author finds it most apposite to quote Atatürk to explain why Islam is the most rational and, thus, the last and most perfect religion: "[I]f something suits logic and reason and serves national and religious interests, don't ask anyone. That thing is religious."[39] And in the nation's classrooms, it is the sponsors of the Turkish Islamic Synthesis who currently define and institute the relation between state and religion.

Clearly, the textbook squarely situates nationalism, the republican regime, and modern sciences within religion. In its attempt to fashion a national collectivity, the seventh-grade primer on religion appeals to secular, rational values and practices; it simultaneously scripts an Islam in terms of modern secular idioms and a secular modernity in terms of Islamic idioms—and all under the auspices of national unity.

Yet it would be amiss to ignore the impact of secular modes of representation in the production of this text. In writing about a national religion the author sought to represent, he brought into being the positivist ideas of natural and political history—out of those historical facts and laws of nature that are taken to be impartial determinants of the Turkish essence, or öz. And no matter how much the author invokes the authenticity of religious and national traditions or writes in a language of impartiality, he had to frame religion according to a secular imaginary. Not the prophet Muhammad and the Qur'an but Atatürk and his reforms are the reference points for rendering fragments of historical events and ideas into a nationalist religious teleology.

The historical narrative that the author of the textbook elaborated did not take into consideration the cognitive and intellectual independence of young readers. Only the author is positioned as the one endowed with the textual wisdom from which children can benefit. His words are particularized, their coloration heightened to accommodate the author's worldview—his didactics, pedagogy, and ideology. Pupils, in turn, are expected to accept the terms of their religious nationalism, to become willing members of the political community projected in the religious text. Yet the act of authoring a textbook invariably brings to bear ideas about the school population, that is, it anticipates responses that will have an impact on the children's subjectivity. Through the religious textbook, the curriculum may strive to forge solidarity among all Muslim citizens irrespective of their religious background and thus omits mention of doctrinal or sectarian differences, but it does not necessarily follow that Turkish citizens who constitute their spiritual world differently will decode the semantics of the curriculum in the same manner.

Many of the themes covered in the religion textbook were accepted as common knowledge in Yayla—with a difference. Although the overwhelming majority of townspeople identified with secular modernity, Sunni Islam, and Atatürk, very few townsmen performed on a regular basis the five daily prayers or attended mosque services. Throughout the region, the adult men from Yayla were known for their laxity in religious practices, whether openly eating in daylight during the month of Ramazan, consuming alcohol, or gambling. In Yayla itself, many quipped that only elderly men—"those with one foot inside the hole"—needed to worry about the next world and pray.

Clearly, the Islamization of the public sphere had not made significant inroads in the town. Religious parties did poorly in elections. In the 1989 municipal elections, the Welfare Party garnered only 54 out of 2,483 votes. At the time of my field research, only six men had recently joined Sufi brotherhoods. Their outward appearances advertised their newly embraced religiosity. Claiming to follow the practices (*sünnet*) of the prophet Muhammad, they dyed their eyelashes and unkempt beard jet black with kohl, covered their head with a turban, wore a collarless shirt, put on nonalcoholic perfume, and made a point of wearing a silver wedding band on their right hand.[40] After two of them opened grocery stores, they were all suspected of receiving money from Iran or Saudi Arabia—two countries popularly condemned as *fanatik*. More upsetting to many was that these members of religious brotherhoods boycotted the state-appointed mosque prayer leaders, whom they accused of improper knowledge of the faith. Not surprisingly, some of these devout townsmen opted to send their children away to unofficial community schools where secular teaching was kept to a minimum.

The differences in religiousness did not escalate into serious confrontations, however. Whenever the topic of brotherhood was brought up, townspeople invariably blamed false religious leaders and their venal politics and

credited Atatürk for trying to rid the country of such leaders. Two apocryphal stories were frequently invoked to prove that the Turkish statesman
was a true man of religion. The president supposedly gathered all the imams
to the capital and demanded that they trample on Qur'ans strewed on the
floor. Almost all complied with the impious order and were immediately
hung as false religious leaders. The few who picked up and kissed the Holy
Book and placed it on a table were retained as imams. Another version has
Atatürk place Qur'ans on chairs and order the imams to sit on them. Once
more, he hangs all those preachers who defiled the Holy Books with their
buttocks.[41] A few townspeople were even convinced of Atatürk's religious
sentiments and linked his holy status to his year of birth. According to the
Gregorian calendar, Atatürk was born in 1881.[42] The Arabic numbers 18 and
81 are ascribed particular sanctity because they appear in the natural folds of
the palms and add up to the 99 Beautiful Names of Allah, the *Esmâ-ül husnâ*.
Nobody found it incongruous that Atatürk's birth year was with reference to
a non-Islamic form of timekeeping. The numbers agreed, and that was sufficient proof.

Turkish Islamic Family Values

In Turkey, women symbolize the dangers and promises of modernity. Gender identity and relations have become privileged signs around which secular and religious public figures configure and articulate a moral vision of the
Turkish state, citizenry, and family. Much of the debate over women focuses
on mass education, and thus girls' schooling stands out as one of the most
heavily charged issues in the country.[43]

Framing the success or failure of the Turkish polity in terms of women's
education goes back to Orientalist observations of the cloistered harem,
which attributed women's low levels of education and literacy rates to a
despotic political culture.[44] Indeed, one could argue that the so-called Eastern Question—the nineteenth-century European discourse about the political decline of the Ottoman state—has been resignified as the Women's
Question in the postcolonial world order.[45] This highly gendered discourse
about the relationship between education, society, and polity was equally
evident in Baloğlu's report. The educator strongly opposed girls attending

religious-track schools, whose curriculum he deemed to be undemocratic and unscientific. His argument went as follows: women poorly trained in secular topics make poor mothers to schoolchildren and thus stifle the country's ability to compete with more technologically advanced nations.

The Turkish Islamists have argued otherwise. To them, the secular educational system had failed to prepare women in their roles of educators at home, and it had contributed to the loss of moral values that had once sustained the patriarchal household. Accordingly, religious state intellectuals and policy makers were of the opinion that they had to step in and prevent further disintegration and instability of the Turkish "national family" (*millî aile*).[46] In response to what they perceived as the onslaught of Western amorality, they set out to re-Islamize the domestic sphere. And just as they positively assessed religious culture to constitute national identity, Turkish Islamists have equally appealed to national values to persuade the nominally Muslim citizens to reestablish the extended patrilineal family and its gendered hierarchy.

The main architect for the revival of the extended traditional patrilineal family was Cemil Çiçek, state minister for Women's and Family Issues.[47] To ensure his pious version of the family, the minister turned to sociology and anthropology to debunk a convergence theory that assumes that economic development inevitably leads to the adoption of a nuclear family system. In his opening remarks at the first conference on the Family and Women (Türk Ailesi Şûrası; 17–20 December 1990) he convened, the minister stated,

> The view that as we advance family structures and psycho-social models of the industrial age are unavoidable is losing favor in our times. . . . Our family is a small model of our cosmos. . . . Since Creation, men and women have not been enemies or objects of rivalry. On the contrary, they feel the need for each another; they are living creatures that complete each other. Let me just express this. Today, some of the functions of the Turkish family have broken down . . . because socio-economic changes have brought about cultural chaos to our country. I just want to make it clear that the Turkish family has the most harmonious basic values in this world; its family relations are the most fitting examples for humankind.[48]

To make sense of the current cultural chaos (*kültürel kaos*), scriptural texts do not suffice. Rather, the minister draws on Western observations of the so-called Oriental family, which he treats as authentic documents of the past, and these observations gain further credibility from contemporary sociological and anthropological research. Terms from sociology and cultural anthropology abound in the minister's discourse on the Turkish Islamic family. Three months before the conference, in an interview he gave with the journalist İnci Hekimoğlu for the liberal daily *Güneş*, not once did the minister use religious terminology. Rather, he tapped into the social scientific language that many of the readers of *Güneş* had acquired at school and in the popular culture.

İH: How are national values evident in family roles?

Çiçek: There are laws that the state passes. But there are sociological laws too. They change according to the group or culture found.

İH: What are the aims of the national policies that you believe are necessary for the family?

Çiçek: They aim at protecting cultural values. For instance, there are relations with neighbors, visits on holidays, and so forth. I'm referring to the revitalization and perpetuation of these inborn traits.

İH: Is there a woman problem in Turkey?

Çiçek: Of course. There is also a problem for men and children. Yet all I see here are articles claiming that women's problems derive from men. There's a tendency to show men and women as rivals to one another. . . . The true problem is the social laws. The more we educate our people, then we will be able to do away with wrong opinions and the bad relations bothering our people.[49]

The fact that Çiçek referred to "sociological laws," and "cultural values" to support his views on marriage, family, and sexuality was not surprising. The minister had made kinship studies a priority of the state, and for this purpose, he set up in 1990 the Institute for Family Research (*Türk Aile Araştırma Kurumu*). Out of a total staff of 150–200 people, the institute employed 40 professional sociologists and anthropologists. One of the major supporters of the Turkish Islamic family model has been Orhan Türkdoğan, an anthropologist known for his folklore research of eastern Turkey. One of the keynote speakers at the conference on the Family and Women, which the religious nationalists organized, Türkdoğan stated, "One must welcome a national policy designed to strengthen and improve the family. The policy aims to retrieve from the old moral family identity those national values which can then be channeled to the new moral Turkish family."[50] The institute ostensibly supports research projects on subjects that anthropologists and sociologists have traditionally studied; namely, one, the Turkish family and cultural change; two, integration of three generations in the family; and three, women's economic role in the country. In fact, most projects were concerned with women's sexuality. According to *Türkiye*, a daily sympathetic to the idea of the extended patriarchal family, the funded programs were concerned with "the period when women begin to take up prostitution and what are the prostitutes' attitudes towards the institutions of spouse, child, and family," "the importance and understanding of chastity in Turkey," or "the problems of working women and how they affect the family institution and family members."[51] All these studies deal in one way or another with independent women—the *feminists*, whom Çiçek accused of trying to usurp men's traditional roles in the family.[52] A month after the conference, the minister reiterated his stance on the war on "enemies of the Turkish family": "In our days, some groups have taken aim at the institution of marriage; they find the continuity and feeling of security in the marital contract irksome and harmful. . . . For a long time, groups which have always nurtured a hostile attitude toward our national culture and whose brazenness has increased want to stamp our society with attitudes contrary to our social values."[53] Accordingly, feminists posed a threat to the nation's biocultural survival. Indeed, the gist of an SPO report on the "Turkish Muslim person model" that received wide press coverage was that "the status of the male head of the household . . . had suffered" since men have abandoned leadership (*reislik*) to their women.[54] This deep-seated fear of an emasculated male citizenry has led to religious nationalists campaigning to push women out of the organized work force and back to the domestic quarters. Otherwise, they argue, women are more likely to end up being degenerate, conspicuous consumers of material goods and sex. To these puritanical moralists, reassertion of male authority requires feminization of women, that is to say, restricting female members of the household to a particular set of activities associated with domesticity (e.g., home economics and child rearing). The solutions they offered were to educate girls in Qur'an courses and İmam-Hatip schools where spiritual family values dominate the curricula and, more generally, publicize the virtues of the extended patriarchal family in the educational system.

The school system invests a great deal of attention in upholding the minister's idealized conception of family and family values. To impart these values, the curricula enlist familial metaphors to create a sense of national unity. As soon as they begin school, children are exposed to a language that systematically couples the images of the family with the political imaginary of republican Turkey. The very first lines that first graders learn to read are "The Turks are one big *family*. Turkey, our *father*land, is this family's home. Our *mother* tongue is Turkish." [55] The idea of the state as paterfamilias and the family as the foundation of Turkish society, which is enshrined in the Turkish constitution, is adumbrated throughout children's elementary school years. Thus, the passage "The Family Is Holy" states,

> The family is the foundation of society. If families are happy, then the nation remains strong. Because the Turkish Nation well understands this, it gives great importance to the family. For the Turkish Nation the family is holy. The Turkish Nation is tied to its customs. It is patriotic, hospitable, honest, and hardworking. Strong family ties have perpetuated these attributes because every person acquires his first education from the family. Families teach children ties and respect to national and spiritual values. [56]

The links between family and nation center on the mother. For one Family Day (once called Mother's Day), which has been commemorated in the Turkish school system since 1955,[57] public school walls were plastered with a poster showing a photograph of an extended family: a middle-age couple, three children, and a set of grandparents. Its caption on top read, "We're Happy, We're Strong"; on the bottom, "Because We Are the Turkish Family." [58]

The sanctity of the family unit entails reasserting a sexual division of labor in the home. Women's major patriotic duty is a motherhood that safeguards the morally laden household and, by implication, the nation at large. Thus, in the third-grade reader, a deeply nostalgic view of woman-as-mother permeates a lesson on family members.

> Turkish women are always next to their men and help them. They administer and manage the home and take care of children in the best manner.

They work to ensure that their children are clean, orderly, hard working, and strong. They nurture and raise them for the country and nation. . . . Women are the basis of Turkish society and its most powerful pillar. . . .

Isn't it from our mothers, grandmothers, and aunts, the first teachers of the family nest, that children first learn about love, respect, mutual help, and solidarity?

Turkish women don't forget the big, heavy and difficult duties and responsibilities which they have borne. Throughout history, they have done and continue to do their duty in the best possible way.[59]

Roles outside the home are rarely invoked. Rather, the focus is on domestic chores. As soon as children begin school, they are exposed to a discourse that systematically establishes domesticity as women's avocation. Witness a passage in the third-grade natural science textbook: "The father is the head of the family. . . . Our mothers clean our house. They wash the laundry. They sew the ripped up seams. They cook our food."[60] The link between domesticity and girls' education is spelled out in Fikret Özgönenç's *Family's Educational Duties*, a popular pedagogical manual for parents: "There is a very close connection between a daughter's schooling and the house chores you have taught her. Should a mother not make her daughter do house chores because her daughter goes to school, studies, and takes exams, then she is taking a very negative approach to the latter's education."[61]

Özgönenç's fears have not come to pass—at least, not in Yayla. In essay after essay on the family, elementary and middle school girls mentioned the heavy, unrecognized labor they bore. Safigül, for example, wrote about domestic chores among girls' lot: "My older sister . . . finished elementary school. She copes with housework. They did not send her to middle school. I have passed into eighth grade. I am 14 years old. Housework falls mostly on me. Right now I spend my days carrying bricks." Not all girls willingly accept the double standards for sons and daughters. Hediye, then enrolled in the business administration program at a regional university, strongly disapproved of parental attitudes that discouraged girls' ability to succeed at school: "The biggest mistakes derive from our mothers. Mothers incorrectly raise their sons. They tolerate more from the boys; boys have the upper hand at home. . . . Girls going to school have to do housework; boys, whether in school or not, never get their hands dirty." Hediye had no intention of returning to live in Yayla. Her less educated peers, however, had fewer options and needed to cope with gendered premises that link maleness with the public sphere, femaleness with the private domestic sphere.

A Chaste Nation

Apprehension over the loss of family values has been mostly directed to young women's premarital chastity. Early on, girls in Yayla are made aware of the moral sanctions against unrestrained mobility, which boys have been granted at birth. This came to my attention when I assigned pupils to write about their community. I had anticipated that they would describe the historical, geographical, and economic aspects of their hometown. Some did. Many, however, chose to write about the legendary origins of the Serpent Cliff (*Yılanlı Kaya*), a rocky projection overlooking the nearby mountain pass, the Cilician Gates, known as Gülek Boğazı. The local townspeople picture the rock as an enormous snake on the verge of overtaking the castle just above it. It is this imagery that shapes the legend about a young girl who suffered the consequences of leaving her home unattended and without permission. I quote in extenso the essay written by Seval, an eleven-year-old fifth grader.

A long time ago there was a good-hearted king. This king had a daughter. One day a fortuneteller came to the king. The king asked the fortuneteller to look at his daughter's fortune. His daughter's fortune was the following: the fortuneteller began to explain and said that one day in the future an enormous dragon-like serpent [*ejderha*] would certainly swallow his daughter and that there was nothing that the king could do to prevent it. Upon hearing this, the king immediately built a castle [*şato*] at the tip of a rocky cliff for his daughter and imprisoned her there. One day, the daughter was bored and escaped from the palace. She played in the countryside and on her return to the palace she sat at the foot of a tree that was next to the mountain pass and fell asleep. From behind her the girl heard strange noises the enormous snake was making and was very scared. The girl who saw that the enormous snake was coming from behind began to escape. Understanding that she would not be able to escape from the enormous snake, the daughter began to implore Allah. She said, "Allah, Allah, either turn me into a bird or a stone." Allah turned both the daughter and snake into stone at the place that they had been. Since that time there is a stone statue of the kneeling girl. The king who understood this said, "Fool [*Kelek*] Külek, you have destroyed my nest." Since that day the name [of the mountain pass] has been Külek.

The legend—a primary, popular interpretation of a toponym—reveals nothing of the historical origins of the community.[62] Yet the narrative elicits in the children a greater sense of identity and continuity with the past than would any chronological account of the community. Its continual viability presupposes and refers to what Richard Harvey Brown calls a "social order of meaning . . . in which a sense of lived connection between personal character and public conduct prevails."[63] What makes the legend meaningful and alive is that, first, it recognizes that girls have intentions and make choices and, second, it confirms a patriarchal moral universe that considerably constrains their ability to freely act. The inanimate stone girl and snake exemplify an ongoing tension between female desire and male-defined social norms and, no less poignantly, the dire consequences of autonomous female agency in society.

The legend has its counterparts in real-time values and consequences. Newspapers regularly carry stories about women who had premarital sex and, thus, dishonored themselves and their families. The conservative daily *Türkiye* periodically publishes a series of confessional letters warning young girls of the dangers of flirting (*flört*). One letter ran with the headline "Young Girls, Don't be Deceived!"[64] Next to the letter was a photograph of a young woman with a black band covering her eyes. (The black band not only suggests anonymity but publicly marks her disgrace.)[65] Lest the young woman's letter misses its mark, the editor of the series adds his own comments: "The young girl E. H. writes that she acted too freely around men. As a result of flirting with a young man she had met on the street, she was taken in with the promise of marriage. The young man violated her, and then abandoned her. She recommends that young girls learn from this a moral lesson and stay away from flirting."[66]

The town of Yayla has not been spared from media coverage of premarital sex. Several townspeople had clipped a newspaper article about a mosque prayer leader who had impregnated a local teenager.[67] He left the village.

The young woman and her family still suffered from public humiliation. One middle-age relative summarized the social ostracism the woman's family suffered with the proverb "the virgin daughter is a castle; if it is destroyed, it is nothing but a worthless rag."[68] This condemnation on female premarital sex is assumed to hold even after death. One of the few devout young men in Yayla told me that several years ago the corpse of an immodest young woman turned black upon interment. The moral of his story was evident: the sinful woman would suffer in the next world.

Anxiety over girls' chastity (*iffet ve namus*) and feelings of shame (*utanma duygusu*) carries over into the curricula.[69] Suspicion of their morality results from assimilating the female body to an immutable nature or a cosmos that adults must control. This naturalness of gender difference finds visible expression at school. To extend schoolgirls' sexual innocence, the Ministry imposes an asexual dress code; ministerial directives ensure that pubescent girls conceal their incipient womanhood. At the time of my fieldwork, all elementary-age schoolchildren, irrespective of sex, were required to wear black smocks with white Eton collars—a uniform found in many European countries. Upon entering middle school, a corporealization of the two sexes' identity is instituted. Boys then wore a shirt, jacket, and tie, while girls continued to wear the black smock as do their elementary school peers. According to several teachers, the differences in uniforms indicated the different adult roles assigned to boys and girls. The boys' dress code mimicked that of civil servants; the terms *ceketli* ("one with a jacket") and *kravatlı* ("one with a tie") are associated with the generic state official. The differences in dress code were also aimed at muting girls' sexuality. According to the ministerial directive on dress code, elementary and middle school girls are forbidden to wear sleeveless, wide-open shirts or any type of jewelry.[70] Most of the focus is on hair, as loose hair connotes promiscuous sexuality.[71] From elementary school on, the school staff ensures that girls either keep their hair short or pull it back in braids or pony tails. Those who fail to comply with this regulation are not allowed to enter the school grounds. I witnessed a woman teacher, who, while personally disapproving of the "very rigid rules in the schools," nevertheless sent home a seventh-grade girl whose hair was untied. Many girl pupils mentioned to me having embarked on a similar "train trip" (*tren yolu*) to the principal's office.

Women instructors, in their capacities as representatives of the state, are also expected to desexualize their bodies. They must adopt a series of semi-otic conventions that simultaneously downplay their physical sexuality and highlight their unsexed role of civil servant. A ministerial directive elaborates what clothes the female staff can wear and in what manner. "Provocative pants that are either extremely tight or too wide are not to be worn. Blouses which are tight, sleeveless, or very open are not to be worn. Skirts with hemlines above the knee cannot be worn. . . . Make-up cannot be conspicuous; perfume is to be used sparingly; jewelry is not be overdone."[72] Understood is that should a teacher exhibit a too ostentatious wardrobe, she is liable to convey a coquetry and artificiality out of line with her professional role and, thus, corrupt her impressionable young wards.[73]

Keyed to this concern over dress code is anxiety over girls' horizons of mobility. As a widely read educator pointed out in his book *Children's Education in the Family*, "parents should pay attention to where their daughters come and go; they must not leave them to wander on their own."[74] In assuming the worse for unchaperoned girls, he cast doubt on their virtue. Boys do not suffer from this societal prejudice. Neither the school system nor society at large expect boys to abstain from having sexual intercourse before marriage.[75] Both men and women in Yayla take for granted and openly joke about a male adolescent's virility; a salient feature of his manliness (*erkeklik*) is his sexual potency. Female sexuality, on the other hand, is not a joking matter. Apprehension over girls' sexual behavior is, moreover, intimately connected to the literacy they acquire at school. As writing extends the space of communication beyond the control of adults, verbal dexterity is associated with sexual forwardness and accessibility. A generation ago, parents feared that a literate girl would correspond with a man and thus sully the family's honor. Older village men repeatedly told me, "We didn't send girls to schools; we didn't want them writing love letters to boys and shaming our family's honor." Illiteracy, accordingly, would prevent girls from being tempted to entice unrelated men into amorous (extra- and premarital) dalliances. Popular prejudice about girls' love letters was reproduced in an anecdote, ironically titled "Progress," which was posted in the elementary school's hallway.

One of the people attending the literacy course in town was a village girl. The girl insisted that she was mainly in love and only wanted to learn how to write her name. As soon as she learned to write her name, she left the course and returned to her village. A year later, she once more applied to the same course. Once more she told the same teacher that she only wanted to learn how to write her name. He then asked her: "My dear, didn't you learn to write your name last year?" "Yes sir, but since then I have married. I changed my last name."

Fears about female literacy may elicit a chuckle in the coeducational school system, but they remain ever a source of anxiety for some conservative circles in the country. The best-selling of all wall calendars is the one published by the Directorate of Religious Affairs. In almost every household in Yayla hangs this calendar, which consists of sheets of paper for each day of the year. Each leaf states the hours of the five daily prayers and quotes a passage from the Qur'an and a saying attributed to the prophet Muhammad, Atatürk, or an illustrious man of religion. On the back side of each leaf is addressed a wide gamut of social issues, including relations between the sexes. For the calendar day of 27 September 1980, the leaf answered the question whether "education incites women to become prostitutes": "There is some truth that literacy can lead to prostitution. There is no inherent relation between knowledge and education with prostitution, but as educational institutions are unable to regulate morals and instill discipline and order, young people's morals can be tainted. Unfortunately this problem is widespread today."

If literacy connotes potential, scandalous openness of a woman's body to the outside world, unfettered mobility is perceived as totally unraveling the patriarchal notions of honor and shame. To walk about (*gezi gezmek*), that is to say, to go from place to place without a purpose in mind, is a male prerogative. Should a townswoman take the liberty to do likewise, she will invariably be described by an expression that impugns her morality: "she wanders about too freely" (*çok geziyor*).[76] As far as most townspeople were concerned, only high society (*sosyete*) women and actresses could operate totally in a mixed-gender environment because many are assumed to sell their sexuality. Indeed, the term "free" (*serbest*) denotes radically different meanings depending on the individual's gender: for men, self-employment; for women, a too free-and-easy manner with men. In the past, trepidation over the mixed-gender environment at school resulted in many parents either not sending their daughters to school or withdrawing them after third grade. Thus, Elif, an illiterate mother in her forties, claimed that she "didn't attend school because there wasn't a school where only girls studied." Since then, attitudes toward coeducation in the town have changed. No household wants an illiterate bride, as illiteracy indexes backwardness. All girls of school age attended the two elementary schools; about a quarter of the graduates enrolled in the local middle school. Most parents, however, rarely considered daughters pursuing secondary, let alone university, education. The general opinion was that girls are destined to remain at home, before and after marriage, and that the purpose of schools was to prepare them for their future adult roles as wives and mothers. Quite a few townspeople summarized this gendered division of education with the popular saying "the father who loves his son gets him a teacher; his daughter, a husband."[77]

Coeducation, female literacy, or the school uniform do not occupy much attention among townspeople. A far more pressing issue is their ability to marry off their daughters. Thus, townspeople welcomed the three-month-long sewing (*Biçki-Dikiş*) course, which opened in the summer of 1990. Some thirty teenagers ostensibly learned the trade of seamstress but, in fact, worked on their wedding trousseaux. Parents were less than enthusiastic over the dress code. As a state-run program, all participants in the program had to wear white blouses, black ties, and long black skirts, the latter of which bared their calves. They also had to keep their hair uncovered. What made the teenagers' immodest appearance all the more disconcerting to many townspeople was that classes were held at the former movie theater, between the central coffeehouse and the mosque, smack in the center of the town. At the graduation ceremony, one of the fathers voiced out loud his disapproval. "We're not in the city. Look at them. Heat is escaping from their bodies. In the city, not here, do women bare themselves in public. . . . Anyways, the girls will be back in their shalwars after the ceremony."[78] Several of the men present smiled at the father's comment and looked toward the left where the adult townswomen were wearing an embroidered headkerchief, long-sleeved blouses, and baggy shalwar pants.

Not all school-age girls accept a patriarchy that denies their ability to freely participate in the public sphere and pursue a career outside the home. Some do invoke a school discourse that celebrates the (male-directed) emancipation of women from traditional gender relations.[79] Gül, who had recently graduated from the local middle school, aspired to attend a high school in the nearby city of Tarsus, but her parents and immediate kin were hesitant about sending her unchaperoned to an urban high school. Frustrated at her own exclusion from full participation in her society, she tackled head-on the collective prejudices of her immediate community.

> We [girls] suffer from prejudices. Just think about it. A woman has no say in front of men; she can't meddle in men's business. They think we live in a totally different society. They are always thinking whether we have soiled our honor. . . . Think about it, why can't a girl go out at night alone? Most boys I know think we're just a piece of hymen [*bir zar parçası*]. . . . A country can't develop with this kind of thinking. A woman must be economically independent. But how does our society react? While a man can do whatever he wants, all the burden and guilt is dumped on us women. . . . I too want to be a modern person.

Her plaint, however truncated, bespeaks a desire to partake in new gender ideals—greater geographic and social mobility—that she and other local girls associate with republican ideals. Self-conscious teenagers like Gül increasingly resent a patriarchal subordination that excludes their participation in male-defined social realms and confines them to the cloistered perimeters of the home. Criticism of the local patriarchy was not particular to young women desiring secular careers. A group of young women, who had recently graduated from a Qur'an course in the city of Tarsus, set about changing patriarchal attitudes toward women and knowledge—through their piety. This was the case with Ayshe, whose drama-filled wedding I shall now describe.

A Dramatic Wedding

A major source of instruction in the national educational system is the school play (*müsamere*). Ever since Ottoman Turkish intellectuals, like Ziya Pasha, governor of Adana, adopted Western drama in the 1860s, theatre has been deemed an effective pedagogical vehicle to foster collective solidarity and patriotism and promote social causes. Likewise, republican educators recognized the importance of school plays for the political sociability of children. As a ministerial directive states, plays are intended to inculcate "love of humanity, nation, and country" all the while stigmatizing those forms of knowledge that the ministry disapproves.[80]

Like textbooks, school plays are intended to link particular ideas and events to collective histories and identities to create a cultural homogeneity with which citizens of different backgrounds identify. The language and knowledge so produced realign individual subjectivities along nationalist lines. There are substantial differences between the two sources of instruction, however. The school play differs from a textbook in that the former relies on the audience watching and listening to an onstage cast, not reading in-text characters. The school play differs from other forms of drama in that playwrights for the school system take their cues from pedagogical directives and goals, not from personal memories or those of other individuals. That is to say, the cast of onstage characters speak to one another to simulate a political imaginary for the offstage listeners and stimulate identification with this imaginary in order that both cast and audience emulate ideal generic heroes and heroines. The speech of characters is heard in terms of what the authorized playwright is allowed to say through the characters and not in terms of the character's own discursive intentions. In this regard, school plays with their stylized speech and didactic messages can be likened to rituals whose (liturgical) scripts are intended to move the audience to redemptive thoughts and feelings that in turn will transform it into a model community.

In Yayla, during the major national holidays, townspeople came to watch their children perform school plays. Most themes centered on patriotism, hygiene, frugality, or identification with the secular reforms, including emancipation of women. In October, the elementary school children put on the one-act play *Republic Day*, as befitting the national day. Each child-character chose what he or she thought was the greatest achievement of the republican regime. The heroine Filiz (which literally means "slender and beautiful woman") singled out coeducation.

Had there not been a Turkish Revolution [i.e., Atatürk's reforms], I would most likely be wearing a large headscarf by age seven, memorizing the Qur'an by nine, but I would be unable to understand any of it [since it is written in Arabic]. I would think that the stars above us were gold nails hammered onto the sky's walls, and that I couldn't do the least thing about the world or my life. That is, I would be no different from an oak tree . . . I would be even worse off. . . . I would live behind thick curtains without even having the most elementary rights. And, the bitterest thing . . . I would not even notice this appalling state of affairs because of my ignorance. Whenever I think of this and compare my life with that of my grandmother and even with that of my mother, I am flabbergasted and happy.

Filiz's soliloquy reinforces a school discourse that constantly associates restrictive dress code with women's oppression, both metonymically representing backwardness. Thus, a passage in a third-grade reader describes how a parent takes pride in her daughter's scouts uniform: "Mother recalled the old days: 'Blessed are those who made it possible to witness [the changes] in our lifetimes. In the past, we covered our faces with a jet black veil. We could not even make out the tip of our nose. And oh that *charshaf* [the long, black, tentlike dress that covers the head and the entire body]! It made us look like a ghost.'"[81] Periodization (as in linking social mores with standard historical periods—primitive, medieval, modern) is a rhetorical means intended to break away from a devalued past. A second-grade primer graphically depicts the opposition between progress and backwardness: one picture shows a black veil and Arabic scribble; opposite it is a picture of an unveiled woman and the Latin character *A*.[82]

Such overarching narratives of progress and emancipation saturate so much of children's historical consciousness that schoolchildren relate individual lives and experiences in terms of modernist discourses about dress. That is to say, the attire that a person wears is taken as an index of their modern or primitive mentality. Thus, in an essay on "Our Modern and Cultured People," Burak, an eighth-grade boy, asserts that "there are still primitive people in Turkey. Their behavior dates back to ancient times. For example, some women wear the veil or *charshaf*. But a cultured person acts in a completely opposite manner." While Burak and other boys understand attire to index historical periods, most girls explicitly link a wardrobe to an entire gamut of social relations between men and women. The unveiled woman comes to signify sexual parity. At least that is what Selda, one of the few women high school students, seemed to argue in her essay.

Whether a person has money or not, she can certainly become modern. For example, let's take the case of a very rich family. Never mind how modern the [male] head of the family [*aile reisi*] seems to be, he doesn't even come close to modernity. He makes his wife wear the veil. She doesn't behave like a wife, but rather like a slave. So no matter how wealthy a person is, if his temperament doesn't lend itself to modernity, money will be of no use. Now let's take the example of a poor family. The man behaves in an appropriate fashion toward his wife and respects women's rights. He gives his wife permission to work outside the home. The woman both respects and loves her husband. There is mutual love.[83]

Except for a few young Qur'an course graduates, whom I will discuss in greater detail below, townswomen do not wear clothes that bear any resemblance to a veil or charshaf. If anything, as Nefide, then in seventh grade, noted in her essay "My People," younger women "have begun to adapt a bit to city costumes." This is most evident at local weddings, when Western dress and shoes with high heels are worn and young women reveal part of their forelock. What was far more radical in Selda's essay was her taking up the idea of companionate conjugal relations whereby men have to accept marriage as a relation between equals so as to achieve domestic happiness. To think of marital relations as one based on partnership, mutual respect, and open communication considerably departs from the Turkish Islamists' nostalgia for an imagined men-in-control family.[84]

The sartorial ideals, as embodied in the character Filiz and praised by Selda, have not impressed all young women, however. Ever since Ayshe, my landlord's sister, attended an unofficial Qur'an course for teenage girls in the nearby city of Tarsus, she has consciously adopted those prerepublican sartorial norms that the school play discredited. She wore an especially large headscarf, completely covering the neck, shoulders, and chest, and a loose-fitting cover-all topcoat (*zar*), worn in all weather to conceal the contours of her body. In local parlance, she belonged to the turbaned (*sarıklı*) women; the turban being the male headdress outlawed as part of the secular reforms legislated in the 1920s. Their religious dress code was not only a response to a society that has pushed Islam to the margins of everyday life. It also created an arena of all-female solidarity.

From what I learned from Ayshe, the lessons at the Qur'an course differed little in format from those she had undergone in elementary school; they consisted mainly of lectures and rote memorization. Her "mother-teacher" (*hoca anne*), a middle-age woman who came from a family associated with the Nakshibendi brotherhood, also led lively discussions on current economic and social transformations in the country, a moral economy based on piety and, above all, a Muslim woman's responsibilities in society. It goes without saying that Ayshe did not think the religious instruction she acquired in Tarsus had rendered her into either an ignorant person or an inert object as the school-play character Filiz suggested; rather, she felt empowered to confront head-on the secular ideals she had been exposed to for five years at the local elementary school.

This confrontation soon took place—at her wedding. Anybody who had heard about how Ayshe had conducted her marital negotiations independently of relatives anticipated that her wedding would be very different from previous ones. They were not disappointed.

A few words on town weddings are in order. Weddings are highly tense occasions. They are more than a celebration of the union of two households; in the words of anthropologist Victor Turner, weddings are "life-crisis ceremonies," in which "many relationships among group members must change drastically, involving much potential and even actual conflict and competition."[85] Townspeople are keenly aware that their attendance, their gift, their household reputation, and their verbal interactions are objects of intense scrutiny and that the outcome can and does affect future relations in the community. The juxtaposition of mournful songs about the bride's departure from her parents' home (e.g., *Kız Anası*, literally, "the daughter's mother") and sexualized dancing suggestive of the nuptial night complement the sublimated social tensions of the wedding. The night before the marriage, "the night of the henna" (*kına gecesi*), in which the bride's hands are smeared with henna dye (popularly understood as symbolizing earthly fertility), some of the bride's female age-peers dress up as mustachioed men and perform skits and dances. At one of these evenings, which I attended, the bride sat in a chair while married and unmarried women, holding up a round tray of henna surrounded by candles, danced circles around her. Periodically, the women smashed the pile of melting henna with their fists, at which moment the bride cried and some of the more brazen married women cracked jokes on the stiffness of the groom's penis and the length of time it will take to break the virgin bride's hymen.

In any case, well before the betrothal, Ayshe had decided to forgo the typical wedding young couples in Yayla celebrated at the time. A serious, if not somewhat dour, person, she disdained the levity of marriage festivities as well as objected to the de rigueur Western white bridal robe and the presence of men on this commemorative day. (To her, male relatives should only be present for the modest, commemorative noon meal.) Her wedding would be different; it would be educational. She took charge of organizing the wedding and this included putting on a play that would foreground her religious convictions and pious religiosity.

I now turn to describing the dramatic turn Ayshe's wedding took. With her former teacher and classmates from the Qur'an course, she performed three skits, all of which constituted an Islamic parable of secular modernity.[86] Before the performance, a procession of classmates led the young bride into a sitting room, turned into a theatre for the occasion. Each woman carried a notebook of hymns from which they chanted verses (e.g., "The people will go on the true path / Islam will embrace the whole world today," "The [civilian] law changes, the Qur'an never") that related far more to public affairs than marriage. Then, while the classmates installed Ayshe in the middle of the divan in the rear of the room, her teacher introduced the program and delegated roles to her former and current students—very much like a headmaster does for elementary pupils about to perform a school play. The sketches follow, as it were, a predetermined logic: from the exteriorized social life of rural women to the more discrete and individualized existence of the educated city dweller and finally extending to the inner psyche, hidden from normal human perception. Moreover, they lay bare a particular social order of meaning in which men and women are held morally responsible for both their outward actions and their most intimate thoughts and feelings. Here, personal character must coincide with public conduct; together, they form the basis of the pious individual and her community of believers.

The first skit concerned the period of betrothal when a bride's mother strives to procure optimal living conditions, including high-status gifts, for her daughter. Two rural families each aspire to marry off their daughters to the same young, rich man. The groom's parents desire a modern spouse—someone who knows when and where to cover or bare her head and other body parts; in other words, a woman who is able to adapt her outward behavior to both secular urban and more traditional rural settings. One bridal candidate and her mother will do whatever is necessary to conform to the wishes of the groom's parents. At the point that the two women are discussing how many television sets they will receive in the dowry, the teacher interrupts the scene to reproach the two characters with rapaciousness. In Turkish, the term for *greed* is constructed from elements that mean "one with a pair of hungry eyes" (*açgözlük*). Following the teacher's digression, the scene resumes, and contrary to expectations, the rich groom chooses the "blind" girl (*kör kız*) who is ignorant of worldly affairs; all she knows is the Qur'an.

To a large extent, the scenario was familiar to all the spectators. Preceding and during a period of engagement, the negotiations between the groom's and the bride's families put the future reputation of both households at stake. And most vulnerable is the bride who joins her husband's household. Should her family be seen as having been too rapacious in contracting the matrimonial alliance, then her husband's relatives will hold her later responsible for the actions of her parents.[87] That was not the point of the skit, however. At least, not for the teacher. At the conclusion of the skit, the teacher paired off greed and self-interest (*menfaat*) against blindness with proper intentions (*niyet*) to argue that obsession over material goods had blinded mother and daughter from recognizing the preeminence of spiritual faith in matrimony and that expert knowledge of the material world had tainted their outward behavior and, as a consequence, their inner state. The blind ignorance of the other bridal candidate, on the other hand, sustained an innocence that successfully transcended the external trappings of an increasingly commodified society.[88] To paraphrase one spectator's synopsis of the teacher's comments, a wedding shouldn't be the culmination of two families bargaining over commodity goods; rather, a mother should worry about the consequences of marital agreement for her daughter's afterlife.

Underlying the mother-teacher's judgment of the bridal contest is a mystical (Sufi) understanding of knowledge, as one derived from divine illumination, which lies beyond the apparent world. In effect, she disparages the secular conceit that empirically observed forms of knowledge are an emancipatory force in society. In the context of state-run schools, the main reference point is the distinction between light (*ışık*), on the one hand, and darkness, on the other, always keyed to mass education and its uneducated Others. Light in all its forms is a recurrent motif by which the official political culture construes the state's pedagogical mission. "There is no returning to darkness; only to become civilized and progressive," the minister of Education Avni Akyol told the audience of a televised opening of a new elementary school in Istanbul.[89] Not surprisingly, since the republic's inception, the torch has been the logo of the Ministry of Education. The symbolic dimension of the torch is vividly captured in Ferid Karslı's semiautobiographical novel, written in the 1930s. It tells the story of a heroic teacher waxing lyrical about what he will accomplish in a desolate village: "I don't suppose we'll find the light of electricity in the village. But that doesn't matter, we're bearing a torch and its light will illuminate not only this region, but the entire nation."[90]

Indeed, the national educational system continues to regularly represent teachers as guiding the common people away from superstitions and ignorance and leading them to enlightenment. One of the duties of instructors, as outlined in *The Elementary School Program* manual, is to "distance the student from false superstitions and beliefs he has received from his family and milieu and from various sources outside school."[91] For educators, seeing with wide open eyes is the prototypical form of knowing. Thus, for example, a poem in a second-grade reader begins with the verses "My teacher is like the sun / Who holds up the light against darkness."[92] In the same class, during Teachers' Day (24 November), second graders graphically represented their instructor as a candle that emits light. The teacher, visibly moved by the pupils' drawings, expressed to me how devoted she was to enlightening the children: "I will surely ignite a light inside these children whose spark of life has darkened in their extinguished hearts . . . ; then they will be the best people in the whole world." In moments of exasperation, I also heard her blurt out, "open your eyes . . . and [do] not remain blind ignoramuses" (*gözünüzü açınız . . . kör cahil kalmayınız*).

In short, the mother-teacher's mystical notion of enlightenment collided with that upheld in the school system and, to a large extent, with that in the society as a whole. In the context of the skit, however, the virtuous "blind" woman, who shunned the material world for an inner spiritual one, won the contest over the groom.

The second skit concerned a university graduate who, upon discovering the Qur'an and its eternal truths, decides to live a life of modesty and set up a devout household. She requires that all prospective grooms agree to four conditions: one, she will cover her head whenever she leaves the home; two, she will teach him to read the Qur'an; three, he shall grow a beard and keep ritually clean; and four, she will wear a bridal outfit that does not give away the shape of her body. In her monologue about the ideal husband, she emphasizes his "faith and practices" and shows indifference to his "family [economic] situation and all that it concerns." Very much in line with the overall ideas of the first skit, the Qur'an graduates question the concept of a couple aimed at biological reproduction of household and familial self-preservation. Rather, this skit suggests a marital love in which husband wife mutually support each other through their common faith.

Once more at the end of the skit, the teacher interjected her thoughts and beseeched the audience to review their ideas about matrimony.

> We say when asking for a woman in marriage, "According to the command of God and the word of the Prophet," but aren't we really thinking whether the groom is an engineer or the son of a doctor? Today's mothers don't ask whether the son-in-law is pious or not. It is inconceivable that someone is a Muslim simply because he recites the confession of faith [*kelime-i şehadet*] in a Muslim country. If someone does blasphemous things, then one cannot call that person a Muslim. . . . It is thus wrong for a pious girl to marry an impious person. The groom has to be the woman's equal in religious matters. He must complement her strong beliefs. Let this skit be an example.

The teacher's comments were clear to all present: active performance of the faith, not religious affiliation by birth, defined the religiousness of a person and his household. Accordingly, a man who doesn't practice his faith removes himself from the Muslim community, and by association, his wife, however devout she herself may be. In upholding the separation of sexes on moral grounds and expecting both sexes to adhere equally to the same moral code, she inverted the patriarchal discourse of the conjugal couple, in which men educate women on how to be proper spouses. Rather, she suggested that should husbands fail to live up to the same moral standards and be spiritual partners, then women have to intervene in the non-Islamic deeds of men and take responsibility for the household's spiritual welfare.

Her provocative suggestion raised long-simmering issues about the double standards regarding the religiousness of women and men in Yayla.

Although most men were lax about their religious practices, almost all expected the women in the household to observe the five daily prayers and the fasts as well as hold gatherings to read the *mevlûd*, Süleyman Çelebi's fifteenth-century panegyrical poem about the birth of the prophet Muhammad, at all major rites of passage (birth, circumcision, military service, betrothal, and death). As a rule, men read only selected passages from the long poem, most often from an edition that has been transcribed into Latin characters. Women, on the other hand, read the text in its entirety and only from copies printed in Arabic characters, which they associate with divine powers.[93]

Collective expectations about women's religiousness derive in no small measure from earlier resistance to coeducation in state-run schools. While mostly boys attended the local elementary school and acquired rudimentary literacy skills in modern Turkish and its Latin characters, girls remained at home and learned to decipher Arabic characters (colloquially called "old writing" or "old letters") from a woman teacher (*kadın hoca*) who was known for her personal sanctity and recitation skills. Emphasis, then as now, was on recitation of the sacred verses of the Qur'an, not necessarily understanding them. As reading out loud from a holy text is perceived as an act of spiritual love (*muhabbet*), female household members literate in the Arabic script are assumed to channel the supernatural world into the privacy of the home. And a household accrues even more prestige when it hosts a major *mevlûd* reading, in which women from a neighborhood as well as from other neighborhoods and communities participate.

Not all private religious gatherings have met approbation from townsmen. As young turbaned women like Ayshe gain direct access to religious texts in Qur'an courses, there has emerged a new style of religiousness that openly challenges a previously unquestioned patriarchy in the community. The Qur'anic injunction that "a woman who does not show respect to her husband does not show respect to God as well," which many husbands often related to me to justify wifely submission, no longer seemed to hold sway over young women. One consequence of this shift in form of religious knowledge is that men's impious activities have increasingly come under critical scrutiny among women and are understood and explained as jeopardizing home and community. Even more threatening to townsmen is that those patriarchal norms that limit women's horizons of mobility outside the home effectively prevent the men from scrutinizing from up close women's meetings. A year before my arrival, some of the husbands feared the worse— that the *mevlûd* recitals were only a pretext for their wives and turbaned female friends to cast spells against their gambling and consumption of alcohol. Fearing that their wives were using religion as an act of defiance, they called in the rural police to close down a meeting, invoking the rarely applied law that forbids religious gatherings in private homes.[94] No woman was arrested, but the religious literature was taken away. The husbands' drastic action had no precedent in the town's history. It did, however, underscore how women's desire to change lives and circumstances threatened local male hegemony.

The third and final skit performed at Ayshe's wedding concerned the impact of a commodity-driven market on the inner psyche. A young woman watches a television commercial advertising Müjde nylons, the most widely sold brand in the country. The spot shows an actress (*artist*) wearing a very open (*açık*) dress that reveals the entire length of her legs. The viewer subsequently goes to bed. In her dream, she sees herself among the dead and a person with an account book, weighing her good and bad deeds. She had sinned when she subjected her eyes to a publicly open film. Upon waking up, she decides to veil herself; she literally closes herself up before men and mass media.

At the conclusion of the skit, the teacher explained why the audience should refrain from watching television, except for those religious programs aired on Holy Nights.

> Television is an infidel's invention [*gâvur icadı*]. Remember that Allah Most High is always watching. At the Day of Judgment your eyes will bear witness of what you watched. Remember that Allah Most Just and Merciful knows what is in your heart. In the Hereafter, he rewards us for our good deeds; he punishes us for our bad deeds. When you watch [Islamically] unacceptable [*haram*] programs that show improperly dressed men and women, then you are committing a sin. Prophet Muhammad, peace be upon him, says, "The furtive glance is one of the poisoned arrows of Şeytan [the Devil], on him be God's curse. Whoever forsakes it for fear of Allah will receive from Him, Great and Gracious is He, a faith the sweetness of which he will find within his heart." . . . The divine dream saved the Muslim woman from the trappings of the infidel West.

Here, the teacher's commentary reinforces a patriarchal discourse that presupposes that young women inherently lack self-control over their bodily appetites (*nefs*). Conversely, an adult man is assumed to have greater faculty of reason (*akıl*) to exercise self-restraint with the opposite sex, to avoid any untoward remarks or looks toward a non-kin woman. Should he fail to have control over his loins (*bel bağlı*), he is said to be a ropeless (*ipsiz*) person—one who has severed moral ties with the Islamic community.[95] According to this sexual division of emotions, young women are liable to imitate the commercial artiste—a French term that popularly connotes not drama skills but rather scandalous openness of the female body and unfettered promiscuity. The model's legs serve as a metonym for lust; the nylons, for an infidel West and commoditized sexuality. To draw out the difference between the televised world of commodities and the spiritual imaginary of piety, the skit takes recourse to a mystical understanding of sight in visionary dreams. Dreams are popularly understood as divinely inspired messages that expose the most private inaccessible pasts of a person and, as a result, provide meaningful, causal connection with the future life of the dreamer. Key to this esoteric notion of vision is blind (to beg the pun) submission to spiritual wisdom and guidance; the novice initiate must withdraw herself totally from the illusions of the everyday world to experience unity with Allah.

This close association between seeking total knowledge and experiencing initial blindness was made evident to me while visiting a Sufi lodge at Mersin; one of my hosts exemplified this relation with a popular expression: "Who is blind? When a man is a stranger in a country [he is blind], whether he has eyes or not" (*Kör kimdir? Garip isterse gözleri olsun*).[96] Accordingly, only in the unconscious state of a dream is revealed the divine light (*nur*)— the relation between a dreamer's past and subsequent experiences. As a result, the novice initiate gains control of what is normally beyond conscious control, gains visibility to the invisible, paranormal world. Thus, it is during the pitch-black nonconscious state of sleep, when an individual oscillates between life and death,[97] that the dreamer reconstitutes her private self in such a way as to adopt a new social identity and reemerge into a new everyday self: from young sinner to a pious, virtuous woman. In Lacanian terms, the surreal dream provides the possibility to see one's past and future self, to "see" at all.[98] The vision that links life, death, and rebirth was a fitting finale for this theatrical performance that wed the material realities with the inner-most thoughts of both cast and audience.

The three skits brought into sharp relief issues common to the performers and their public: uncertainty about the appropriate gendered forms of behavior as women increasingly participate in the public sphere and market-place; ambivalence about deeply rooted codes regulating gender and generational relations; and unease at public discourses that have pushed a spiritual cosmography to the margins of everyday life. To reverse this societal trend, the turbaned women turned the wedding into a didactic forum: a dramatic introduction to an alternative, moral order and its particular understanding of gender relations, household, and market, which most of the audience was neither familiar with nor had participated in. The aesthetic conventions of the school play, which they had been exposed to in the secular school system, lent themselves to telling the "life" story of the Qur'an course graduates of the women belonging to the local piety movement. They took on the role of the storyteller who translates individually lived-out experiences (*das Erlebnis*) into a collective experience for the listeners. Or as the German-Jewish literary critic Walter Benjamin wrote in his classic essay "The Storyteller," "storytelling . . . does not aim to convey the pure essence of the thing, like information or a report. It sinks the thing into the life of the storyteller, in order to bring it out of him again."[99] Likewise, the young women's performance was intended to convey edifying lessons that would invigorate (or to them, re-Islamize) the moral fiber of the community.

It could be argued that all three skits reinforced patriarchal values of husband-worship, family nurturance, and female self-abnegation. After all, the performers accepted the differences in creation between men and women and reaffirmed patriarchal distinctions between male and female spheres of action. Yet the kind of companionate marriage they promoted in the wedding was at odds with gender relations typical of the immediate audience. What may have seemed at first a conservative perspective of gender relations can be arguably construed as defining a spiritual femininity in opposition to male control of women's physical being. The pedagogical roles that the young women assumed for themselves reveal an attempt to regender local society in ways that acknowledge the young women's own personal agency. Normally, male heads of household take upon themselves to be custodians of virtue, to bear authority, responsibility, and accountability over all women and male juniors; unmarried women, in turn, are expected to behave in a submissive manner. This was not the case in Ayshe's wedding. By virtue of their cumulative education, first in the local elementary school, later in the postprimary Qur'an course, Ayshe and her classmates identified themselves as not only servicing the needs of men and children within the domestic sphere but also having the requisite spiritual knowledge to challenge taken-for-granted ideas about gender identities and relations and, more importantly, the authority of older men and women. As Dale Eickelman points out, due to widespread literacy and universal education, young people in the Islamic world no longer rely on the authority of representatives of the "high" tradition to draw meaning out of faith.[100] The Qur'an graduates assumed the role of authority figures, very much like the virtuous young woman in the second skit. Their conscious engagement with the Islamic heritage provided them a sense of agency—an ability to publicly articulate an individual ethics whereby each person is responsible for his or her own actions. In insisting upon segregation of the sexes throughout the wedding ceremonies and expecting both sexes to adhere to a Qur'anic morality, the turbaned bride and classmates had unsettled a patriarchal code that allows men to limit women's expansion in social space.

Suffice it to say, the performers failed to convince the audience of their holiness through the performance, even for those with an affinity for the values espoused. It is one thing for actresses to realize themselves in their roles; it is another matter to expect the audience to identify with the actresses' condition. Women from the same community articulate an ensemble of contingent subject positions at variance with one another precisely because of the ambiguous connections between a particular social vision and a specific gender regime, on the one hand, and the contingent, fluid social situations that comprise the day-to-day understanding of gender, on the other. Thus, if many of the older women seemed confused over the semantic meaning of the performances, they were neither ignorant nor indifferent to the issues dealt with in the skits. A sense of poverty and helplessness, more of which I will discuss in the next chapter, pervades everyday thoughts. Nonetheless, the elderly were taken aback at having unwed women tell them how to conduct marital alliances and show disrespect with their refusal to defer to the older, unlettered women and their moral norms.

Several times during the performance, the mother-preacher asked the "old billies" (*kartlar*) to step outside the room since "they are clueless and can't learn anything new." Going further, as several interviewees told me, she repeatedly invited elementary and middle school–age girls, who were sheepishly standing on the threshold, to sit up front next to the performers. Some of these girls recounted to me how they envied the freedom that the pious young women displayed. Others, many of whom attended the secular-track high schools and universities, were less kind; they treated the Qur'an course graduates as obscurantists or arrogant upstarts. In sum, the dramatic performance had failed in having the entire audiences identify with the virtuous premises of the sketches: collective redemption through personal shame, renunciation of materialist aspirations, and reintegration as pious women. Quite a few of the older women present considered Ayshe and her friends to be troublemakers intent on unleashing divisions among the townswomen and between the townswomen and their spouses, brothers, and fathers. Not an accusation to be taken lightly, given that local women have to daily confront long-standing patriarchal prejudices that blame women for instigating social chaos. Yet whatever reservations some of the audience had about the young performers, townswomen were moved to reflect upon the relationship between gender and modernity as well as to engage with their own gendered position in the community. To this end, the Qur'an course women graduates created an aesthetic space for women to actively participate in ongoing debates about the relation between gender and faith in an increasingly commodified society.

Envoi

Religion is a critical signifier of difference among Turkish citizens. In the context of growing anxieties about Turkey's place in the West, the Turkish Islamists have struggled to create a homogeneous and morally exclusive polity. As privileged interpreters of state-society relations, they have appealed to indigeneity and cultural authenticity to promote a syncretism of religion and nationalism in the educational system. The religious values, which they designate as culture, were all designed to cast Turkish citizens as a normatively cohesive, archetypically moral and patriarchal people. Culture-specific essentialist generalizations (e.g., "Turkish women") permit a conflation of history and culture, which together come to define a generic Turkish citizenship that simultaneously exemplifies the essence of Islam and defies historical contingencies of a nation. History is eliminated, as the future is merely the reassertion of the past. Or as Véronique de Rudder points out, "differences of a cultural nature sometimes shed into natural differences between cultures . . . which, furthermore, tends to naturalize culture, to turn culture into nature, into a new 'race.'"[101] Here, Islam is equated with Turks; Islamic civilization becomes a mirror image of Turkish history. Any deviations from this idealized ethnos can be explained away as historic accidents resulting from crude imitation of the secular West since, according to this logic, almost all Turkish citizens originally grew up with the same values and practices. This nostalgia for residual cultural forms becomes the basis for an insurgent engagement with contemporary global secularism.

Treating culture as a moral descriptive category to forefront certain social identities among citizens was not particular to religious nationalists. Secular industrialists and businesspeople deployed the concept of a *democratic* culture to structure, legitimate, and valorize their neoliberal economics. After all, the economic well-being of citizens is as visceral a national issue as religious identity, both of which are highly gendered. I recall here that Turkish Islamists were of the opinion that secular humanism has induced an emasculation of society, such that dominant masculine motifs of self-control and reason were giving way to self-gratification, selfishness, sexual license, and promiscuous consumption—all of which were assumed to produce a feminized public sphere. The women graduates of the Qur'an course were equally critical of a hedonist materialism taking hold of local society. They did not share the Turkish Islamists' anxiety over gender boundary crossing and the consequent loss of male privilege, however. On the contrary, they challenged a local patriarchy that colluded with the logics of capitalism and an emerging culture of consumption. They attacked the collusion of women with a secularist lifestyle precisely because of what they perceived to be the head-on collision between a patriarchal gender regime and the spiritual world of Islam. It was this collision that spurred the young pious women to reject the neoliberal market economy and its materialist trappings—issues that dominated the social imaginary of the townspeople of Yayla and are the topic of the next chapter.

Notes

1. Verena Stolcke, "Talking Culture: New Boundaries, New Rhetorics of Exclusion in Europe," *Current Anthropology* 36 (1995), p. 2.

2. Niyazi Berkes, *The Development of Secularism in Turkey* (Montreal: McGill University Press, 1964), p. 6.

3. İsmail Kaplan, *Türkiye'de Milli Eğitim ideolojisi ve siyasal toplumsallaşma üzerindeki etkisi* (İstanbul: İletişim, 1999), p. 306.

4. For a trenchant critique of secularist approaches in Turkish scholarship, see Serif Mardin, "Projects as Methodology: Some Thoughts on Modern Turkish Social Science," in *Rethinking Modernity and National Identity in Turkey*, ed. Sibel Bozdoğan and Reşat Kasaba (Seattle: University of Washington Press, 1997), pp. 64–80. Highly sophisticated scholarship on the rise and influence of religious views in Turkish politics and society has emerged in recent years. E.g., Nilufer Göle, *The Forbidden Modern: Civilization and Veiling* (Ann Arbor: University of Michigan Press, 1996); Alev Cinar, "National History as a Contested Site: The Conquest of Istanbul and Islamist Negotiations of the Nation," *Comparative Studies in Society and History* 43 (2001), pp. 364–91; Navaro-Yashin, *Faces of the State*; Ayse-Nur Saktanber, *Living Islam: Women, Religion and the Politicization of Culture in Turkey* (London: I. B. Tauris, 2002); and Jenny White, *Islamist Mobilization in Turkey: A Study in Vernacular Politics* (Seattle: University of Washington Press, 2002).

5. For an overview of this religious nationalist movement, see İlhan Tekeli, "Türk-İslam Sentezi üzerine," *Bilim ve Sanat* 77 (1987), pp. 5–8; Bozkurt Güvenç et al., *Türk-İslam sentezi dosyası* (İstanbul: Sarmal Yayınevi, 1991); for a good analysis in English, see Binnaz Toprak, "Religion as State Ideology in a Secular Setting: The Turkish-Islamic Synthesis," in *Aspects of Religion in Secular Turkey*, ed. Malcolm Wagstaff (Durham, UK: Center for Middle Eastern and Islamic Studies, University of Durham, 1990), pp. 10–15.

6. Güvenç et al., *Türk-İslam sentezi dosyası*, pp. 187–90.

7. Quoted in Güvenç et al., *Türk-İslam sentezi dosyası*, p. 88. The report was titled "Study on Methods and Responsibilities to be used in Establishing Cultural Elements and Politics" ("Kültür unsurlarının ve kültür politikalarının tespitinde uygulanacak yöntem ve sorumluluklar hacında inceleme") and dated 20 June 1986.

8. Quoted in Güvenç et al., *Türk-İslam sentezi dosyası*, pp. 74–75.

9. Quotes respectively from Toprak, "Religion as State Ideology in a Secular Setting," p. 13 and Güvenç et al., *Türk-İslam sentezi dosyası*, p. 54. Both authors are referring to T. C. Başbakanlık, Devlet Planlama Teşkilatı, Millî Kültür: Özel İhtisas Komisyonu Raporu Yayın No. DPT: 1920-OIK: 300 (Ankara, 1983), p. 527.

10. Minister of Education Hasan Celal Güzel commissioned Bozkurt Güvenç, then professor of anthropology at Hacettepe University, to write a report comparing Turkish and Japanese cultures. The minister refused to publish it since Güvenç, who

favors viewing Turkey as complex mosaic of diverse identities, did not support the Turkish Islamists' arguments about a singular national culture (private communication, Ankara, August 1986).

11. Associating a distinct, sovereign national consciousness with a "spiritual domain of culture" has been a central feature in many non-Western nationalist movements since the nineteenth century. It goes without saying that this derivative discourse elides doctrinal or sectarian differences within the religion. See Partha Chatterjee, "History and the Nationalization of Hinduism," *Social Research* 59 (1992), pp. 147–49.

12. "'Din bilgisi' dersi programlarının yürürlükten kadırılması; 'Din ve ahlâk bilgisi' dersinin konulması," *TD* 45 (29 March 1982), p. 156.

13. Gregory Starrett, "Margins of Print: Children's Religious Literature in Egypt," *Journal of the Royal Anthropological Institute* 2 (1996), p. 127.

14. School textbooks continued to portray Turkish people with Aryan features. In an interview he gave to the newspaper *Cumhuriyet* (10 July 1989), the minister of Education Avni Akyol publicly condemned the graphic representation of "white" Turks in textbooks: "There are pictures in which neither you nor I exist. All the children in textbooks have round blue eyes and blond hair. Because our children can't find such persons in their midst, they will look at these books and say, 'Goodness gracious, who's this person?'"

15. For a detailed analysis of biology and history textbooks from the 1930s that stressed the "whiteness" of the Turkish people, see pp. 36–40 in my "Education and the Politics of National Culture in a Turkish Community, ca. 1990," PhD diss., Department of Anthropology, University of Chicago, 1996.

16. Although the curriculum has long dropped the proto-Aryan thesis, the main outlines of the Turkish History Thesis continue to be taught in the school system, albeit in a slightly more attenuated manner. At a school play that I attended, one of the stage characters shouted out "The Turkish Nation did not spring from a small lineage but raised hundreds of lineages and, since time immemorial, has sowed the seeds of civilization to the entire world."

17. Necmeddin Sadık, *Sosyoloji, liseler için yeni programa göre* (Ankara: Devlet Matbaası, 1936), p. 47.

18. Cihad Tunç, *Ortaokullar için din kültürü ve ahlâk bilgisi* 2 (İstanbul: Millî Eğitim Basımevi, 1987), p. 94.

19. Tunç, *Din kültürü ve ahlâk bilgisi* 2, p. 93.

20. Tunç, *Din kültürü ve ahlâk bilgisi* 2, p. 51.

21. This nationalist representation of Islam is also found to be the case in television programming. As Emilie Olson notes, during the month-long Ramazan fast, the "religious programs [on television] were presented in the context of Turkey's *national* heritage, not in the context of the pan-Islamic community"; see her "Muslim Identity and Secularism in Contemporary Turkey: 'The Headscarf Dispute,'" *Anthropological Quarterly* 58 (1985), p. 167; her emphasis.

22. Tunç, *Din kültürü ve ahlâk bilgisi 2*, pp. 96–97. Other religion textbooks ascribe Turkish ancestry to illustrious Muslim scholars, including the philosopher Averroes (Ibn Rushd) and the great theologian Gazzali; see Jacob, *L'enseignement religieux*, p. 377.

23. Tunç, *Din kültürü ve ahlâk bilgisi 2*, p. 60. Other religious manuals mention praise from Lamartine, Bismark, John Davenport, and Thomas Arnolds; see Jacob, *L'enseignement religieux*, p. 399.

24. Veysel Gani, "Osmanlı eğitim sistemi," *Millî Eğitim* 85 (1989), pp. 49–55.

25. Amiran Kurtkan Bilgiseven, *Millî eğitim sistemimiz nasıl olmalıdır?* (İstanbul: Türk Dünyası Araştırmaları Vakfı, 1986), p. 11.

26. In his popular column for the conservative daily *Türkiye*, Ali Güler set out to prove the scientific bases of the evil eye (*nazar*): "Today, science accepts that rays come out of certain people's eyes. When some people see something they like, rays coming out of their eyes harm animate and inanimate things. . . . There are people whose evil eye causes misfortunes in society. Experience has shown that the evil eye influences more often women and children." "Göz değmesine bâtıl inanış denir mi?" *Türkiye* (7 October 1990), p. 9. His explanation notwithstanding, the only cure the journalist could conjure up was reading certain passages from the Qur'an or carrying an amulet.

27. Binnaz Toprak, "The State, Politics and Religion in Turkey," in *State, Democracy and the Military: Turkey in the 1980s*, ed. Metin Heper and Ahmet Evin (Berlin: Walter de Gruyter, 1988), p. 131. The curriculum presented only creationism. Turan Güven, an assistant professor of embryology at Ankara University and once vice president of the ultra-right-wing paramilitary student organization Ülkü Bir, was placed in charge of authoring the ninth-grade biological textbook. In an interview with the liberal weekly *Tempo* (29 October 1989), he defended his creationist views: "Ninety-nine per cent of the people in Turkey are Muslim. . . . The views in biology lessons must reflect our people's beliefs and philosophy. Or are we only to take all our views from the West? Don't we have our own views?"

28. Quoted in Kirby Page, "Nationalism Interprets Islam," *Christian Century* 47 (1930), p. 114.

29. Tunç, *Din kültürü ve ahlâk bilgisi 2*, pp. 24–25.

30. Tunç, *Din kültürü ve ahlâk bilgisi 2*, p. 101.

31. Tunç, *Din kültürü ve ahlâk bilgisi 2*, p. 44.

32. Tunç, *Din kültürü ve ahlâk bilgisi 2*, p. 121.

33. See, for example, Michael Meeker's discussion of radical Muslim intellectuals who aspire to recapture the pristine Islamic community; "The New Muslim Intellectuals in the Republic of Turkey," in *Islam in Modern Turkey: Religion, Politics and Literature in a Secular State*, ed. Richard Tapper (London: I. B. Tauris, 1991), pp. 189–219.

34. Distinguishing superstitions and false belief from true religion concerned the pre-Ottoman state. Then officials, acting in the name of the state, upheld canonical

law and punished those individuals accused of leading astray the Muslim community. The current school system takes a radically different approach; it intervenes by promoting those beliefs, practices, and ethics to which believers *willingly* give assent because they belong to the natural order of things and thus naturally befit the Turkish people.

35. "'Din ve ahlâk bilgisi' dersinin konulması," *TD* 45 (29 March 1982), p. 156. Four years later, another directive repeated the wording verbatim; see "Din kültürü ve ahlâk bilgisi dersi öğretim programına ait genel ilkelerin kabulü," *TD* 49 (20 October 1986), p. 402.

36. It is important to bear in mind that the author chose to use neologisms such as *bilimsel* ("scientific"), *akılcı* ("rational"), *aktif* ("active"), and *ilerleme* ("progress") in evaluating positively a religious-inspired modernity. Conversely, school textbooks and ministerial directives draw on a vocabulary based on Arabic cognates to denounce "false" (read, nonscientific) interpretations of the Islamic faith. For example, a directive on teaching Atatürk's principles attacks "superstition, sophistry, and ignorance" (*hürafe, safasata ve cehalet*). "Temel eğitim ve ortaöğretim kurumlarında Atatürk inkılap ve ilkelerinin öğretim esasları yönergesi," *TD* 45 (18 January 1982), p. 38.

37. Tunç, *Din kültürü ve ahlâk bilgisi 2*, pp. 44, 88. In Egypt, the state promotes a similar functionalist role to Islam; see Starrett, *Putting Islam to Work*, pp. 155–56.

38. Tunç, *Din kültürü ve ahlâk bilgisi 2*, p. 89.

39. Tunç, *Din kültürü ve ahlâk bilgisi 2*, p. 120.

40. Older men normally sport a round trimmed beard (*çember sakal*).

41. It is well known that Atatürk died of cirrhosis of the liver—not an issue in Yayla where most adult men consume alcohol. Religious critics, who disapproved of his drinking, frequently mention an apocryphal story, in which the statesman supposedly ordered a minaret torn down since it obstructed the view of the Bosphorus strait from his favorite bar; see Ruth Mandel, "Turkish Headscarves and the 'Foreigner Problem': Constructing Difference through Emblems of Identity," *New German Critique* 46 (1989), p. 32.

42. In 1926, the Kemalist regime introduced the Gregorian calendar as part of a series of reforms on measurements, including the twenty-four-hour clock, the meter, and the kilogram. These reforms were touted as "international" because the rational calibrations were deemed to transcend national or communitarian identities. See Bernard Lewis, *The Emergence of Modern Turkey* (Oxford, UK: Oxford University Press, 1968), p. 270.

43. In 1990, about 71 percent of the 9.5 million illiterate citizens over six years old were women and girls. State Institute of Statistics, *Statistical Year Book of Turkey, 1993* (Ankara: Devlet İstatistik Enstitüsü Matbaası, 1993), p. 69.

44. See Iver B. Neumann, and Jennifer M. Welsh, "The Other in European Self-definition: An Addendum to the Literature on International Relations," *Review of International Studies* 17 (1991), pp. 327–48.

45. See Lila Abu-Lughod, "Do Muslim Women Really Need Saving? Anthropological Reflections on Cultural Relativism and Its Others," *American Anthropologist* 104 (2002), pp. 783–90.

46. On the eve of World War I, with the emergence of a Turkish nationalism, the Muslim upper classes began to identify with the new or national family (*yeni/millî aile*), which corresponded to the monogamous educated couple. Zafer Toprak, "II. Meşrutiyet döneminde devlet, aile ve feminizm," in *Sosyo-kültürel değişme sürecinde Türk ailesi*, ed. Ezel Erverdi (Ankara: T. C. Başbakanlık Aile Araştırma Kurumu, 1992), p. 229.

47. Cemil Çiçek hails from Yozgat, a large town in central-eastern Anatolia known for its conservative electorate. While a student at the Faculty of Law at Ankara University during the 1970s, he belonged the Union for National Struggle (*Millî Mücadele Birliği*), a religious-inspired paramilitary organization.

48. "Aile, hükümetten kurtulamıyor," *Güneş* (18 December 1991), p. 4.

49. "Kadının çalışması riskli," *Güneş* (27 September 1990), p. 12.

50. Orhan Türkdoğan, "Aile yapıları, *Türk Edebiyatı* 202 (1990), p. 42. Elsewhere, in the flagship journal of the Ministry of Education, Türkdoğan was quoted bemoaning a "youth growing up without religion, taking on a materialist worldview and a consumerist life style, and becoming estranged from the nation." Mustafa Aksoy, "Akif'e göre aile, eğitim ve aydınlar," *Millî Eğitim* 95 (1990), p. 42.

51. "Türk ailesinin profili çıkarılacak," *Türkiye* (5 October 1990), p. 7.

52. Cemil Çiçek, "Aile, nikâhı ve nikâha saygıyı esas alan bir müessesedir," *Türk Edebiyatı* 202 (1990), p. 7.

53. "Aile, hükümetten kurtulamıyor," *Güneş* (18 December 1990), p. 4.

54. Ali Boratav, Hatice Seçkin, and Emre Koyuncuoğlu, "Aile nasıl kurtulur?" *Nokta* (11 November 1990), p. 70. Necmettin Turinay, who heads the Institute for Family Research, voiced similar fears, saying that "women's functions have developed as a result of them taking on responsibilities handed over from their fathers and husbands." "Seçilme nedeni analşılamayan başkan," *Güneş* (28 September 1990), p. 10.

55. *İlkokul Türkçe ders kitabı 1* (İstanbul: Karacan Yayınları, 1989), p. 1; emphases mine.

56. *İlkokul hayat bilgisi 3* (İstanbul: Millî Eğitim Basım, 1990), p. 30.

57. The connection between Mother's Day and Family Day is self-evident in Turkish. The word *aile* can mean either the entire family unit or only the married woman. For example, open-air tea gardens are divided into two sections, one for men only (*erkeklere*) and one for the family (*aileye mahsus*), where women and children sit.

58. The "married" couple in the photo shoot worked for the Family Information Center, which is run by Turkish Islamists. Although the campaign was designed to celebrate the extended patriarchal family, the "grandparents" turned out to be residents of an old-age home; see "Aile nasıl kurtulur?" *Nokta* (11 November 1990), p. 70.

59. Aydoğdu, *Türkçe ilkokul 3*, pp. 55–56.

60. Hüseyin Hüsnü Tekışık, *Hayat bilgisi ünitelerine kaynak kitap 3* (Ankara: Tekışı k Matbaası ve Rehber Yayınevi, 1983), p. 26.

61. Fikret Özgönenç, *Ailenin eğitim görevleri* (İstanbul: Remzi Kitabevi, 1972), p. 75.

62. The local legend has its counterparts elsewhere in Turkey. All over the country are localities with the name of Kız Kalesi, the Maiden in the Castle. No matter how impregnable or isolated the castle, the snake ultimately strikes the king's daughter.

63. Richard Harvey Brown, "The Position of the Narrative in Contemporary Society," *New Literary History* 11 (1979–80), p. 545.

64. "Genç Kızlar Aldanmayın!" Türkiye (28 September 1990), p. 8.

65. Black bands are also used to cover the nipples of foreign tourists, whose pictures decorate the back pages of national tabloids (e.g., *Bugün*); the bands often miss their designated targets.

66. "Genç Kızlar Aldanmayın!" Türkiye (28 September 1990), p. 8.

67. Hürriyet (4 July 1983).

68. Kız dediğim kaledir, yıkılırsa çürük çaput olur.

69. "Temel eğitim ve orta öğretimde ahlâk dersleri programı," *TD* 37 (22 July 1974), pp. 301–2. Female chastity is equally associated with upholding the nation's honor during times of warfare; see Chapter 5.

70. "Milli eğitim bakanlığı ile diğer bakanlıklara bağlı okullardaki görevlilerle öğrencilerin kılık–kıyafetlerine ilişkin yönetmelik," *TD* 45 (1 February 1982), pp. 63–64.

71. See Carol Delaney, "Untangling the Meanings of Hair in Turkish Society," *Anthropological Quarterly* 67 (1994), pp. 159–72.

72. "Kılık–kıyafetlerine ilişkin yönetmelik," *TD* 45 (1 February 1982), p. 64.

73. This concern over sexual promiscuity of women teachers has dogged the educational system since the 1930s. In 1934, the ministry first published a directive that forbade women teachers from dressing like "movie stars," which would otherwise tarnish "their pedagogical role"; see Ramazan Gökalp Arkın, *İlkokul öğretmenine temel kitap: köy ve şehir öğretmenlerinin, öğretmen olacakların ve ilköğretimle ilgililerin kitabı* (İstanbul: Türkiye Yayınevi, 1966), p. 636.

74. Halil Fikret Kanad, *Ailede çocuk terbiyesi* (İstanbul: Millî Eğitim Basımevi, 1969), p. 161.

75. In a university study on normative attitudes to sexual behavior of men and women, 84 percent of the male respondents said that men should experience premarital sex, whereas 76 percent considered it wrong for women to lose their virginity before marriage. Of those men surveyed, about 76 percent had some sexual experience before marriage, most often in a state-regulated brothel; see "Erkekler cinselliği bilmiyor," *Güneş* (8 October 1990), p. 5. Women's responses to the survey were similar: 77 percent stated that men should have premarital relations, and only 21 percent thought that it was "possible" for women but "for sure wrong" to have sex

before marriage; see "Kadının cinsel sorunu kocasının kaba kuvveti," *Güneş* (11 December 1990), p. 1.

76. The family excursion (*gezi*), a recent urban custom, rests upon men's ability to move freely outside the home; the married couple acts as a unit, in which the wife benefits from her husband's freedom of mobility.

77. *Oğlunu seven hocaya, kızını seven kocaya verir.*

78. The term he used for heat was *hararet*, which connotes sensuality and lust and implies disruption of the social order.

79. See Yesim Arat, "The Project of Modernity and Women in Turkey," in *Rethinking Modernity and National Identity in Turkey*, ed. Sibel Bozdoğan and Reşat Kasaba (Seattle: University of Washington Press, 1997), pp. 95–112.

80. Quoted in Arkın, *İlkokul öğretmenine temel kitap*, p. 496.

81. Aydoğdu, *Türkçe ilkokul 3*, p. 65.

82. İsmail Aydoğdu, *Türkçe ilkokul 2* (Ankara: Öğün Yayınları, 1986), p. 17.

83. When Selda wrote this essay, a husband still had legal authority over his wife. He was not only legally empowered to decide where the family resided and whether his wife could work outside the home but he also had the right to demand that his spouse perform household duties. In December 1990, women succeeded in having repealed from the Civil Law the clause that "the man is the head of the household." In theory, wives no longer needed their husbands' permission to work outside the home. The victory was not easily won as conservative politicians mounted a campaign to quash the initiative. In an interview given to the men's magazine *Kadınca* (October 1990), the minister of Justice Oltan Sungurlu stated that "if we let women have leadership we'll go up in smoke." In invoking a popular expression that refers to the end of a patriline (popularly symbolized as a hearth), the minister was suggesting that independent women would extinguish the nation.

84. Already by the turn of the twentieth century, middle- and upper-class Istanbul households favored companionate marriages together with more independent roles for wives; see Alan Duben and Cem Behar, *Istanbul Households: Marriage, Family and Fertility, 1880–1940* (Cambridge, UK: Cambridge University Press, 1991), pp. 195–200.

85. Victor Turner, "Dewey, Dilthey, and Drama: An Essay in the Anthropology of Experience," in *The Anthropology of Experience*, ed. Victor W. Turner and Edward M. Bruner (Urbana: University of Illinois Press, 1986), p. 41.

86. As men were not allowed to be within earshot of the wedding, my description relies on details of the sketches related by several women who attended the event.

87. See Nükhet Sirman, "Friend or Foe? Forging Alliances with Other Women in a Village of Western Turkey," in *Women in Modern Turkish Society: A Reader*, ed. Sirin Tekeli (London: Zed, 1995), p. 208.

88. On the acquisition of a modern identity through purchase of commodities, see Chapter 4's "Home and Time."

89. TRT, *Evening News* (17 September 1990).

90. Ferid Karslı, *Bir köy öğretmeninin anıları* (Ankara: Köyhocası Basımevi, 1935), p. 134.

91. Millî Eğitim Bakanlığı, *İlkokul programı*, p. 107.

92. Karayiğit and Karayiğit, *Çukurova için hayat bilgisi*, p. 49.

93. See Nancy Tapper, and Richard Tapper, "The Birth of the Prophet: Ritual and Gender in Turkish Islam," *Man* 22 (1987), pp. 69–92.

94. More often, this law is applied to non-Muslim groups, like the Jehovah's Witnesses.

95. The trope of the rope derives from a well-known passage in the Qur'an (sura 3:103), "And hold fast, altogether, by the rope which God [stretches out for you] and be not divided among yourselves and remember with gratitude God's favor on you."

96. The Qu'ran makes explicit the connection between Allah, his universal message, and light (*nur*); consider sura 4:174, "For we have sent unto you a light that is manifest," and sura 24:35, "Light upon Light, Allah guides those whom he will unto his light."

97. Two common proverbs associate sleep with death: "sleeping is the little death" (*uyku küçük ölümdür*) and "sleeping is the brother of death" (*uyku ölümün kardeşi*).

98. Jacques Lacan, "Of the Gaze as *Objet Petit a*," in *The Four Fundamental Concepts of Psycho-Analysis*, ed. Jacques-Alain Miller (New York: Norton, 1978), p. 105. The Turkish word *rüya* means both "dream" and "vision."

99. Walter Benjamin, "The Storyteller," in *Illuminations*, ed. Hannah Arendt (New York: Shocken, 1985), p. 91.

100. Dale F. Eickelman, "Mass Higher Education and the Religious Imagination in Contemporary Arab Societies," *American Ethnologist* 19 (1992), pp. 643–55.

101. Véronique de Rudder, "L'obstacle culturel: la différence et la distance," *L'homme et la société* 77–78 (1985), p. 45.

CHAPTER FOUR

Nation and Market

The class that has the means of material production at its disposal has control, at the same time, over the means of mental production, so that thereby, generally speaking, the ideas of those who lack the means of mental production are subject to it.

—MARX AND ENGELS   *The German Ideology*

It is not only a matter of what history does to the body but what subjects do with what history has done to the body.

—ALLEN FELDMAN   *Formations of Violence*

Nationalism, which is most often identified with a moral political order binding all citizens, is equally linked to economic development. Citizens are called upon to pursue and contribute to collective prosperity as the nation's wealth is understood as dependent on the productive organization of labor. Economics and collective identity intermesh. To further these aims, national educational systems propose to create a new economic order in civil society, to prepare children—the future labor force—for an industrious working life. And to a large extent, the curricula undertake to reshape children's character and behavior in order that they identify with productivity, self-motivation, punctuality, and diligence. Otherwise, the logic goes, an impoverished nation is fated to die along with its poorly trained workers.

This Darwinian world pitting nation against nation clearly emerges in Minister of Education Mustafa Üstündağ's 1974 directive on social sciences for elementary and middle school pupils: "Nations compete with each other over prosperity . . . , and the Turkish nation must be at the forefront of this

125

competition. . . . Pupils must understand . . . that all of mankind takes part in a war of life and death."[1] This apocalyptic scenario continues to guide policy makers' understanding of the relationship between education, nation, and market in Turkey. The 1990 TÜSİAD educational report makes frequent reference to Turkish high school students losing ground compared with their peers abroad and, thus, Turkish industry's inability to compete successfully with industrialized nations, particularly in the field of computer technology and biotechnology. Loss of a "competitive advantage" (*rekabet üstünlüğü*) in the global market is pinned to the "rapid progress in science and technology," to the "extraordinary speed with which the accumulation of knowledge and technology increases and goes out of date."[2] To achieve and sustain competitive advantage in the face of international competitors, the report advocated that the Ministry of Education increase technical and vocational programs that are responsive to global market forces, to apply market principles to the school system.[3] In short, education must stress economic, rather than merely moral, citizenry.

The report provided the business community with the legitimacy to extend their influence in state educational policies. The TÜSİAD industrialists, who advance a worldview that equates democracy and social progress with free markets, were concerned about the country's ability to produce the next generation of working citizens for economic globalization. The high rate of joblessness among high school and university graduates laid bare the failure of the national educational system to prepare students with marketable skills. Blaming officials and politicians for overemphasizing religious instruction facilitated a pedagogical discourse that made government educational policies accountable to the operational logic of global capital markets. Economic and political spheres are blurred, as nongovernmental business organizations like TÜSİAD command the state's attention all the while recognizing and expecting the state's prerogative to intervene in their favor. This is possible because all parties assume the separation of the means of ownership from the political administration of a country. As a result of this liberal conceit, the state is vested with the authority to create a new economic order in civil society.

This concerted effort to link the goals of national education with the demands of the market economy reflects a worldwide trend "towards the empowerment of finance capital vis-à-vis the nation-state."[4] For much of the twentieth century, the republican regime had orchestrated what Barrington Moore would call a "revolution from above"—namely, the transformation of an agrarian bureaucratic society into a capitalist one, the formation of middle classes whose structural position and loyalty were to be firmly tied to state projects, and the material improvement of the countryside.[5] Following the 1980 coup d'état, there was a shift to neoliberal economic policies. Then, under pressure from international financial organizations, in particular the World Bank and the International Monetary Fund, successive governments abandoned early policies that favored small-scale farmers, import-substitution industries, and parastatal industries; rather, they have committed themselves to reducing the role of the state in the economy, eliminating inefficient (state) enterprises, curbing the strength of trade unions, downsizing public expenditures and social services, attracting foreign investment, and most importantly, promoting industrial exports for foreign currency.[6]

The transformation of the economy from one based on a protectionist model to one based on a more market-oriented one has made the national school system one of the prime sites of social change. With a drive for greater efficiency and productivity, the industrialists seek to implement educational policies that correspond to what they consider to be the economic needs of the country.[7] In the name of progress, they aim at creating the conditions under which discourse about economic choices and relationships can be realized first at school, later in the workplace. To promote these aims, the TÜSİAD report invokes the metaphors of choice, competition, individual competence, and freedom to impress upon the public the inexorable necessity of a neoliberal polity and society.

So far, the free-market consumerist approach to education remains the privilege of the moneyed classes alone. Villagers and inhabitants of small towns like Yayla remain excluded from the business community's neoliberal imaginary. More often, they are understood in terms of irreducible essences such as underdevelopment, poverty, folklore, and otherworldly religiosity. According to this logic, they remain to a large extent mired in ongoing traditions. Therefore, they are incapable of exercising any meaningful role in national policies and, especially, in their children's education. Presumably, the different national elites (officials, industrialists, journalists, scholars, and the military) alone have the intellectual capacity to educate the rural public.

Through state institutions like the school system, they have greater clout to formulate and thus disseminate their ideas about culture and economics, about progressive urban lifestyle and backward rural livelihood. It is with this understanding of the countryside that educators seek to instruct the rural masses in how to lead rational lives both at home and at work, to properly use body and time, and thus, be capable of participating in the country's economic modernization.

All the same, villagers and small townspeople are not simply passive subjects to state-directed changes. Drawing on publicly sanctioned norms and sentiments about the public good, economic activity, and community membership, they engage with those cultural forms disseminated during their school years. At issue is how children and parents maneuver between their own historical subjectivity and the expectations originating outside the community.

In this chapter, I examine how the more utilitarian functions of the curriculum, which are intended to train an economically more active and responsible labor force, remain the only choice for most children in Yayla. The curriculum focuses on themes established well before the neoliberal turn in public policy: socializing pupils to a rational work ethic, inculcating progress and progressive time, and limiting urban migration and family size. Thus, I explore how townspeople, young and old, engage with extralocal definitions and evaluative commentaries about modernity that impinge upon their economic sense of self, other, and world. In Yayla, children and adults feel caught between an immediate space of poverty and a horizon of consumerism, between a villageness that they shun and an extralocal urban/e world that seems beyond their reach.

"From Boom to Bust" Demographics

In his concluding remarks in the TÜSİAD report, Baloğlu emphatically states that "the most important factor affecting national education is related to population."[8] To the educator, overpopulation hampered the educational system. This, in turn, prevented economic modernization of the country and, thus, its competitive power in the world. The factors most commonly blamed for this demographic imbalance were urban migration and the high rate of fertility.

The importance of the concept of population for administrators and policy makers worldwide cannot be overestimated. As Foucault pointed out, closely linked to modern state formation has been specifying and rearranging social relations on the ground into statistically defined populations.[9] Administrations attempt to impose homogeneous social categories on social groups, in line with state interests. This is possible since the notion that collective identity can be numerically represented has taken hold of modern governance. This notion requires the presumption of fixed, mutually exclusive differences that reduce social complexity to irreducible elementary units—an instantiation of methodological individualism, which privileges the idea of coherent self-identical subjects. Those seemingly primordial features (language, religious affiliation, gender) selected for categorizing populations are thought to represent an objective reality existing outside discourse. It is the belief in the neutrality of these categories that enables political regimes to not only quantify the social composition of peoples but, more importantly, institutionally impose the authority of statistical qualification to rationalize collective identities.

Statistical categories and operations do not occur in a political void. The use of statistics displays intentions to impose a particular form of knowledge on the subjects of observation.[10] That is, they are organized around concepts, categories, and associated narratives through which self, other, and world are symbolically mediated. And the statistical conventions of measurement, repetition, and analysis, which draw upon commonsensical ideas about the nature of social reality, in turn, generate new orders of knowledge, new objects of intervention, and ultimately, new forms of subjectivity.[11] The constant reiteration of similar categories not only links people of various demographic and biographical conditions into a coherent group but also reinforces a sense of unity and continuity. Conversely, this reiteration provides the means to spell out the discontinuities between different communities, all the while defining hierarchical relations between them.[12] Such statistical transformations create a singular zone of continuous sovereign jurisdiction. Classifying populations into categories is as much prognostic as diagnostic. Population, thus, has become the subject of governance as well as the object of government intervention, with policies that regulate birth, migration, or fertility rates.

Like many other countries, Turkey has experienced a huge population shift in the past century. The percentage of the population living in the cities has more than doubled in forty years, from 25 percent in 1950 to 62 percent in 1990. Over the same period, the populations of major cities like Istanbul, Ankara, and Adana have multiplied several times. The demographic changes result from the massive exodus of people from the rural areas of the country. Out-migration in itself is not a new phenomenon, however. Before the 1950s, unmarried men often left the village for long periods to earn money for their wedding dowry.[13] Since then, migration has changed considerably in form, as entire families have moved to urban centers, returning to their home communities only during vacations and holidays. Likewise, the majority of households originating in Yayla now reside in the nearby cities of Tarsus and Adana.[14]

Policy makers try to grapple with the problems that emerged in these burgeoning urban sprawls, like low educational levels, limited income, marginal jobs, and cultural differences. Baloğlu, for example, blamed the migration to the cities for being the key factor for producing problems with the educational infrastructure, including double-shift lessons and overcrowded classrooms.[15] Migrants unsettle a metropolitan imaginary that privileges the vertically integrated, highly organized, and efficient city. These blemishes have also become the objects of curricula. Shantytowns, located on the margins of the city, epitomize an out-of-control, chaotic poverty whose inhabitants, according to a second-grade life science textbook, are liable to suffer from poor health and pursue a life of crime: "If we don't help some of the poor [living in shantytowns], they will get sick . . . ; maybe they will die. Some of them . . . might become criminals who get used to stealing. Some may even develop bad dispositions."[16] Thus, through the primary school curriculum, policy makers have set about stemming the rural-to-urban migration and the dangers it poses to the economic well-being of the country. In the third-grade primer, for example, correspondence between a recent migrant and his village friend provides an opportunity to promote idyllic images of the Turkish countryside all the while persuading inhabitants of rural communities to keep away from the chaos and pollution of urban centers.

> I received your letter that you sent recently. You wrote that you and your family are sick of village life and want to move to the city. You ask about my thoughts on this subject.
>
> My brother, we moved here believing what was told to us. The truth is that I have not been able to find here any one of the things we had hoped

for. Here, the water doesn't flow gushing and foaming white as in the village. Above all, there are no clear ice-cold springs. Where are the very green fields and the air that we couldn't satisfy ourselves enough? Where are the toadflaxes, crocuses, daisies, and poppies out of which we made crowns?

Do you remember how we counted the stars while lying on top of roofs on hot summer nights? Sometimes we weren't able to share the bright stars. Now I am satisfied with the least faint star. The stars have all disappeared; the city smog has hidden them. And people and vehicles are all mixed up with one another on the narrow streets, squeezed in between tall buildings. Everything here is done in great agitation and haste. How happy is the person who makes it safe and sound to his home.

In short, I have tried to explain city life. Now the decision whether or not to move to the city is up to you and your family.[17]

A large thought bubble dominates the graphics accompanying the text. Sitting at his desk, the city boy imagines a pastoral scene in which a horse and lamb graze on green pastures, against the background of village houses and mosque. Nostalgia is not enough to stem the rural exodus. The last passage of the same textbook describes a model teacher who successfully drew on traditional social and economic relationships to prevent farmers from abandoning their home community.[18]

While these textbook passages draw on a sense of loss to locate the village in a pristine state and static tradition, they also tap into the notion of exile (*gurbet*), a long-standing trope used to characterize the once pastoralist community's winter encampments in the lowlands. Movement back to the highlands, as local storytellers were fond of narrating to me, began with nostalgia for the home community, specifically, for a glorified sex life. This story was typically related thus: the moment that all the young brides simultaneously complain to the fathers-in-law that their husbands lack the strength to have sex in the malaria-infested muggy swamps of the lowlands, the order is given to move the herds to the mountains, where the men would regain their virility from the clean air and pure water and their wives sexual satisfaction.

Yayla still conjures up health and vitality for both local residents and summer tourists, but out-migration to the insalubrious cities in the plains continues unabated as parents seek better educational opportunities for their children. Orhan, then an eighth grader at the local middle school, seriously considered attending a high school in Tarsus. In an essay on the "Cultural Situation" (*Kültürel Durum*), he described urban centers and their inhabitants imbued with education: "In the cities there are many elementary schools, many [regular-track] high schools, vocational schools, and private colleges offering specific studies; in the large provincial centers, universities. All these schools have many classrooms, thousands of students and hundreds of teachers. Most city people graduate from high schools. There are few who only completed elementary school. There are quite a lot of university graduates. . . . There are many cultured people in the cities."

As households place greater emphasis on advanced education for boys than for girls, Orhan was more likely to be sent to Tarsus to further his schooling than his female peers. He was also more likely to become a permanent migrant and might not assume the responsibility for providing for his parents in old age. That is to say, sons gain and take their education outside the community and often adopt the nuclear model of family, which channels almost all financial and economic resources to the conjugal couple and their children. As a result, parents are reassessing a generic subordination of women, which actively shaped and informed local educational strategies respectively for boys and girls. Daughters are less likely to move far from their home community and thus are found to be more dependable.[19] The reversal of attitude toward daughters has contributed to a dramatic increase in enrollment of young women in the local middle school; some parents were even sending their daughters to city high schools.[20] One consequence was an emerging rift between those girls who attended secondary school and members of their age-group whose parents did not see the benefits of educating their daughters beyond elementary or middle school. The former saw themselves as using their knowledge for gainful employment and even spoke about postponing marriage till they accrued some financial leverage with regard to their future husbands and mothers-in-law. Conversely, they disparaged their less educated peers whose educational options were more restricted. Thus, for example, Şeyma, who was enrolled in a city high school, wrote in an essay that "Most of the families don't educate their daughters. When they turn 15 or 16, they are married off. There is a saying 'don't educate your daughter and you won't regret it later.'"[21]

But a far more pressing issue than the rural-to-urban exodus or adult sons abandoning their parents and taking up residency in urban centers has been the high growth rate of the country's population. As Baloğlu argued in his report, "Every twenty-five years the population of the country doubles. In the year 2000, there will be an increase of 23 million. This increase is a heavy burden on the educational system. . . . One of the main factors for the widening gap between Western countries and Turkey is this rapid population increase."[22] In 1927, the first census of the Turkish Republic, there were only 13.5 million people. The twelfth quinquennial census in 1990 counted over 56.5 million. That is, in six decades, the country's population had increased fourfold. Moreover, over 20 percent of the population is ten years of age or under. To make matters worse for national policy makers, the annual increase of jobs (1.5 percent) outstrips the annual increase in population (2.4 percent). According to the TÜSİAD report, this demographic imbalance hinders Turkey's candidacy for the EU as member states generally link the fertility rate with a nation's modernity level and specifically fear that millions of unemployed Turks would flood European labor markets.

Following the 1960 military coup, the state changed its perception of high birth rate from that of a boom to a bust.[23] As a result, it reversed its pronatal policy and began to aggressively tackle the explosive birth rate. Family planning became state policy. In 1965, the Health Ministry established a General Directorate of Family Planning: the government legalized the sale of contraceptives, the dissemination of information on birth control, and abortions in case the mother's health was in jeopardy. In 1983, abortions (up to ten weeks after conception) on demand became legal.[24] Even though the annual population increase dropped from 5.3 percent to less than 2.5 percent, governments were unable to provide sufficient numbers of teachers for the overcrowded school system. To adjust to the annual population increase, the state needed to hire 25,000 primary and secondary school teachers and build 20,000 classrooms. Every year, 500,000 more pupils enroll in primary schools and an additional 150,000 students enter high school.[25] Likewise, as Baloğlu noted in his report, construction of school buildings had not kept pace with the country's demographics; whereas the number of elementary students nationwide increased by 22 percent between 1977 and 1987, the number of schools increased by less than 11 percent. To overcome the shortage of school buildings, Kenan Evren, the junta leader turned president, ran a national campaign, "Build your own school." Private donations and community contributions exceeded all expectations; by 1986, one third of the total investments in construction of school buildings came from private citizens.[26] At Yayla, overcrowded classrooms had not been a problem since 1978, when a prominent businessman funded the construction of the Dilek Günay elementary school and, thereby, put an end to double-shift lessons.

Needless to say, a sense of perennial crisis pervades any discussion of the impact of demography on the national educational system. Thus, Minister of Health Cevdet Aykan's public statement in 1972, that "unless we are able to realistically solve the problem of population growth rate, there will burst forth much sorrow, confusion, and horrible behaviors," still troubles policy makers and educators alike.[27]

A concerted effort has been made to reduce the high birth rate in the countryside. Strapped for funds, the government has enlisted the private sector to socialize and educate the public in family planning. (The national curricula dealt with neither sex education nor family planning.) In 1986, TÜSİAD established the Turkish Family Health and Planning Foundation, which provides financial support for programs, including nationwide television advertisements and films (e.g., *Berdel*) that promote small families. Sustaining the businesspeople's fears of a population out of control are the figures of the ultravirile rural man and overfertile woman. The obsession with the sexuality of Islamic societies, first advanced in the West, has been transferred to the Turkish countryside. Or as Baloğlu declared, "There is a close link between birth rate and level of education. Families with low levels of education have many children; conversely the more education that a woman has, the lower her family size. . . . Education on birth control and family planning is our utmost duty."[28]

To provide rural women with information on maternal hygiene and family planning, the state has trained and appointed midwives to rural communities. Emine, for one, worked as a midwife for a total of fourteen years, the last nine at Yayla. A city person, she had initially disliked living in a relatively remote community. Nor did the local women readily take to her. Not only was she an outsider, she was a single woman at the advanced age of twenty-three. As she put it, local women were uncomfortable confiding intimate sexual issues to a person who, in local parlance, "remained on the shelf." Two months into her service, her dubious status changed for the better as she married the mayor's son, principal of one of the local elementary schools. Since their marriage, she has taken advantage of her husband's extensive kin ties. Emine claimed to have persuaded village women to actively limit the number of children. Besides supplying women with birth control materials, she sent women to undergo abortions at the public hospital in Mersin. In her position as both midwife and mother in a prominent family, she saw herself as "best able to sensitize the population to family planning needs" by explicitly coupling local poverty with ignorance of modern contraceptive methods. In other words, she invoked her expert medical opinion to determine what the proper number of children for a household was. To Emine, only citizens "lacking culture" had large families and thereby jeopardized their children's future well-being. It goes without saying that she saw her family (a boy and a girl) as setting an example to the entire community. (As an aside — her husband, Halil, told me that he would have had more children had the first two been girls.)

Not all have approved of the current trend for smaller-sized families. Turkish Islamists have found birth control to be killing off the country — materially and spiritually. They too used state organizations, most notably the State Planning Office and the Institute for Family Research, to halt the declining birth rate. The economist Nevzat Yalçıntaş, head of Intellectuals' Hearth, argued that a decline in the number of citizens born in Turkey would hurt the country's competitive advantage in manpower.[29] Accordingly, demographic interests of the nation took precedence over bodily autonomy and rights of individuals. Moreover, religious nationalists correlated the drop in the birth rate with moral corruption of the polity. At the 1990 Family and Women conference, which the Turkish Islamists organized, Emin Işık, a conservative woman journalist, stated: "The first signs of decrease in population are in societies where prostitution and promiscuity prevail."[30] She specifically pinned sexual license to the plethora of pornographic films originating from the West that hit the Turkish market in the 1970s.[31]

Indeed, opponents to family planning branded regulated fertility as a foreign conspiracy. The same journalist described the Family Planning Foundation (which TÜSİAD finances) as one of the "organizations originating from abroad, intent on destroying Turkish generations in the mother's womb, by obtaining large quantities of means of birth control." The presence of the London-based International Planned Parenthood Foundation, which supplies Turkey with contraceptives, and USAID, which promotes family-planning programs, further fueled the foreign conspiracy theory.[32]

Not surprisingly, those religious nationalists, who sought to reinstitute the patriarchal Islamic family system, campaigned for the repeal of the Family Planning Law and, in particular, of abortion on demand.

The townspeople have been drawn into the debate over reproductive politics. This came to my notice in a sermon that a guest preacher from a devout community north of Yayla delivered at the mosque during the morning service of the Festival of Sacrifice (*Kurban Bayramı*).[33] The preacher, Ahmet, who sympathized with much of the political agenda of the Turkish Islamists, condemned all Muslims who intentionally limit the size of their families. "Let us say it outright, family planning jeopardizes Islam. It prevents the Turkish nation from multiplying. . . . Birth control is the work of communists and world Zionists and their Christian allies in Europe. We have the means to provide the same standard of living as in America with 100 million people [that is, double the present population]." He then went on to blame women who for selfish motives preferred a consumer culture to the hard work of setting up a family. "There are women who spend all their time outside the home, and spend millions on beauty salons, make-up, and clothes. They find devotion to raising children to be a foolish waste of time. They do not hesitate to take poison so as to remain beautiful and not bother giving birth and raising children for the benefit of the Turkish nation." He ended his censure with a passage from the Qur'an (sura 151): "do not kill your children out of poverty, for we provide food for you and them; avoid what is shameful . . . , and do not take a life, which God has forbidden." In other words, triumph of nation and faith depends on sustaining a high birth rate among believers, on men regaining control over an unbridled femininity—with a twist, however. His standard for religious modernity was the secular United States and its standard of living.

The preacher failed to sway his listeners. The specter of an underpopulated nation did not move them. Yet he had succeeded in bringing up collective unease over the relation between reproductive practices and gender relations, on the one hand, and the laity's identification with Islam, modernity, and nationalism, on the other.

Many men and women in Yayla also considered any form of (artificial) family planning to be a sin (*günah*) because it challenged faith in Allah's ability to sustain believers. In any case, according to the midwife, only about one fourth of the townspeople used modern contraceptive methods, whether the IUD or pill for women or condoms for men. From my own conversations with men, it became clear that most were averse to using a condom since sheathing the sexual organ would reverse the process of male adulthood and sexuality. Popular wisdom holds that circumcision literally opens up the male-bearing seeds (semen); the circumcised boy is then said to be "without a sheath" (*kabuksuz*). Following circumcision, boys leave the more enclosed (*kapalı*) domestic quarters of their mothers and sisters and begin to participate in open (*açık*) arenas (e.g., coffeehouses, public thoroughfares), the prerogative of adult men. Women are equally uncomfortable about artificial methods of contraception; many consider the introduction of foreign elements into their bodies as tainting the uterus. Not surprisingly, as in the rest of the country, the overwhelming majority of couples in Yayla prefer coitus interruptus.[34] Moreover, as the midwife Emine complained to me, some heads of household still measured virility by the size of their family. Ibrahim, a shepherd, for example, wanted to father up to ten children. His wife Durdane thought otherwise and risked her life by inducing abortions. Emine supplied Durdane with contraceptives and finally persuaded the recalcitrant husband that birth control was preferable to raising two children without a mother. In fact, as Emine pointed out to me, about a quarter of all pregnancies ended in abortions—most often self-induced; this figure for Yayla conforms closely to those from a national survey done in 1988.[35]

In fact, it was largely on the initiative of townswomen that family planning and modern contraception became established in the community. While men explicitly practiced an (ascetic) form of birth control, women tacitly bore the burden of pregnancy and abortion. According to women I interviewed at the clinic, sometime in the early 1970s a mobile team came to explain family planning and methods and informed the women about birth control pills and IUDs. The headman of the largest neighborhood strongly opposed the visit, telling the team that "nobody in our town is interested. Everybody is satisfied with having children." Word about the visit got around, and the townswomen forced the headman to recall the team: "We attacked him all over; we gave him blows on the head with mallets. . . . 'Who do you think you are? It's our lives. Let us see you give birth for once.' He gave in."

State intervention unleashed a latent demand for birth control. Following visits of other mobile teams and finally the appointment of a permanent midwife in the mid 1980s, townspeople were intent on imitating their urban peers and desired to limit childbearing to two children. Whenever I asked how many children a person wanted, both men and women would lift up two fingers and say "two are enough." This was the case for young parents, most of whom have three or four children. One middle-age mother explained the shift to regulated fertility, from quantity to quality of family members: "Now we say two is enough. Who has the strength to take care of more? We used to unload them one by one. In the cities, women knew better. Food and clothes cost money. We're so poor that we have a hard enough time educating two children. 'One is good, two is enough, three is trouble, and four is only good for the Gypsy' [*bir iyi, iki karar, üç zarar, dört çingeneye yarar*]."

For many townspeople of Yayla, more prolific social groups are seen to incarnate uncontrolled sexuality. Gypsies are assumed to be a "people without a [holy] book" (*kitapsız*) and therefore act more like animals than human beings.[36] That is, they are unable to restrain their carnal appetites and, thus, have more children than they can support. Animal characteristics are also imputed to nominally Muslim "backward" populations like the Kurds, many of whom live in the economically less developed eastern provinces of the country. One of my neighbors, the blacksmith, for example, accused them of lacking the faculty of reason (*akıl*) since they breed without regard to the number of their offspring.

Associating large families with animal behavior is not limited to Gypsies or Kurds. Some of the elderly townsmen imputed upon themselves bestial characteristics, since they had been clueless about the importance of birth control. Mehmet, my blacksmith neighbor's father, then in his late eighties, reminisced about a conversation he had with a British engineer who had come to Yayla to oversee the paving of the mountain pass road during World War II.[37] The engineer had asked how many children he had, to which Mehmet had answered ten, by lifting up both hands. The Englishman had responded by putting up two hands behind the head. Mehmet had understood that the foreigner was mimicking the ears of a donkey and inferred that he was saying "are you a donkey or what" (*eşek misin*). I suggested that perhaps the Englishman had been mimicking rabbit ears since rabbits in English culture are known for their prolific breeding. The villager insisted that the foreigner had associated him with the donkey. Then as now, donkeys connote utter stupidity, as in the expression *eşek gibi*, which roughly translates as "thoughtless." At least in retrospect, Mehmet was not upset at the Englishman but rather at himself. The moral being the following: had he sired a smaller family, he could have afforded to educate the children, who in turn would have been better able to financially support him in old age. In other words, having fewer children would have allowed parents to devote more resources to each child.

In any case, as children's upbringing has become increasingly individualized and commoditized, procreation and modern contraception are increasingly a choice deliberated by couples. Evaluating fertility in terms of scarce resources (education) and social mobility (villageness as opposed to an urban lifestyle) has become the norm.[38] Children's well-being is now perceived to depend on responsible parenting. As Selda, then a high school student, in an essay on modernity defined the poor yet modern couple as one oriented to their children's future needs,

> The husband behaves appropriately with his wife and respects women's rights. He gives his wife permission to work [outside the home]. The woman both respects and loves her husband. There is mutual love. They can only have as many children as they can support, not as many as they can produce. For me this is modernity.

Like many adult townspeople, Selda held up the differences in number of young dependents as a yardstick to judge whether a household is modern or backward. I asked her how many children a modern couple should have. She did not want to give absolute numbers; to her, a couple should have as many children as they can feed, care for, and educate.

The decisions townsmen and townswomen take for rearing fewer children should not be automatically read off as wholesale adoption of the modernization paradigm and its underlying notions of rational choice and cost-benefit. While all are aware of the shift from a familial mode of production to a capitalist one, not once did I hear anyone connect the size of a family with either freedom of action or individualism (as in personal realization of an autonomous self separate from a larger entity such as the family). That is, local notions of personhood, body, fertility, and sexuality do not simply buckle under from the capitalist penetration in local society. The choices that couples in Yayla have made over the size of the family took on a variety of meanings, which emerged from multiple understandings of life courses and life strategies. For a few households, extensive patrilineage, virility, un-

ease with contraceptives, and religious prohibitions on regulated fertility
were still persuasive arguments; for many, however, the small family was a
requisite to survival in an increasingly expensive world. Either way, the different responses to family size revealed attempts at drawing meaning out of
the most personal and intimate of experiences, the sexual act.

Clearly, there was no consensus over the relation between fertility, household identity, and national well-being or, for that matter, on the ideal number of children. What is evident is how national debates over biological reproduction and demography provided justification for intervention in the
household and underscored a struggle over the political subjectivity and
bodily practices of the Turkish citizenry. The liberal industrialists saw the
demographic issue as one going from boom to bust. The Turkish Islamists,
on the other hand, considered a reduced population growth to sap the vitality of the polity. All sides, however, thought that current demographic
trends were of imminent public concern: the wrong numbers will stump national development. Demographics have become a politically charged issue
as rival political lobbies battle over the sovereignty of the citizen's bodies.

The sexual act has become a public concern precisely because, as I have
shown in the previous chapter, all participants construe the family as the primary and fundamental unit of society. What model family best serves the social, economic, and political needs of the country is thus intimately connected with ideas about procreation. Yet however much the neoliberal
industrialists and the religious nationalists differed on reproduction politics,
both were of the opinion that the state has the legitimate right to intervene
in the citizen's sex lives. Thus, centers of political and economic power increasingly encroach on citizens' bodies in ways unimaginable only a few generations ago. If the state expands a couple's reproductive options by providing contraceptives and legalizing abortion and sterilization, it nevertheless
regulates through legislation a politics of reproduction and thereby defines
sexual agency for citizens. After all, both the midwife who supplies women
with contraceptives and the medical specialists who decide on abortions
must work within the framework of the law. In other words, the state increasingly determines the series of choices and decisions that shape couples'
reproductive strategies.

These interventions into the domestic sphere instantiate what Michel
Foucault calls "bio-power"—the processes whereby the state gains access to

the body and intervenes in individual private lives to control, monitor, and manage the "organic" life of the polity.[39] In effect, it reduces the sexual lives of men and women to reproductive functions alone. And fundamental to state attempts at regulating the citizens' sexuality is emphasis on the conjugal couple that acts independently of larger social networks, be it kin or other community members. In fact, both neoliberal industrialists and the Turkish Islamists expect husbands and wives to comply with the exigencies of the social body by assuming responsibility for their bodies and sexual practices and thereby become responsible citizens: either to limit or reinvigorate their fertility.

Home and Time

A salient feature of modernity has been a perceived inability to arrest time, to get a handle on what Elizabeth Grosz calls "the continual eruption of the new."[40] Likewise, keeping up to date, living in sync with the developed world has obsessed Turkish policy makers and educators alike for the past 150 years.[41] Very often, mention is made of the need "to catch up with the times" (*çağı yakalamak*), "to skip an era" (*çağ atlamak*), "to not remain behind" (*gerisinde kalmamak*) technologically more developed nations. Thus, at a televised speech he delivered on the occasion of the opening of the 1990–1991 school year, Prime Minister Yıldırım Akbulut declared, "Turkey will very soon catch up with the present era in the field of education as in all other undertakings."[42] A week later, the minister of Education Avni Akyol qualified Akbulut's optimism. The minister warned his audience that "we must raise the level and quality of education if we are to catch up and not remain behind the times."[43] In this race against time, groups and activities are ordered into a scheme of different historical eras, ranging from the Stone Age to the Space Age.

Forging national identities through the ideological prism of incremental progress prevails in the curricula. Both textbooks and teachers repeatedly break down behaviors and thoughts into primitive (*ilkel*), barbaric (*barbar*), medieval (*ortaçağ*), and modern (*modern*) mind-sets. The shift to modernity is most often credited to Atatürk who, according to the eighth-grade history textbook, for example, set out to "modernize a backward society" by ridding it of all "ties, understandings, and beliefs dating from the Middle Ages."[44] Moreover, teachers, who see themselves as enlightened agents of modern knowledge, often take the opportunity in class to label local social mores and norms they disapprove as "medieval."

The evolutionary discourse propagated at school finds expression in the media coverage of the living conditions and domestic practices of villagers and townspeople. Mass-circulation dailies and television programs regularly cover stories about subterranean habitations. The conservative daily *Tercü-man*, for example, ran an article on the underground dwellings of a large village in Siirt, a relatively poor province in southeastern Turkey. The headline read "The Cave Age at the Threshold of the 21st Century."[45] The writer did not mince words on what he thought about the village: "In a period in which the world lives out the Space Age, primitive cave life still exists." Four months later, the liberal weekly *Nokta* published a lengthy article on the cave dwellings of a small town in central Anatolia; the title of the piece was none other than "The Cave Age."[46] Such characterizations of rural homes are not new. Since the turn of the twentieth century, journalists regularly relegate village architecture, interior decoration, and associated behaviors to a prehistoric era.[47] Or as Anne McClintock describes it in the context of Western imperialism, an "anachronistic space," a space figured as "prehistoric, atavistic, and irrational, inherently out of place in the historical time of modernity" has taken hold of the imagination of the Turkish media at large.[48]

This taxonomic breakdown of lifestyles has equally influenced how businesses target different consumer publics. A market research team with whom I met on a visit to Istanbul had finished a three-year project titled Research on Values and Life Styles. Intended for advertisement agencies, the report drew up a consumer profile of eleven million high school graduates, ages fifteen to thirty-five. Inspired by Daniel Lerner's classic *The Passing of Traditional Society: Modernizing the Middle East* (1958), the team identified two main groups, the moderns and the transitionals: the former were further subdivided into pace-setters, seekers, and new Europeans; the latter into the simple, the faithful, and the strugglers.[49] While the report avoided stigmatizing terms like *primitive* or *prehistoric*, it considered the transitionals to be "ten to fifteen years behind Europe" and, thus, unsuitable targets for a modern consumer lifestyle.[50] In effect, the research team dismissed the overwhelming majority of Turkish citizens—the urban poor, villagers, and devout Muslims. All the same, advertisers market historical time to the entire population. For years, Turkish consumers have been exposed to a discourse that harnesses the country's destiny with European modernity. Advertisements in the press, radio, and television regularly play up the fear that Turks are lagging behind Europe. When, for example, Honda released its new car model, the Hatchback, it approached potential buyers with the opportunity to "turn on the engine at the same time as Europe" and, thereby, become "a modern European."[51]

Thanks to market initiatives, media interventions, and school discourses, belonging to the modern era has become as much a local obsession as a national cause. The townspeople of Yayla, young and old, most often associate modernity with a material culture that suggests a more urbane, contemporary lifestyle, and more specifically, the well-furnished urban home and associated domestic practices they studied at school.

Connecting domestic architecture with a particular historical period spills into daily conversations and informs public identities. This connection was brought to my attention when a coffeehouse owner, Zekeriye, took me to visit his relatives living in the nearby village of Kenzin. In the course of a conversation at an open-air coffeehouse, a middle-age man began describing his community by stating, "we're medieval" (*ortaçağız*). I had not expected this response, and thinking that I had misheard him I asked him to repeat. Once more he said, "we're medieval." Others present nodded in approval. He then elaborated, "There is nothing here. We still get our water from the fountains outdoors. We have only two grocery stores and one barbershop . . . and the mosque does not even have a minaret. We have one single multigrade elementary school while at Yayla there are two primary schools and one middle school. They are more up to date (*çağdaş*)." He finished the comparison between the two communities on an equivocal note: "Here the people come from manly stock, there from schools" (*burada erden, orada mektepten*). Upon my return to Yayla, patrons at Zekeriye's coffeehouse did not consider their neighbors in the next village to be manlier but all did agree that the townspeople were better schooled and, hence, more attuned with modernity.

Discursively using historical time as a social and spatial means to differentiate with neighboring groups is quite common in Yayla as well as throughout Turkey. Popular wisdom is that the further east one travels in the country, the more primitive (the neologism *ilkel*) the population. The distinction between eastern and western parts of the country is, moreover, recursively replicated onto the neighborhoods of Yayla, producing what linguistic anthropologists Susan Gal and Judith Irvine suggestively call an "orient within the Orient."[52]

Kozu, geographically the most western neighborhood in Yayla, is derisively known as "Little Istanbul" (*Küçük İstanbul*).[53] Among most townspeople, Istanbul elicited mixed reactions. It was widely perceived as embodying both the best and the worst of the West. The higher standard of living and the better services were offset by what many townspeople found to be an ostentatious and pretentious lifestyle devoid of morals. Kozu residents embraced the term with enthusiastic pride, however. Almost all the inhabitants of this neighborhood migrated to the nearby cities of Tarsus and Adana, where they found work in administration and factories, and returned to their homes in Yayla only during the summer vacation.[54] Consciously adopting a more urbane identity, they have constructed anew their ancestral homes using concrete foundations, allocated rooms to particular functions, put up windows facing the street, and replaced flat earthen roofs with sloping corrugated iron. All of these changes confirmed as it were their urbanity. Conversely, the residents from Kozu considered the homes in the other neighborhoods to epitomize rural backwardness and disorder. These sentiments were very much present in a schoolboy's essay on his hometown. Then a middle school boy whose family had recently migrated to Tarsus, Bülent described Yayla as "still underdeveloped. There is no difference between the East and us. . . . Most of the houses are made out of earth. That is, the homes date from old times [*eski zaman evi*]. The narrow streets, the ramshackle houses one on top of the other . . . impart to the settlement a disorganized appearance." The old homes to which Bülent was referring are two-story structures built from stone, wood, and earth, in which the ground floor is most often used as a stable and storage areas while the upper floor is reserved for the living quarters. At the heart of the house is the second-floor covered balcony, the *hayat* (literally, "life" since it is the living hub of the home) from which one enters the other rooms. Whenever weather permits, almost all household chores, meals, and entertainment take place there. One side of the balcony opens up to a terrace; the other side leads to separate rooms. A generation ago, when extended families were still the norm, each room was intended to be an independent living space for a couple and their children. A single room was thus designed to meet all the needs of the household. There one slept, ate, entertained, and even took a bath. To meet the different functions of the room, at mealtimes a large tinned copper tray is brought out; bedding (mattresses, blankets, and quilts), stored either in a recessed cupboard or on top of a dresser, is taken out when necessary, as are cushions when visitors drop by.

At the time of my fieldwork, the topsy-turvy village look of the town was perceptibly changing as housing cooperatives consisting of two-story (*dubleks*) summer homes made out of concrete and brick were being built in the more traditional neighborhoods. Intended for middle-class people escaping from the sweltering heat of the lowlands, each housing unit had a living area of ninety square meters: on the bottom floor, forty square meters for the kitchen, bathroom, and toilet; on the second floor, the bedroom, living room, and balcony. All had indoor plumbing and bathrooms. In addition to these housing complexes, colossal villas, locally called "castles" (*şato*, from the French *château*), were being built on the northern outskirts of the town. Despite misgivings about outsiders living in their midst, most townspeople welcomed the modern homes; as one elementary school girl enthusiastically wrote, the new housing complexes "impart a modernizing orientation to our small town." By the time I finished fieldwork in February 1991, over 120 summer residential units were in the last stages of completion.

Enthusiasm for the modernity of the new summer residences reflects a general shift in attitudes to domestic architecture and practices, both of which serve to mark and create social distinctions within the community. Homes have become competitive displays by which male heads of household make public their ability to construct a modern home and furnish it with the latest household goods, in other words, to exhibit mastery of the signs of modernity. No homeowner wants to be perceived as backward thinking.

As garnering status in the community becomes increasingly tied to the public visibility of the house's exterior, families are building homes along the lines of those in the Kozu neighborhood. Because postmarital residence is virilocal, priority is given to construction of homes for sons.[55] "To get married" and "to marry off one's son," respectively *evlenmek* and *evermek*, derive from the Turkish word for "house," *ev*. Townspeople refer to a bachelor as a man "without a roof" (*damsız*), and no thought of marriage is entertained until the groom's side provides separate domestic quarters for the couple. Following the visit of a suitor who lacked the resources to build a home for her daughter, a middle-age mother bluntly told me why she refused his suit: "He can't even set up a tent of his own. No roof, no cunt (*dam yok am yok*)." She was referring to the *çardak*, a makeshift structure consisting of wooden posts and a roof of branches, which families set out in their gardens in the summer months. Besides providing living quarters, the groom procures cloth and cotton for the bedding, one or more carpets, a (convertible) couch, and gold jewelry.

Transformation of the lived-in space of homes had been less rapid. Male household heads were less inclined to purchase electrical appliances and Western-style furniture. Women, beholden to a patriarchal subordination, which excludes them from participation in male-defined social realms, have taken the lead in remodeling the interior of the home. Much credit, they argued, goes to the school curricula, which elevated their status of future homemaker from tradition-bound housewife to an informed manager of household. No longer were female pupils expected to follow customs and imitate older women in the community but rather to follow the written directives in their home economics primers to transform the home into a social space of citizenship. Nation and home have become mutually constituting entities, in which properly ordered domesticity is a very public matter. Until 1969, all fourth- and fifth-grade pupils were required to take a course in family lore (*aile bilgisi*); subsequently, the life sciences curriculum in second and third grades and that of natural science in fourth and fifth grades have taken up many of the themes first introduced in family lore classes.[56]

Before townspeople received television broadcasts in 1974, schooled children, and in particular girls, were to be emissaries of the idealized home; their older peers, subjects for social change. Textbooks provided the only (very grainy black-and-white) images of the new domestic order, in which every household activity was allocated to a specific room and its corresponding furniture.[57] I will briefly discuss Zehra, the heroine of the fourth-grade *Family Lore* primer (1959) that Hatice, a woman in her early forties, had kept since her elementary school days. Living in a conservative small town in Anatolia, Zehra decides to remodel her family's home and remold domestic practices according to her textbook. She replaces the floor mattresses with beds; the dinner platter with a dining table.[58] Zehra proudly declares to herself, "I will set the table as I learned in my lesson in Family Lore."[59] By virtue of her superior education, she takes up the authoritative role normally held by the matriarch of the domestic unit, the paternal grandmother. She teaches her mother and grandmother how to run a modern home. Grandma still serves food on the floor; Zehra's mother takes out the dinnerware from her bridal trousseau only at the arrival of a guest. Zehra changes all that; on her own initiative, she sets a table on which every household member gets their own separate dish and silverware; she tops off her interior decorating with a vase of flowers set in the middle of the table.[60]

The curricula did not immediately effect changes in the children's homes, however. Given that Yayla was hooked up to the national electricity system only in 1973, passages from the 1950s textbooks that praised the virtues of electric appliances would have been meaningless. "Without lifting up any dust, an electric vacuum cleaner spotlessly cleans the house in a short time. Isn't that great!"[61] Before connecting to the grid, the only electricity in the town was from generators that a few coffeehouses used to run radios. Otherwise, townspeople relied on oil lamps for lighting. The material poverty of rural communities like Yayla was such that pressured kerosene lamps went by the name of *lüks*, French for "luxury."

In the past generation, the situation has considerably changed. The once forbiddingly expensive household articles have become tangible means for establishing social standing in the community. Possession and presence of objects, not their everyday use, provides their owners the respectability to distance themselves from all that is associated with poverty, villageness, and backwardness. As French philosopher Jean Baudrillard aptly points out in his discussion on consumer culture, "a need is not a need for a particular object as much as it's a 'need' for difference (the *desire for social meaning*)."[62]

Much of the burden for the purchase of this modernity has fallen on brides and their families. Beginning at puberty, girls begin to prepare their trousseaux, which are intended to supply some of the needs of the future household. A generation ago, a woman's trousseau fit in a hope chest or two. Then, it would include a few rag rugs, one or more woven rugs, embroidered and laced headkerchiefs, embroidered linen, a mattress, a quilt, and long rectangular pillows. Today, in addition to these items, which require much time and effort in their preparation, the bride must acquire electric appliances, furniture, and manufactured goods to materially constitute her identity as a modern homemaker and wife.

Setting the standard for outfitting a completely up-to-date home are well-off newlyweds. An apt example was the public display of the new household of the mayor's nephew. Ersin, the groom's father who runs a successful chicken coop, had outfitted the bedroom with a king-size bed, a double closet, a make-up table, a large mirror, and a chair; the main sitting room with a long rectangular table and eight upholstered chairs, a matching cabinet display with glassed-in shelves, and a convertible couch. The financial outlay by the bride's side was no less impressive. Her relatives furnished the kitchen with a small table, chairs, a washing machine, a toaster-oven, a refrigerator, gas burners, two sets of aluminum and porcelain dishes, plastic containers, pots, and two pressure cookers. Her family also bought several electrical appliances, including a refrigerator, an iron, a sewing machine, and a vacuum cleaner. Neighbors and age-mates of the bride who came to view the public display of the new household were impressed. They had a visual reference upon which they could plan a trousseau and marital agreement. Other than the groom's father, nobody commented on the furnishings making all the rooms appear cluttered and cramped. What did bother some of the young women present was the amount of time and labor that the bride and her family had spent on the traditional form of bedding. Pointing to the pile of ten long pillows and four square ones, one of them blurted out, "Who is planning to have so many children these days?" Self-evident in her remark was the close link between neoliberal discourse on fertility and family size, on the one hand, and modernity and the type of home, on the other. Another adolescent, known for her wit, punned on the word *yük*, which means both a cupboard for bedding and a burdensome load. She inverted the expression "it is light but valuable" (*yükte hafif pahada ağır*), which is often used in reference to jewelry that the groom's family provides the bride. To her, the traditional embroidery and bedding were "heavy and worthless" (*yükte ağır pahada hafif*). The light banter aside, the bride was very pleased with her new household and turning toward me remarked, "We are like Europe" (*Avrupa gibiyiz*).

For young townswomen, the near-unanimous desire to modernize the domestic interior was unequivocally associated with liberation from the stigma of "villageness." The repudiation of rural conditions is dependent on the Manichaean division of a future from past home amenities; the latter were now viewed as unessential, burdensome, and worthless. This desire to model and realize oneself after the good life of Europeans was captured in an essay seventh-grader Orhan wrote about his community: "Most of the people who live in the mountainous areas make a living from farming. The people who live in big cities want to imitate the Europeans. In the last years they have become like them. The other people want to imitate those living in the big cities." Emulation did not reflect the reality of most townspeople, however. Despite incurring the risk of being taken as unmodern, few households could afford to own the material culture that has come define modernity in Yayla. All-purpose rooms remained the norm and most domestic practices still conformed to what media and curricula would consider as typical of out-of-date homes; the overwhelming majority of families continued to take out mattresses at night and eat their meals around a platter set on the floor. Furniture was limited to a convertible couch and dresser. And the only appliances all families owned were a television set and a refrigerator. In short, few houses matched the ones described in the children's third-grade natural sciences reader: "Every house consists of a reception room, bedrooms, a guest room, a kitchen, bathroom, and toilet"; even the financially comfortable newlywed couple had not allocated "a separate bedroom and study" for children.[63]

Despite the seeming disconnection between domestic ideals and realities, schoolchildren figure their home environment in a language that tangentially links them with modernity. In essay after essay on the home, pupils listed status-laden electrical appliances all the while eliding basic household items central to the management of the home. Moreover, pupils, irrespective of their families' economic and social status, consistently used French-derived household terms, which they acquired at school, to describe their house's salient features. Selda, a fifteen-year-old high school student, for example, took pride in her house's *hall*, *salon*, *vestiaire* (cloakroom), *toilette*, *buffet*, *vitrine*, *climatisateur*, *garderobe*, *garage*, and *crème* (paint). The cloakroom Selda mentioned is none other than the second-floor covered anteroom (*hayat*); other children referred to it as an "open-air *salon*." The conscious choice of foreign vocabulary does not mean that homes have been converted into a series of functionally differentiated rooms; nor do pupils claim new domestic practices are under way with acquisition of Western appliances and furniture. Yet the enumeration of material objects and the use of foreign terms, I would suggest, provide linguistic prompts that fuel aspirations for the desirable features of consumer society. In a school culture that brandishes modernity as the goal of every citizen, the townspeople and their children have begun to materially and linguistically possess household signs of modernity to shape and manifest a self aligned with a progressive, dynamic history.

Body and Time

The race against time is also a will to obliterate a collective memory about lethargy and indolence—a diagnosis that Western observers of the late Ottoman Empire used to indict Turks as incapable of adapting the work ethic of an industrial society and, thus, out of sync with the developed world. The prognosis was worse: sickness and death. Since then, a fear that time is being wasted and should be seized has gripped policy and opinion makers in Turkey.[64] A central motif of the national educational system is to keep up with the speed (*hızına ayak uydurmak*) of development and innovation, to turn pupils into fast-paced productive laborers for the economic needs of an industrial nation. The curriculum has responded to the challenge and is committed to a Fordist industrial order with its emphasis on punctuality, regularity, and speed. The overall aim is to generate a new consciousness among schoolchildren about the relationship between forms of knowledge, agency, and time. The logic goes something like this: a well-run and efficient student body is the basis for a well-run and efficient labor force and nation. Thus, for children to become industrious adults they must assume a purposeful and rational use of their bodies. In Sartrean terms, this corporeal style of being becomes a lifelong national project.[65]

New orientations to body and activity are closely related to the logic of accumulative, linear, and continuous time. Like its counterparts in other countries, the Turkish school system calculates every task and subject matter in clearly seriated and delimited amounts of time. The school schedule or calendar, as Bourdieu observes, "is made up of commensurable islands of duration, each with their own rhythm . . . depending on what one is *doing*, i.e., on the *functions* conferred on it by the activity in progress."[66] Thus, the Ministry of Education decides how much body of material pupils can absorb in a day as well as the optimal amount of knowledge they must acquire by the end of the year. Thus, instructors are expected to teach x amount of y subjects in z time.[67] Textbooks follow the rhythm of accumulated knowledge that the ministry allocates to each subject matter.

Time consciousness is ever present in the classroom. The calendar of annual events hangs behind the teachers' desk; the monthly schedules lie on top of their desks; the daily time sheets are written down in their notebooks. On the rear wall of the classroom, school children refer to the lesson unit (*ünite köşesi*) to keep abreast of the topics they will cover during a month. Furthermore, absolute time determines children's success or failure at school. The educational system rewards those pupils who master a given task on time: the yearend exams assess the child's ability to achieve specific goals and activities within the determined completion-time target.

The school system not only organizes space and time into uniform and quantified units to increase productivity at the institutional level it also zealously husbands time to produce a work ethic at the individual level. Emphasis is on strict compliance to a standardized schedule of activities. The plangent battery-operated bell, which first marks morning roll call and then breaks up the rest of the school day into forty-minute class periods alternating with twenty-minute recesses, regulates the simultaneity of activities and modulates the movement of the entire student body. A pupil who fails to respond to the bell and comes to class late, and thereby disturbs his or her classmates, is a theme frequently broached in primary school primers. To counter such antisocial behavior, children are repeatedly implored to "work in a planned [*planlı*] manner and on time," to "adhere to a daily work schedule [*program*]," "to not waste time in things that do not concern them." The concern with time takes on greater importance in fifth grade, the last year of schooling for most boys and girls, many of whom are expected to contribute their labor to household resources. It is fitting that the last reading passage fifth graders study in their primer is titled "Work and Time." Success hinges on a work ethic based on proper management of one's time: "A person's daily life is orderly and successful if he does his work punctually. . . . In any case, if we look around ourselves, we see that successful people are those who are responsible and hard-working."[68] Conversely, children who fail to follow a schedule, loiter, or play truant are assumed to be most prone to lead delinquent adult lives and, thus, unable to effectively participate in the national economy.

Scheduling and punctuality are not the only temporal issues addressed at school. For generations, schoolchildren as the future workforce have been socialized toward directed movement, perpetual activity, and uniform mechanical acceleration. Schools treat the body as a signifying medium wherein the timely performance of tasks is taken to be a sign of a well-disciplined nation. The transformation of students' bodies into machines of speed is most poignantly captured in Talip Apaydın's memoirs, in which he reminiscences about a lecture his school principal at an agricultural teachers' college gave in 1938 about the ability of modern people to maximize their time. The principal quoted from a diary of a Turkish "man of science" who had undertaken a railway journey from the Hejaz to Germany.

> In Arabia, the people lie . . . under the tree shade at the track's side, and sleep snoring loudly. Nearing Syria I saw that people would sit; on their faces there was laziness, apathy. In Anatolia they'd stand on their feet but they were still lazy and indifferent. They would slowly drag their feet wherever they went. Our train entered Bulgaria; the people's walk changed. I saw that they walked swiftly. We came to Austria; the people were more spirited. At last we arrived in Germany; the people didn't walk, they ran. They ran so much that they built escalators; a person would go up on one side and return in the opposite direction; escalators took someone wherever he had to go faster. . . . My comrades, from Arabia to Germany one can see the link between people's demeanor and their level of civilization. We [Turks] are not a foot-dragging people; and we must not be one. We must forge a new character for our nation. Then we will elevate ourselves. We will then save ourselves from backwardness! . . . Not only in our walk, but also in our speech, reading, working and . . . yes, even in our eating, we will always be quicker and quicker! We are two hundred years behind Europe. It's not enough to walk; to catch up to Europe we must run! To close this gap as quickly as possible we must run in everything we do.[69]

The railroad tracks define distance and cultural space in terms of time. In juxtaposing the panoramic series of embodied practices with an ascending level of civilization, the diarist, and by implication the principal, chronologically orders peoples into a scheme of different work ethics: the Anatolia of "indifferent" villagers suffers from indolence and underdevelopment; Germany, the most Western destination, epitomizes fast-paced modernity. The railway journey suggests a parable of modernity in which the dynamic body metaphorically drives the force of history itself. Pedagogical engineering of the body is thus made to appear global, natural, and essential.

Reworking children's bodies along the principles of classical mechanics remains ever a salient issue in the school system. To increase student productivity, the entire pedagogy is geared to time-saving strategies as well as to timely and speedy completion of tasks. Specific duration of a task becomes a norm around which pupils must meet. The guidelines on dictation for elementary school students, for example, link children's speed to their cognitive development: "It is appropriate for second graders to write an average of ten syllables a minute; third graders, thirteen; fourth graders, fifteen; and fifth graders, seventeen. Students must not be allowed to deviate from this standard."[70] The same logic holds for assessing or, more specifically, measuring children's reading performance over time. Government directives correlate grade with overall composition of text. From first to fifth grade, the number of texts and pages in Turkish primers children are expected to read progressively increase as the size of font decreases.[71]

Attention to acceleration of the body is not limited to in-class performance. It is closely associated with perpetual activity in the adult world of work. Thus, to believe a fourth-grade reader, for example, successful citizens "run against the stopwatch."[72] The illustration accompanying the text reinforces the idea of willfully accelerating bodily motions: in sharp contrast to the light shade the illustrator applies to the people waiting at a city bus stop, strong colors highlight two figures—one, a businessman looking intently at his watch; the other, a youth running down the street with his briefcase. The image of racing ahead has equally taken on importance in political campaigns. Thus, a full-page advertisement, which the government party (ANAP) took out on the eve of the 1989 municipality elections, ended on an optimistic note: "We are running at full speed into the next century. We have the largest investments in the world. We arouse the jealousy of friends and foes throughout the world. We set an example to Europe and America in many areas."[73]

Pace the literary critic Frederic Jameson, the "waning of the great high-modernist thematics of time and temporality" has yet to occur in the political culture of Turkey.[74] Politicians, educators, and townspeople all invest temporal categories with phantasmic meaning: they associate a progress-oriented modernity with ideas about worldliness, consumption, and innovation. And crucial in fostering this modernity is teaching schoolchildren to think about time as progressive, rational, and manipulatable and thereby to develop an up-to-date mind-set.

This evolutionary discourse has come to populate the imagination of the schooled public. The categories of mechanical, industrial, and progressive time have become guiding principles for all domains of social praxis; they provide powerful terms of comparison between the town and other communities in the country, as well as give substantive coherence to future aspirations. Thus, for example, in an essay on "Our Modern and Cultured People," two seventh-grade girls consciously linked time discipline to the level and type of education an individual receives. "Modern and cultured people pass their time reading books and newspapers. . . . These kinds of people abide to a schedule (*programlı*)." "In our society educated people are perceived as cultured. . . . Cultured people are never idle. These individuals abide to a plan (*planlı*) and schedule. They are able to look forward all the time." In short, rational time management functions as a trope through which local schoolchildren believe that the better educated population has the ability to will body and time to transform industrious life strategies into productive life courses.

At the time of my fieldwork, few townspeople and their children enjoyed the material amenities of a modern consumer culture and lifestyle and even fewer saw themselves as actively participating in a historically dynamic society. All the same, the idea of progress has come to inhabit everyday conscience. Thus, a middle-age townsman expressed his frustration over the gap between national ideals about time, which he shared, and the local realities that he experienced: "The world is changing and developing quickly. Turkey is finding its place in the world. Our eyes are on the West. . . . We don't want to be left behind." Unlike the two middle school girls, he did not attribute the uneven experience of modernization and modernity between the townspeople and "modern and cultured" people to better assimilation of the curricula but to the unequal distribution of educational possibilities in the country.

"Orphans" of the Father-State

"We owe a lot to villagers and farming families. We must always show respect for their calloused hands and pure sentiments. They have done the most for this country. As Atatürk said, '*The real master of this country is the villager.*'[75] Thus, this passage in a third-grade life science reader seeks to positively represent the rural inhabitants of the country. Elsewhere in the same reader, villagers are described as "very tied to their traditions. The most ancient Turkish customs are observed in villages. Pristine Turkish words are still spoken in villages."[76] Treating villagers as the unadulterated (but voiceless) sign of the nation dominates the curricula. Villages and small towns like Yayla come to embody an allegory of national wholeness and unity; they are assimilated with an undivided Turkey possessing a unitary self and a singular will. Rural communities are thus represented as best preserving the *öz*—the timeless cultural essence of the Turkish nation.

The townspeople of Yayla were far from impervious to the neoliberal economic policies in the country, however. They were only too aware that they had lost effective control over the means of production: commercialization had undermined the old basis of the household economy and forced adults to reorient their productive activity toward a commodity market and consumption of manufactured goods.[77] At the same time, irregular menial work, high unemployment, and hyperinflation since the 1970s had adversely affected their ability to cope with the costly upkeep of a family in a consumer-oriented economy. Uncertainty about the viable reproduction of the household had become a constant concern. Earning a viable living was difficult, as is securing their children's future livelihood. In reaction to this, parents and children both suggested that the state should take responsibility for extending opportunities to the underprivileged. Access to privileged education had become the parameter by which townspeople measured the effectiveness of the state to meet their economic expectations for secure salaries.

Only a generation ago, most of the townspeople herded goats and sheep or raised camels; then, there were over thirty thousand head of goat and sheep. Others made a living from cutting wood in the forest or worked as wage farmhands in the lowlands. Since then, the economic situation of Yayla had drastically changed. Governments have considerably limited exploitation of the forests, and major cotton farms require less manpower on account of mechanization. More dramatic a change in the local economy has been in animal husbandry. By 1990, there were less than one thousand head. The once honorable profession was most often described as vile (*rezil*), due to the solitude and uncomfortable working conditions. For sure, young women were quite adamant about not marrying a shepherd, whom they considered to be uneducated and clueless about worldly affairs (*dünyadan haberi yok*). Nor did they contemplate spending their lives milking or bringing fodder. Fazıl, then a twenty-five-year-old shepherd and bachelor, was quite pessimistic about the prospects of finding a bride; he quipped that "the pine needles will have all fallen" before he married. Indeed, all manual labor was frowned upon, and the nationalist trope "the villager as master" did not appeal to local sentiments. If anything, the youth had distanced themselves from any association with villageness, which brought to mind perpetual underdevelopment and endemic poverty. Rather, they identified with the concept of the gentleman *efendi*—the literate, urbane state official who mediates the allocation of social positions and power from state to citizen.

As such, many families sought more comfortable and secure jobs for their children, which have altered their understanding of the state's responsibilities and education. The goal of most parents has been ensuring a steady income with social benefits (e.g., medical insurance and pension) for their children, or what they call a "life guarantee" (*hayat garantisi*). One consequence has been a change in local perception of education. Only thirty years ago, schooling was perceived as being for those few who needed literacy skills to fulfill bureaucratic functions or master religious instruction. Thus, many parents withdrew their children after they had acquired rudimentary reading and writing skills in third grade. As a rule, parents in Yayla were retaining their children in school till completion of fifth grade. This was not always the case in other communities, and the curriculum has done its utmost to raise awareness of the benefits of the elementary school diploma. Having in mind those parents who withdraw children early, the third-grade life sciences reader states, "Those individuals who do not finish elementary school will have difficulty obtaining a job. Those who do not have a diploma do not always find employment. . . . They can't become a school janitor, a guard, a driver, a nurse, a mailman, a factory worker, a sergeant, or a private in the army."[78]

Formal education has increasingly become perceived as the only means for securing long-term employment, such as clerical positions in government or jobs in large factories. Or as Safigül, who was entering middle school, simply put it, "Our people have realized that schooling provides income, that is, it secures a profession." The desired jobs required either a high school diploma or vocational training, neither of which is available in the small town. In other words, schooling has become the means for transforming a villager (*köylü*) into a civil servant (*memur*). Parents have thus increasingly invested in their children's education and send them to schools in larger cities. In turn, sons (and increasingly daughters) are expected to support their parents in old age. To gain this security, adult members of the community have been regarding the entire political apparatus as the framework within which economic and social rights are to be obtained. In return for fulfilling their civic duties and obligations, including payment of taxes and military service, parents were demanding that the state provide security—namely, "life, dignity, honor, and property" (*can, ırz, namus, ve mülkiyet*). To many townspeople, the means to this security is education.

The promise of a better future through public education had not been kept, however. The lack of equipment and teachers in the local middle school had inadequately prepared the townspeople's children for the more demanding high schools in the cities. During the 1988–1989 school year there were no instructors for either Turkish or mathematics; the following school year, the school had not been able to recruit someone to teach Turkish.[79] Middle school students were well aware that teachers, most of whom come from urban areas, were reticent about spending a few years in a relatively isolated, poor mountain community. Thus, Orhan who was then in seventh grade and planned to attend a high school in Tarsus was of the "opinion [that] the education is insufficient. In some classes, teachers instruct not in their subject of expertise. Because of the lack of instructors, the students' rate of success is normal (*normal*)." Here, *normal* does not imply a median standard but rather invokes a normative situation that cannot be altered in the immediate future. The lack of qualified instructors resulted in a high rate of attrition; only a third of the entering class of sixth graders succeeded in graduating middle school. Not surprisingly, only a handful of local children ever attended university. Nor did high school and university diplomas necessarily help secure employment. A common complaint among the townspeople is that the "schools produce youth with diplomas without a job or a profession." Even competition for menial factory jobs was stiff. At the time of my fieldwork, youth unemployment was estimated to be between 20 and 30 percent. Understandably, townspeople were apprehensive about the future viability of their households.

Both the townspeople and their children were keenly aware of the connection between the quality of education and the income of households. The overwhelming majority of rural families possessed neither the cultural nor the financial wherewithal to prepare their children to enter magnet (Anatolian high) schools or send them to private colleges; in other words, they could not exercise choice in their children's education. Except for the few gifted pupils who received academic scholarships to magnet or private schools, most children at Yayla did not have access to the knowledge and skills that would ensure them social and economic advancement; unlike their more privileged peers, they would not be admitted to prestigious university programs and obtain lucrative jobs. Thus, in an essay on "Modern and Cultured People," Murat, then a sixth grader attending a private school in the city of Tarsus, distinguished the "educated" urban professionals from the "uneducated" villagers and small townspeople.

> Our modern and cultured people . . . command respect and have much experience. The mothers and fathers educate their children so that they become well-read professionals, like a lawyer, doctor, or judge. Educated people own modern cars, houses, and villas . . . and have disposable incomes. Their children are educated in the best conditions and at the best [i.e., private] schools; they grow up and have a good profession. . . . They earn a lot of money, too.
>
> Most village families are not educated. Nor do they educate their children. When they grow up, the children are as ignorant as their mother and father. Their children become laborers, porters, and garbage men. . . . The sons [who graduate from elementary school] go to middle school or work with their fathers or become apprentices.

Indeed, pupils attending rural schools like those in Yayla were at a clear disadvantage both during their schooling and, later on, in the job market. And as Murat condescendingly observed, the inequality of educational opportunities reproduces disparate opportunities for professional and social advancement, which in turn produces distinctions between different types of school and between the pupils who attend them. The situation for graduates of "regular" (düz) public high schools was not much better; as Çağlar Keyder points out, they "prepare students only minimally to work in modern industry or in any professional slot associated with the increasing complexity of economic life."[80] And despite the repeated calls from industrialists to siphon off students from the regular track schools to vocational ones, the enrollment figures in the latter schools remained low as they suffered from a lack of equipment and staff and, worse, poorly trained students for the industrial workforce.

Education has become a symbolically charged commodity that profoundly informs the subjectivities of schoolchildren. While the curriculum expected pupils to identify with the dominant cultural values inculcated at school, children at Yayla who failed admission to a postprimary school often tapped into the meritocratic ideology of the educational system and took the blame for failing to meet the system's expectations. Most frequently, they pinned their failure to personal cognitive deficiencies (*kafam çalışmiyor*, which literally means "my head doesn't work").

Others, on the contrary, felt that the system had shortchanged them and understood their failure not as a personal predicament but rather a communal one, largely based on family finances. Thus, Selda, a middle school pupil, expressed her frustrations at the difficulties rural families must overcome to educate their children.

> Right now the conditions for studying in Turkey are not easy. For example, a child from a poor family has little success in her studies if her struggling working family does not have the [financial] means. In order to attend a magnet school and graduate with a job she must place well in the [national] exams.[81] Only the rich can send their children to private schools and [the Tarsus] American College. . . . Also, most universities cost money, just about all of them. Besides expenses like books and pocket money, one has to pay tuition. If the child has to work, then she can't study. And, nobody will simply hire an uneducated person. Such are all the problems here. If only the Ministry of Education would stretch out a helping hand to us youth.

Private and magnet schools inscribe a worldly life unavailable to less moneyed pupils like Selda. Indeed, the phenomenal increase in the number of private schools suggests that significant numbers of the middle classes find that public schools have failed to provide those skills and habits necessary for participation in a neoliberal economic order.[82] In 1990, the pupil-teacher ratio at private schools was seventeen to one instead of the fifty or sixty to one in state schools. More importantly, the language of instruction for most subject matter was in either English or German, the two most marketable languages in the country. Indeed, children attending all tracks were aware that employment in import-export firms, tourism, and the stock exchange required mastery of one or more foreign languages. Or as a student attending a regular high school stated, the graduate of a private or magnet school "brings foreign currency into our country and thus helps out the country"— the height of achievement in a neoliberal economic order.

In sum, the current educational tracks with their differentiated skills and credentials situated their respective graduates on different rungs in the national scale of labor, ranging from unemployed, menial laborer to stock-market trader. To a significant extent, the type of schooling children underwent defined their collective identity and personal worth: they either embodied a dynamic modernity or a stationary poverty.

Yet it would be wrong to assume that the children's guardians, the adult townspeople of Yayla, either adopted a fatalist attitude or schemed to overthrow the social and economic order. Rather, they longed for the return of pre-1980 state policies that, according to them, supported entitlement to jobs and provided basic educational needs for their children. In this regard, they framed the political and economic implications of education in the language of patriarchy.

Taking up the patriarchal motif of the "father-state" (*devlet baba*) to emphasize the lack of paternal care on the part of statesmen to resolve the current disparities in education and income was very common. All figures of authority, whether state officials or employers, were construed as patriarchal figures who must provide physical and material support to the economically more vulnerable sectors of the population. In fact, many male adult heads of household willingly situated themselves as dependent on state munificence in the form of jobs for support.[83] According to many townspeople, the state was no longer acting as the compassionate father figure who addresses the economic and educational inequities in the country. On the contrary, townspeople spoke about how the country's political leadership has spurned them, treating them as unwanted stepchildren. They referred to themselves as orphans abandoned to their own wiles.

This perception of an increasingly indifferent state stems, I believe, from popular notions of kinship and the symbolic language of patriarchy. In Yayla, as in many communities in the circum-Mediterranean region, many older townspeople hold to a monogenetic theory of procreation, specifically, that men engender both males and females. That is to say, the male seed alone determines the progeny's physical and moral attributes. Women, on the other hand, are likened to an agricultural field. This theory of procreation is best summed up by Nermin Erdentuğ, who conducted fieldwork in eastern Turkey in the 1950s: "Women are a field, a soil in which the male seed develops."[84] More importantly for my argument here, the degree of kinship between siblings affects the children's share in patrilineal rights. Children having the same father but born from different mothers are considered full siblings (*öz kardeş*); they then equally share the family's patrimony, to wit, the saying "one seed, separate field" (*bir tohum ayrı tarla*). Conversely, in theory, the step-sibling (*üvey kardeş*) born of a different father cannot inherit from the household.

It was with this patrilineal understanding of inheritance that Arif, a truck driver then in his forties, complained about the meager allocation of resources in the local schools at Yayla.

> I look at the situation of the big cities, and I look at ours here. I say this much difference in [the quality of] education cannot be so. A father would not even make such a distinction between his real child and his stepchild. . . . The government does not act at all as a father. . . . They, the politicians, only come at election time; between elections they don't take care of us; they don't give us our due (*bize bakmaz bize hak vermez*).[85]

The truck driver suggested that city dwellers enjoy the status of "real" siblings precisely because, unlike the rural inhabitants, they receive state munificence. Here the state was defined as a male genitor; the local households, unprotected and vulnerable dependents competing for patrimonial largesse.

Framing this competition over resources in education was not limited to the distinction between real and step-siblings. The use of the symbolic language of monogenetic procreation extended to the unfavorable treatment children are expected to receive from their stepmother. Should a man remarry, the new wife is assumed to look after the interests of her own children, to the point of mistreating the first wife's children. An irresponsible father was one who allowed his children to suffer what is popularly known as "treatment typical of a stepmother" (*üvey analık mualemesi*). Such an interpretation of the relations between a woman and her stepchildren was often inflected in discussions on the inadequate education that children receive. Illustrative of this type of argumentation was the complaint about the local school system that Ahmed, a shepherd in his late forties, made: "Aren't we also children of this country? Yet we don't receive anything from the state. . . . Why don't they send us enough teachers to educate our children? The father-state does not act like a compassionate father should. It treats us as a stepmother would." For Ahmed, the nation's political leaders had jettisoned a personalized contract of rights and duties between households and the state. It did not imply an impersonal government grounded in an individualistic conception of society. What made the Turkish state the most viable mode of organizing political power to this shepherd was his faith in the state's ability to provide physical and economic security to all households, including his own. Should the citizen feel that he has not reaped the benefits expected of the state, he will accuse its representatives of having abandoned him. Or as an unemployed farmhand put it, "an orphan cuts his own navel-string."

Indeed, these archaic images of patriarchy provided many townspeople meaningful frames of reference for understanding the contemporary political economy. Household heads perceived that the state had abandoned its paternal duties to mete out just and equitable treatment of all citizens and most often blamed this abandonment on the shift to a free-market economy. Depreciation of real wages and services, privatization of public sector industries, and substitution of agricultural subsidies with value-added taxation on produce had jolted the townspeople's confidence in the state. It was against this background of economic malaise that, on the eve of the national municipality elections, the right-of-center opposition party, the True Path Party (Doğru Yol Partisi, or DYP) took out a full-page ad in the newspaper *Milliyet* attacking the government's economic policies. Claiming to be committed to social justice (*adalet*), including resolution of economic inequities, the DYP advertised itself as the party that would save the citizens from "unemployment, high cost of living, poverty, and inflation."[86] The government ANAP party countered, and threatened to drastically reduce services to any municipality that went over to the opposition. The threats notwithstanding, townspeople of Yayla expressed their discontent with the neoliberal economy and voted for DYP. ANAP placed a distant third, after the left-of-center Social Democrats.

Equally disenchanted with the neoliberal economic policies were those religious nationalists who had supported the religious-oriented National Salvation Party (*Millî Selamet Partisi*, or MSP) during the 1970s and joined ANAP after the 1980 coup. Necmettin Erbakan, the chairman and founder of MSP, was committed to reconciling spiritual equality among Muslims with the economic inequalities in Turkish society. To this aim, he advocated integration of technology and Islamic social justice, application of spiritual values for a work ethic commensurate with industrialization.[87] While strongly opposed to socialism and its materialist interpretation of relations of production, Erbakan and his electorate were keen on preventing and eliminating all forms of economic exploitation through redistribution of wealth. In this moral economic order, wealthier citizens are willing guardians of the poor, who in turn support entrepreneurial profit and recognize the right of private property. The eighth-grade religion textbook, for example, draws on Qur'anic idioms to argue that workers' compliance with the capitalist economic system is revelatory of their faith in Islam and patriotism: "A worker's duty is to do the work given to him in the best manner possible. Thus, from the effort [*hak*] that he has put into his work, he secures for himself a lawful [*helal*] way of earning a living. Through his labor, he contributes to the development of the country." And to ensure a docile labor force, the passage ends with the following warning: "The worker . . . can deceive his employer here and there . . . but he cannot fool Allah."[88]

Thus, these religious-minded backers of capitalism felt that the neoliberal industrialists had betrayed them with the publication of the TÜSİAD report, which criticized the growth of religious education in the country and discredited the alliance between market and faith. This sense of betrayal found expression in an editorial of the conservative newspaper *Türkiye*: "My honorable industrialists: İmam-Hatip graduates can't be anarchists or state enemies. Our dear businessmen: know that these graduates guard your capital without expecting anything in return for their food. . . . The believer respects labor and capital. . . . Why do you oppose the nation's conscience, beliefs, and centuries-old customs? Why do you prepare reports meant to insult this nation?"[89] Other supporters of religious-track schools took a less conciliatory tone to the industrialists' educational report and suggested that they were intent on exploiting the poor Muslim worker. The Islamic daily *Zaman*, for one, ran a cartoon in which two businessmen sporting white bow ties with their black tuxedos were upset at a well-known hadith (a religious saying attributed to the prophet Muhammad) posted outside a Qur'an course: "Give the worker what he deserves before the sweat of his brow dries up." One of the businessmen lifts his clenched fist in the air and shouts: "Look at what's happening! If we don't shut down these [Qur'an] Courses, our workers will see the light." The other businessman calms him down, "Don't worry. We will immediately fabricate an educational report."[90]

Envoi

To many sectors of the population, the government's neoliberal economic policies prevented them from gaining full economic citizenship—namely, the right to employment, adequate protection against market vulnerability, and a decrease of inequalities of opportunity. In short, the state failed to provide for the material welfare of its citizens. Lacking the freedom and opportunity to determine their own economic life strategies, insecurity about the future prevailed among lower-income parents and children, who make up the overwhelming majority of the country and Yayla. Those children, who were unable to further their education, were presented with the singular choice of irregular menial work or long-term unemployment. In effect, the neoliberal capitalist regime that purportedly embraces true choices (in the plural) reinforced their status as second-class citizens.

As the state failed to provide basic educational services that facilitate children's entry into the labor force and thus create full employment, many citizens felt that the state had reneged on its fatherly responsibilities. Thus, the very educational institutions that legitimated the political economic domination of the neoliberalists created the conditions for resuscitating a discourse in which the rights of citizens to a livelihood were elevated over the sovereign rights of the market.

The sense of social and economic injustice was all the more exacerbated as young and old identify modernity with the consumer culture disseminated in the school system, media, and advertisements. They perceived their lives as somehow organized around, and in relationship to, an inability to partake in the modern way of life of wealthier citizens. The tension between their poverty and the extralocal modern ideals—a Hatchback, a fully furnished home, a university education, and a liberal profession for their children—had driven many to reflect on whether the school system had failed them or whether they failed to live up to the system.

What was clear to all was that the neoliberal economic order had created new forms of social exclusion. As a result of their uneducability, rural children had become "othered" in popular discourse as a counterpart to the cultured urban citizens. Caught between a fundamentalist morality and a market amorality, the only remaining fatherly figures many townspeople looked up to (and then with some reservations) were the military—the subject of the next chapter.

Notes

1. "Temel eğitim IV., V., VI., VII. ve VIII. sınıflar sosyal bilgiler programının kabulü hakkında," *TD* 37 (2 December 1974), pp. 570–71.

2. Zekâi Baloğlu, *Türkiye'de eğitim*, pp. 1, 14.

3. Implicit in this neoliberal educational discourse is what Giovanni Arrighi calls the superiority of the "capitalist logics of power" over a territorialist one; see his *The Long Twentieth Century: Money, Power, and the Origins of Our Times* (London: Verso, 1994), p. 36.

4. David Harvey, *The Condition of Postmodernity: An Enquiry into the Origins of Cultural Change* (Oxford, UK: Basil Blackwell, 1989), p. 168.

5. Barrington Moore, *The Social Origins of Dictatorship and Democracy* (New York: Beacon, 1966), pp. 433–52.

6. See Robert Bianchi, *Interest Groups and Political Development in Turkey* (Princeton, NJ: Princeton University Press, 1984), pp. 268–74; and Ayse Bugra, "The Place of the Economy in Turkish Society," *South Atlantic Quarterly* 102 (2003), pp. 453–70.

7. Like the international financial organizations, the Turkish business community subscribed to "human capital theory," which posits that education raises an individual's skills and abilities and therefore his or her productivity in the workplace. Or as George Psacharopoulos and Maureen Woodhall, two major spokespersons of this pedagogical approach, argue, "schooling fosters the type of behavioral change that is conducive to economic growth." See their *Education for Development: An Analysis of Investment Choice* (New York: Oxford University Press, 1985), p. 314. This theory of education (and society) fails to consider issues of class, race and ethnicity, and gender, all of which are closely linked to asymmetrical relations of power in a society.

8. Zekâi Baloğlu, *Türkiye'de eğitim*, p. 171.

9. Michel Foucault, "Governmentality," in *The Foucault Effect: Studies in Govern-*

mentality, ed. Graham Bruchell, Colin Gordon, and Peter Miller (Chicago: University of Chicago Press, 1991), pp. 87–104.

10. Bernard S. Cohn, "The Census, Social Structure and Objectification in South Asia," in *An Anthropologist among the Historians and Other Essays* (New Delhi: Oxford University Press, 1990), pp. 224–54.

11. Concerning the use of statistical categories and procedures for governance, see Ian Hacking, "How Should We Do the History of Statistics?" in *The Foucault Effect: Studies in Governmentality*, ed. Graham Burchell, Colin Gordon, and Peter Miller (Chicago: University of Chicago Press, 1991), pp. 181–96; and Alain Desrosières, *The Politics of Large Numbers: A History of Statistical Reasoning* (Cambridge, MA: Harvard University Press, 1998).

12. On the use of the present tense and the totalizing phrase (e.g., "villagers are/do/behave . . .") as powerful rhetorical devices to establish authority over another society, see Mary Louise Pratt, "Scratches on the Face of the Country; or, What Mr. Barrow Saw in the Land of the Bushmen," *Critical Inquiry* 12 (1986), pp. 119–43.

13. E.g., Nermin Erdentuğ, *Hal köyü'nün etnolojik tetkiki* (Ankara: Türk Tarih Kurumu Basımevi, 1954), p. 7; and Resat Kasaba, "Migrant Labor in Western Anatolia, 1750–1850," in *Landholding and Commercial Agriculture in the Middle East*, ed. Çaglar Keyder and Faruk Tabak (Albany: State University of New York Press, 1991), pp. 113–21.

14. In 1990 the official census counted six thousand inhabitants in Yayla, but the majority of the officially registered population lived elsewhere. Townspeople estimate that 40 percent of the town's inhabitants actually reside in Tarsus, 15 percent in Adana, and a few families in the port city of Mersin. These estimates correlate roughly with the municipality records as well as with the dispersion and genealogical charts of twenty extensive lineages that I drew. As I will elaborate in this chapter, many families moved to the cities during the school year so their children could avail of better educational opportunities. Thus, the town's population swelled from three thousand during the school year to well over ten thousand during the summer recess.

15. Zekâi Baloğlu, *Türkiye'de eğitim*, p. 25.

16. Karayiğit and Karayiğit. *Çukurova için hayat bilgisi*, p. 72.

17. *İlkokul Türkçe ders kitabı 3* (Ankara: Türk Tarih Kurumu Basımevi, 1990), p. 72. Policy makers also make use of audiovisual media to exalt the bucolic village to school-age children. At the Second Turkish Children's Songs Contest, which aired on national television, the winning song, "To Boris, from Ali the Immigrant Child" ("Göçmen Çocuğu Aliş'ten Boris'e"), affirmed indigenous authenticity with its metaphors of longevity and continuity:

Granny Ayshe tell me
What place is Anatolia
Test a person once

No longer will he miss his home
Thank God
That place is Anatolia
Grandpa Hasan tell us
What kind of place is Anatolia
If there's carp in the stream
If there are five prayers a day
If there is a bard in every village
That place is Anatolia

TRT (21 March 1990). The song was written in the wake of the massive forced migration of ethnic Turks from Bulgaria, then still under communist rule.

18. *İlkokul Türkçe ders kitabı 3*, pp. 109–10.

19. See Deniz Kandiyoti, "Women's Place in Turkish Society: A Comparative Approach," *Current Turkish Thought* 30 (1977), p. 11.

20. In 1990, female students made up 38 percent of all high school students, 30 percent of university students. State Institute of Statistics, *Statistical Year Book of Turkey, 1993*, p. 69.

21. Perhaps to emphasize her point about parents' unwillingness to educate their daughters, Şeyma considerably altered the popular expression "Keep your daughter in line or you will regret it later."

22. Zekâi Baloğlu, *Türkiye'de eğitim*, p. 17.

23. As a result of devastating wars preceding and including the War of Independence, the republican regime had enacted draconian laws against any form of birth control.

24. According to the 1983 Population Planning Law (sections 5 and 6), up to ten weeks after conception, women may request abortion on demand provided that they obtain consent of either their husband or legal guardian. After ten weeks, two specialists must make a case that there is a risk to the woman's life or a risk to fetal health. In either situation, women are asked to reveal intimate aspects of their sexual lives, including information regarding the use of contraceptives. According to townswomen, the interviews are particularly trying as medical workers are prone to make demeaning comments on the women's inability to assume responsibility for their sexual behavior—an attitude that reinforces the supposed backwardness of rural society. Not surprisingly, many women prefer to terminate their pregnancies on their own rather than to submit to intrusive interrogations.

25. "Sınıflar, doldu taşıyor," *Güneş* (17 October 1990), p. 5. For the 1990–1991 school year, 10,600,000 primary and secondary students enrolled in 61,400 schools: 6,900,000 pupils in 51,370 elementary schools; 2,340,000 in 6,540 middle schools; and 1,360,000 students in 3,500 regular-track high schools and vocational schools; see "Yeni ders yılı ve Akyol'un çabaları," *Türkiye* (28 September 1990), p. 14.

26. Organisation for Economic Co-operation and Development (OECD), *Turkey* (Washington, DC: OECD Publications and Information Center, 1989), p. 65.

27. "Turkish Family Planning Association Seminar," *Population Planning News* 13 (May 1972), p. 1.

28. Zekâi Baloğlu, *Türkiye'de eğitim*, p. 19.

29. "Beş senede beş saat," *Türkiye* (16 October 1990), p. 4.

30. Emin Işık, "Geleneksel aile yapımızı neye borçluyuz," *Türk Edebiyatı* 202 (1990), p. 36.

31. Pornographic films were popularly known as "the sex market" (*seks fuarı*). In 1979, of the 195 films produced in Turkey, 131 were pornographic in content. Giovanni Scognamillo, *Türk sinema tarihi: ikinci cilt 1960–1986* (İstanbul: Metis Yayıncılık, 1987), p. 31.

32. Walter Holzhausen, "The Population Problem in Turkey (as Seen from the Perspective of a Foreign Donor)," *Nüfusbilim Dergisi/Turkish Journal of Population Studies* 9 (1987), p. 66.

33. The festive day commemorates the prophet Ibrahim's sacrifice of a ram as a divine dispensation released him from the intended sacrifice of his only son Ishmail for his belief in Allah. Following prayer services in the mosque, a feast of the slaughtered meat stresses communal ties; about a third of the meat is given to needy neighbors.

34. H. I. Goldberg and A. Toros, "The Use of Traditional Methods of Contraception among Turkish Couples," *Studies in Family Planning* 25 (1994), pp. 122–28.

35. Hacettepe Institute for Population Studies, *The 1988 Turkish Population and Health Survey* (Ankara: HIPS, 1989).

36. In conversation, townspeople often indexed mention of Gypsies with "excuse me" (*affedersiniz*), a term used before mentioning animals in a conversation.

37. At the time, Turkey was officially a neutral country but, following the battle of Stalingrad, in which the Soviet armies successfully repelled the German army in February 1943, the British prime minister Winston Churchill convinced the Turkish government to have the strategic road going through the Cilician Gates repaved and thus prevent the Axis powers from invading the country from the south. Turkish officials had long considered fascist Italy, which had occupied the nearby Dodecanese islands since World War I, a potential threat to the country's security.

38. See W. Penn Handwerker, "The Modern Demographic Transition: An Analysis of Subsistence Choices and Reproductive Consequences," *American Anthropologist* 88 (1986), p. 402.

39. Michel Foucault, *The History of Sexuality, Volume 1: An Introduction*. (Harmondsworth, Middlesex, UK: Penguin, 1981), pp. 104–7, 140–46.

40. Elizabeth Grosz, *Becomings: Explorations in Time, Memory and Futures* (Ithaca, NY: Cornell University Press, 1999), p. 28.

41. İlber Ortaylı, *İmparatorluğun en uzun yüzyılı* (İstanbul: Hil Yayın, 1983), p. 11.

42. TRT, *Evening News* (17 September 1990).

43. TRT, *Evening News* (24 September 1990).

44. İsmet Parmaksızoğlu, *Ortaokullar için Türkiye cumhuriyeti inkılâp tarihi ve Atatürkçülük* (İstanbul: Millî Eğitim Basımevi, 1988), pp. 121–22.

45. "21. yüzyılın eşiïnde mağara devri," *Tercüman* (25 March 1989), p. 3.

46. "Mağara devri," *Nokta* (30 July 1989), pp. 20–21.

47. E.g., Tüccarzâde İbrahim Hilmi, "Aile hayatımızda Avrupalılaşmanın tesiri," in *Avrupalılaşmak, felaketlerimiz esbâbı* (İstanbul: Matbaa-ı Hayriye ve Sürekâsı, [1332] 1916), p. 56. Less frequently used is the archaeological sensu stricto term *Stone Age* (*taş devri*). Thus, in an attempt to shock his urban readers, Mahmut Makal, a village teacher from central Anatolia, for example, described "the squalor, the primitive conditions in this village—they're indescribable. . . . It might be the Stone Age, which one only reads about in history books!" See his runaway best-selling *A Village in Anatolia* (London: Valentine, Mitchell, 1954), p. 162. The American term *Space Age* has taken hold of public discourse since the first moon landing in 1969. At the local grocery stores, a commonly sold disposable razor is called Space Age. See Paul Magnarella, "Turkish Townsmen View Apollo," *Middle East Journal* 26 (1972), pp. 181–83.

48. Anne McClintock, *Imperial Leather: Race, Gender, and Sexuality in the Colonial Contest* (New York: Routledge, 1995), p. 40.

49. The terms are respectively *çağdaşlar, geçişler, yolaçanlar, arayanlar, yeni Avrupalılar, sadeler, sadıklar,* and *çabalayanlar.*

50. Değerler ve Yaşam Biçimleri Araştırması, *Values and Lifestyles Research. Part II: Quantitative* (İtanbul: Doğrudan Pazarlama A. Ş., 1989), p. 24. For a similar breakdown of the population into traditional, transitional, and modern types, see Daniel Lerner, *The Passing of Traditional Society: Modernizing the Middle East* (New York: Free Press, 1958), p. 165.

51. *Nokta* (12 August 1990), inside back cover.

52. Susan Gal and Judith Irvine, "The Boundaries of Languages and Disciplines: How Ideologies Construct Difference," *Social Research* 62 (1985), p. 981.

53. Historically, the Ottoman capital city of Istanbul represented urban/e (*medenî*), polished society as opposed to the uncouth hinterland (*taşra*) outside the city; see Ulrich W. Haarman, "Ideology and History, Identity and Alterity: The Arab Image of the Turk from the Àbassids to Modern Egypt," *International Journal of Middle Eastern Studies* 20 (1988), p. 177.

54. Before Yayla gained municipality status in 1954, there were two villages, Kozu and Çukur, about a twenty-minute walk apart. By 1990, only five families remained year-round in Kozu.

55. As a rule, the principle of ultimogeniture holds; namely, the youngest son inherits the bulk of the family's land holdings, including the home, as he is expected to support his parents in old age.

56. At the summer state-run sewing course, which I discussed in the previous chapter, the teenage girls were also taught how to manage a hygienic home; for ex-

ample, they were instructed to serve separate dishes for each family member. Since the 1940s, the Ministry of Education has tackled the absence of women in the school system with itinerant courses in sewing and embroidery. With the intent to teach hygiene, child rearing, and modern management of the home, the courses were "aimed at women of all ages not only young village girls." "Köy kadınları gezici kurslarının öğretim faaliyetleri h," *TD* 7 (9 October 1944), p. 61.

57. Townsmen had fleeting glimpses of urban home life from the occasional films shown in the generator-powered all-male movie theater. Introduction of "Frankish" (*alafranga*; that is, Western) domestic practices including table manners was a pedagogical topic for the children of the Ottoman elite at the turn of the twentieth century. İsmet Kur, *Turkiye'de süreli çocuk yayınları* (Ankara: Atatürk Kültür Merkezi, 1991), pp. 125–26.

58. The standard *Elementary School Program* manual expects instructors of fourth- and fifth-grade natural sciences to make sure that "every student builds a wooden bed with simple materials in the school shop . . . and have the families do the same." Most families still use mattresses stuffed with cotton, which they put down on the ground when going to sleep. Millî Eğitim Bakanlığı, *İlkokul Programı*, p. 87.

59. *Resimli yeni aile bilgisi sınıf 4* (İstanbul: Biryayınevi, 1959), p. 72.

60. While the home economics textbook implies that food is served directly on the floor, the grandmother would have certainly marked off the eating space with a cloth especially designed for meals.

61. *Resimli yeni aile bilgisi sınıf 4*, p. 96.

62. Jean Baudrillard, "Consumer Society," in *Jean Baudrillard: Selected Writings*, ed. Mark Poster (Cambridge, UK: Polity, 1988), p. 45; his emphasis. On accruing social capital through purchase of household objects, see Richard Wilk, "Learning to Be Local in Belize: Global Systems of Common Difference," in *Worlds Apart: Modernity through the Prism of the Local*, ed. Daniel Miller (London: Routledge, 1995), pp. 110–33.

63. Tekışık, *Hayat bilgisi ünitelerine kaynak kitap 3*, p. 27.

64. As historian İlber Ortaylı points out, nineteenth-century reformers were always "in a hurry." See his *İmparatorluğun en uzun yüzyılı* (İstanbul: Hil Yayın, 1983), p. 11.

65. Jean-Paul Sartre, *Being and Nothingness*, trans. Hazel E. Barnes (New York: Philosophical Library, 1956), p. 59.

66. Pierre Bourdieu, *Outline of a Theory of Practice*, trans. Richard Nice (Cambridge, UK: Cambridge University Press, 1977), p. 105; his emphasis.

67. Modern pedagogical systems worldwide measure and quantify school knowledge in terms of time units. In hours, the Turkish elementary schoolchild will have studied over five years the following: life sciences (1820); social sciences (820); natural sciences (780); Turkish (1600); religion (80); mathematics (960); art or shop (520); music (200); and physical education (320).

68. *İlkokul Türkçe ders kitabı 5*, pp. 167–68.

69. Talip Apaydın, *Karanlığın kuvveti: Köy Enstitüsü yılları* (İstanbul: Ararat Yayınevi, 1967), p. 54.

70. Millî Eğitim Bakanlığı, *İlkokul programı*, p. 146.

71. "1940–1941, 1941–1942, 1942–1943 ders yıllarında ilkokullarında okutulmak üzere yazdırılacak okuma kitapları şartnamesi," *TD* 1 (13 February 1939), p. 20.

72. *İlkokul Türkçe ders kitabı 4* (İstanbul: Media Print, 1990), p. 95.

73. *Milliyet* (25 March 1989).

74. Frederic Jameson, "Postmodernism, or, the Cultural Logic of Late Capitalism," *New Left Review* 146 (1984), p. 64.

75. Tekışık, *Hayat bilgisi ünitelerine kaynak kitap 3*, p. 119; emphasis in original.

76. Tekışık, *Hayat bilgisi ünitelerine kaynak kitap 3*, p. 113.

77. Deniz Kandiyoti, "Women and Household Production: The Impact of Rural Transformation in Turkey," in *The Rural Middle East: Peasant Lives and Modes of Production*, ed. Kathy Glavanis and Pandeli Glavanis (London: Zed Books, 1989), p. 183. It goes without saying that noncapitalist modes of production, be it informal cooperation between domestic units, subsistence farming, or the patriarchal household division of labor, persist alongside capitalist modes.

78. Tekışık, *Hayat bilgisi ünitelerine kaynak kitap 3*, p. 36.

79. Because middle schools are the junior section of academic-track high schools, teachers instruct only the subject matter they mastered at either a teachers' college or a university. Despite a law stipulating that teachers must begin their careers in less developed parts of the country, there is a surplus of sixty thousand teachers in the wealthier western half of the country while the poorer southern and southeastern provinces lack forty thousand instructors. OECD, *Turkey*, p. 24.

80. Çağlar Keyder, *State and Society in Turkey: A Study in Capitalist Development* (London: Verso, 1987), p. 216.

81. Given the stiff competition for entrance into one of the 110 magnet schools (Anatolian High Schools) in the country, the more moneyed families sent their children to private courses; less wealthy households sufficed with buying preparatory books. In 1990, only 12 percent of the 174,878 fifth graders who applied won a place. "Özel okullar sınavında Hıristiyan, Musevi ve yabancılar dikkate alındı," *Güneş* (22 May 1990), p. 1.

82. Between 1985 and 1990, the number of private schools increased from 243 to 556; student enrollment rose from 59,000 to 126,000.

83. Nükhet Sirman, "State, Village, and Gender in Western Turkey," in *Turkish State, Turkish Society*, ed. Andrew Finkel and Nükhet Sirman (London: Routledge, 1990), p. 25.

84. Nermin Erdentuğ, *Hal köyü'nün etnolojik tetkiki*, p. 69; see also Carol Delaney, *The Seed and the Soil: Gender and Cosmology in Turkish Village Society* (Berkeley: University of California Press, 1991), pp. 30–36.

85. Contained in the term *hak* is the idea of obligation and reciprocity.

86. *Milliyet* (25 March 1989). In Turkey, the names of political parties often have symbolic meaning. The True Path Party refers to the straight and narrow road the faithful were enjoined to follow (in Arabic, the *al-sirât al Mustaqî*), to wit, the Qur'anic passage (sura 3:101) "Whoever holds firmly to God will be shown a way that is straight." Before the 1980 coup, the party was known as the Justice Party (JP), the immediate successor of the outlawed Democrat Party (DP), whose popular leader Adnan Menderes was, to many of his followers, unjustly hung by the military. The rural electorate pronounced *democrat* as "Demir Kırat," the white horse of the seventeenth-century legendary hero Köroğlu who had fought venal Ottoman officials in the countryside three centuries earlier. Both the JP and the current DYP use the white horse as the party's emblem.

87. Binnaz Toprak, "Politicization of Islam in a Secular State: The National Salvation Party in Turkey," in *From Nationalism to Revolutionary Islam*, ed. Said Amir Arjomand (Oxford, UK: Macmillan, 1984), p. 126. To a large extent, voters of the MSP had suffered from economic dislocation: first, small merchants, traders, shopkeepers, and artisans whom the larger industrial combines had squeezed out of business; later, poorly remunerated civil servants and workers. See Jacob M. Landau, *Politics and Islam: The National Salvation Party in Turkey* (Salt Lake City: Middle East Center, University of Utah, 1976), p. 51.

88. Cihad Tunç, *Ortaokullar için din kültürü ve ahlâk bilgisi 3* (İstanbul: Millî Eğitim Basımevi, 1986), p. 139.

89. "Yeni bir irtica müfettişi: TÜSİAD," *Türkiye* (1 October 1990), p. 2.

90. *Zaman* (22 September 1990), p. 8.

CHAPTER FIVE

Nation and Army

Historians of ideas usually attribute the dream of a perfect society to the philosophers of the eighteenth century; but there was also a military dream of society; its fundamental reference was not to the state of nature, but to meticulously subordinated cogs of a machine, not to the primal social contract, but to permanent coercions, not to fundamental rights, but to infinitely progressive forms of training, not to the general will, but to automatic docility.

— MICHEL FOUCAULT *Discipline and Punish: The Birth of a Prison*

Not once did the TÜSİAD report mention the military's direct involvement in national education. This is all the more surprising given that, following the 1980 coup, military leaders set out to deliberately mobilize and manipulate public opinion by carrying its conception of political education into schools. To this end, they considerably tightened the institutional links between the armed forces and the national educational system, including stricter control of personnel, children, and curriculum. In a concerted effort to consolidate national unity through schools, the military closely collaborated with the sponsors of the Turkish Islamic Synthesis.[1] The National Security Council, where the commander in chief and various military commanders made critical decisions in tandem with members of the executive branch of the civilian government, was largely responsible for increasing the number of religious-track schools and approving greater religious instruction in the secular-track school system.[2] Thus, it is highly significant that the report is silent about the central role the military has played in shaping educational policies.

This silence, I believe, is closely related to an unacknowledged homology and symbiosis between formal schooling and military training in modern state formation. Associating education with warfare, pedagogy with military campaigns, and teachers with an officer cadre has been a standard practice in nation building. Universal conscription and universal education have been the two most crucial vehicles in creating the fraternal notion of the nation, congruent with a fixed and bounded territory. Historically, the moment that the Ottoman state began to actively adopt Western forms of knowledge in the late eighteenth century, education has been closely linked to defense, and these links became even more pronounced following the Franco-Prussian débâcle of 1870. Then, French policy makers pinned the Prussians' military success on literacy and sponsored literacy campaigns to produce better trained and more patriotic soldiers. As historian Alan Mitchell points out, French nation-builders believed that political allegiance resulted best from a concerted effort at militarizing the citizenry through schools: "In addition to the popular mystique about the army becoming the school of the nation. . . , the inverse proposition consequently developed that the schools should prepare pupils for military service."[3] Likewise, army and school are an inseparable pair of terms in nationalist rhetoric in Turkey. Already in 1921, in the midst of the War of Liberation, the official newspaper *Hakimiyet-i Milliye* (*National Sovereignty*) frequently quoted the Prussian field marshal Helmuth von Moltke's dictum that the Prussian headmasters, not the generals, had defeated the French in 1870.[4]

Since the founding of the Turkish Republic, collaboration between military institutions and civilian pedagogical ones has evolved with the country's social, political, and cultural transformations. The 1980 coup provided the generals with an opportunity to actively collaborate in shaping the national curriculum and, more specifically, to inculcate the "military dream of society" among schoolchildren. After all, a major activity of a state is war making; but conscription alone does not create soldiers willing to sacrifice themselves for the state.[5] Yet other than Ayşe Gül Altınay's pathbreaking study of the high school military course, little attention has been given to the various ways the Turkish military has worked through civilian schools to foster its own agenda.[6] For the most part, scholars assume that martial ideals are centuries-old traditions and customs.[7] The few studies that do address the pedagogical roles of the armed forces have confined their scope to discussing rudimentary education of conscripted soldiers, thereby reinforcing the military's self-image of praetorian responsibility.[8]

With the aim of explaining the coup leaders' apolitical intervention in the school system, this chapter investigates how the ideology of a military nation has been actualized through the curriculum and the children's responses to this imagined, militarized polity. To instill a spirit of law and order and self-sacrifice in the student body, the armed forces have propagated filial reverence for Atatürk, the father of the country, and a syncretism of military secularism and religious militarism to combat communists and all other political and social entities that challenge the primacy of Turkish nationalism.

Military Interventions

Many townspeople welcomed the military intervention in 1980. To them, only the army could restore order in an otherwise chaotic political situation. During the 1970s, often called the "years of anarchy" (*anarşi yılları*), civilian politicians had failed to contain civil disorder. Yayla had its share of violence, as Marxist and neofascist youth skirmished over the political imaginary of the country. At the time of my fieldwork, political graffiti was still visible under the whitewash of buildings and water tanks. On an abandoned building in the center of the town one could make out the Marxist slogan "The Only Road is Revolution-Federation of Revolutionary Youth" (*Tek Yol Devrim-Dev Genç*). Likewise, irredentist nationalists belonging to Path of Ideal Association (*Ülkü Yolu Derneği*) left their mark: they totally trashed the summer home of a national politician belonging to the left-of-center People's Republican Party in addition to spray painting slogans throughout the town.[9] By the time I had arrived in Yayla, eight years after the coup, things had quieted down, but visceral memories continued to haunt the community.

A town guard, whom I will call Ramazan, illustrated the political impasse with a story about a traffic accident: "When two taxi drivers begin to fight, they expect a person of authority to intervene so that they can go on with their business. When nobody intervenes, don't they say, 'Isn't there any man here?' (*Burada erkek yok mu*)." Framing polity and governance in gendered terms is not particular to Ramazan. In the town guard's allegory, the lack of effective leadership implied the emasculation of the state and, by association, that of the (male) citizenry. And as many townspeople recalling the period preceding the coup told me, as a result of the lack of effective leadership and power (*iktidar*) among politicians, the nation at large suffered from impotence (*iktidarsızlık*). The generals, I suggest here, tapped into the concept of *father-state* (*devlet baba*), which I discussed in the previous chapter. That is to say, they drew on a paternalist understanding of power holders as custodians of the people's welfare to legitimate their intervention. Thus, the generals justified the coup by claiming that the civilian politicians were unable to govern the country and effectively deal with the breakdown of law and order. In other words, politicians had abandoned the nation for partisan politics and thus failed to carry out their paternal responsibilities. Worse still, the junta argued, was that the educated youth had become disdainful of authority and reproduced parliamentary disorder on university campuses and in secondary schools. In turn, townspeople of Yayla often understood the military intervention not only as instituting stability and order but, more importantly, also as restoring the moral bonds linking citizens with the paternalist state.

This concept of *father-state* remains a central feature in the official politics of national culture and finds expression in the curriculum. Thus, children learn that the prerepublican sultans had failed to live up to their fatherly responsibilities. During the two weeks that school children study the foundation of the republic and its founder Atatürk, they are taught why the current republican regime replaced the former Ottoman sultanate. The sultan's cowardice, selfishness, and pursuit of pleasure (all understood as nonmasculine traits) kept the country backward, oppressed, and exploited by foreign powers. These negative traits serve to legitimate the abolition of the sultanate. Furthermore, the curriculum projects a keen sense of the sultans having abandoned the Turkish people, and this visceral point is emphasized throughout grade school. Second graders, for example, read that

> before the Republic, . . . there were no roads, schools, factories and ports in our country. Our commerce was in the hands of foreigners. We bought all of our needs from abroad. All our money went outside the country, too. As

a result our people were poor and unprotected. . . . The nation was without a head, the country was without a protector (*millet başsız, yurt sahipsiz*).[10]

National salvation, according to this official historical narrative, began only when Mustafa Kemal (Atatürk) led the Turkish people to victory in the War of Liberation (1919–1923). Thus, from the moment children attend school, they are taught to be grateful to this illustrious leader, who not only successfully expelled foreign armies but also began the modernization of their country.[11] The theme of Atatürk as savior of the Turkish nation was dramatically adumbrated at one of the local elementary schools in Yayla. The children performed the play *The Nation's Children* (*Ülkü çocukları*). Nejla, the fourth-grade character, spoke to the audience.

If you don't mind let me read a passage from our national history which I have just learned. You'll see how beautiful it is. A Turkish poet [Namık Kemal] says at the moment the fatherland is at its lowest point,

"The foe thrusts his knife into the heart of the land. There was no one to save our ill-fated mother."

Our Great Forefather [Atatürk] changed [the last two lines] in the following manner:

"The foe thrusts his knife into the heart of the land. But yes, one is found to save our ill-fated mother."

The children on stage clapped immediately following her words.

It is with this patriarchal rhetoric of a hypermasculine leadership and a feminized geo-body that the military command has consistently cast itself as a virtuous, disciplined, and meritocratic corps disinterested in ideological or personal competitions. To this effect, the coup leaders considered themselves to be the legitimate ideological successors of Mustafa Kemal Atatürk, that is to say, the politically neutral guardians of not only the country but also the republican regime itself. National unity, thus, took precedence over noninvolvement in civilian politics.[12] This corps identity provided the military with the legitimacy to police the political culture of the country.

Central to the generals' rhetoric was the notion that a stable political regime had to be restored. The army had intervened before, but this time the generals made sure to position themselves as the chief cultural brokers of the national polity. And this included the national educational system. At the core of the new curriculum was a nationalism predicated on Atatürkism (*Atatürkçülük*), the principles of the soldier-statesman Atatürk. All pupils, from first grade on, must learn the military command's version of the life and thoughts of Atatürk.

> In keeping to the existing program's aims and according to the pupils' level of knowledge and age, all elementary school pupils must be made to love Atatürk consciously in their work in and outside the class. It must be made clear in sincere ways how they are tied to His works. . . . Identification with Atatürk and His works must not be limited to a specific lesson. At all opportunities, Atatürk's personality, the important events of the War of Liberation, Atatürk's Reforms, Atatürk's principles and views, together with Our Great Leader's aphorisms must be made known. The pupils must be made conscious of Atatürkism.[13]

The underlying principle was that only a military-sponsored nationalism would prevent anarchy from returning to the country.

Reverence for Atatürk is evident in the schools in Yayla. The school day begins with children reciting the pledge of allegiance, Our Oath (*Andımız*), the second stanza being "O great Atatürk, you have provided us with this day / In the country you founded and the goals you showed us, I swear that I will walk forever on the path you opened up."[14] The walls of hallways and classrooms are decorated with his portraits, which also appear on all covers of textbooks, including the primers on religion. At the Yayla middle school, opposite the main entrance is a wall with the label "Atatürk's Principles." In the center of the wall hangs a portrait of Atatürk in civilian clothes. To the left and right of the portrait hang three golden framed plaques with quotes from the six fundamental principles enshrined in the 1937 constitutional amendment; namely, republicanism, nationalism, populism, statism, reformism, and laicism. At the adjacent elementary school, right next to the principal's office, was built a mound of rocks upon which stands Atatürk in a silhouetted, well-known pose overlooking his troops at Kocatepe, the hill from which the military statesman began the expulsion of foreign armies during the War of Independence; next to this silhouette is a wooden post advertising the six principles.

Atatürk is equally represented in the curriculum. No subject omits mention of him: in math class, second graders calculate the anniversary of his death; in music and art class, middle school students sing his praises and draw his image; in foreign language classes, children master his biography.[15] In their primers, Turkish children devote many class hours to reading about his exemplary life, love of the common people, devotion to the country, and commitment to education. In the first-grade primer, one seventh (six out of forty-seven) of the reading passages are devoted to Atatürk; in the fifth-grade primer, one fourth (thirteen out of fifty-two). This concerted effort at having children identify with the statesman begins early. According to a ministerial directive, six-year-old kindergarten children are expected "to pronounce correctly the name of Mustafa Kemal Atatürk, recite the names of his family members, know his place of birth, recognize several of his pictures, appreciate his heroism, know the date and place of his death as well as his tomb."[16] Devotion to the personhood of Atatürk reaches its peak on the anniversary of his death (10 November 1938). At 9:05 a.m., the time he died, the student body and teaching staff show respect for his memory with one minute or more of silence. The second-grade life science textbook captures well the annual commemoration of Atatürk's death.

> At school we decorate *Atatürk's bust* with flowers. . . . In class, we clean the [framed] *portrait of Atatürk* and decorate it with paper and flowers. Together with our teachers we gather at the ceremonial site. At exactly *five past nine* we stand at attention in order to show respect for *Our Father* for *three minutes*. At the same time, all motor vehicles in the country blow their horns for *three minutes*. Citizens in our villages, towns and cities stand at attention for *three minutes* for the *Great Father*. . . . Flags are lowered to half mast on *November 10*; throughout the day radio and television broadcast programs about *Our Father*.[17]

The year-after-year study of the statesman's life and thoughts is explicitly intended to structure the political consciousness of children. A year and a half after the coup, in his report on public institutions and national unity, the defense secretary attached to the Ministry of Education stated as much: "National education aims at raising a perfect Atatürkist youth who is morally tied to his country; it aims at raising a just, honest, positivist, enterprising, competent, hardworking, honorable, and respectable youth faithful to customs and traditions."[18] Understood is that the educational system will beget a future nation of Atatürks for the childless statesman. In first grade, children read out loud that "we will work hard and show that we are Atatürk children (*Atatürk çocukları*)."[19] Underlying the familial metaphor is that schoolchildren should behave as if they were living extensions of the dead statesman. Ahmet Üst's poem "My Dear Teacher," which is included in the fifth-grade reader, exemplified this emulation of the statesman. The poem ends with "MY TEACHER, take me and make me into a MUSTAFA KEMAL!"[20]

None of the children whom I came to know questioned the cult of Atatürk. Over and over I heard them praise him as the greatest Turk who ever lived; a few were convinced that he was the world's greatest man. All showed gratitude for what he had accomplished, especially for liberating the country from foreign occupation during the War of Independence. Thus, in an essay on "The Turkish Person," which I had assigned, thirteen-year-old Muhteber wrote, "The past of the Turkish people is full of victories. Our forefathers were very brave people and sacrificed themselves for their fatherland. In this way many people became martyrs. Atatürk was a very brave, knowledgeable, and very good commander. He would think more about his country than about himself. He bequeathed the 23 April Children and Hegemony Day to the children. The duty that falls on us is to advance on the road he took." Her statement affirmed a sense of purpose and collective memory that confirmed membership in the nation all the while constraining the individual child to conformity. Her essay also revealed how much Atatürk's military career and the War of Independence were neither incidental to nor illustrative of but rather central to the creation of a uniform national identity in the educational system.

A Nation of Soldiers

School curriculum in Turkey places much emphasis on the fraternal person of the citizen-soldier, who metonymically embodies the united, sovereign national community. Accordingly, the educational materials used in primary schools emphasize heroic episodes of Turkish military history, self-sacrifice for the nation, and pride in war heroes.[21]

Central to these martial virtues has been devotion to the national flag, whose white crescent and five-pointed star are placed on a red background. Since 1939, two years after the Turkish parliament legislated the dimensions and spiritual importance of the flag, reading primers for elementary schools have been mandated to include passages that "inculcate feelings of respect and ties to the national flag."²² In elementary school primers, the flag appears eight or nine places; most often it is shown hoisted over the map of the country. The iconographic representation is intentional. It not only marks out territorial sovereignty but also is intended to structure children's patriotism and loyalty to Atatürk and the state. Thus, argued the military-appointed advisor on education at the opening of the 1981–1982 school year, "It is our most sacred and unchanging duty to wave our Flag, the Turkish Nation's symbol of independence, in all of our schools, educational institutions and every corner of our Fatherland. The flag is the symbol of the Republic, which Great Atatürk entrusted [to the Turkish people]. Atatürk gave willingly his blood and life . . . for the flag. Under its shelter, our Nation has always and everywhere found unity and solidarity, trust and belief, and its national strength and liberation."²³ The level of instinct that these feelings are supposed to operate on is made evident in the third-grade reader that was in use during the 1988–1989 school year. In the reading passage "For the Flag," children are taught that the future of the nation is contingent upon retrieval of the regiment's flag from enemy hands. The narrated event occurred during the Turkish War of Liberation, but the moral is for all times: the flag is more valuable than the present-day children's lives.

> —Sergeant Hasan: I am not worried that the enemy is closing in on us and will kill us. I regret that the regiment's flag will pass into the hands of the enemy. . . . [His corporal Turgut dies retrieving the flag.] The flag wrapped tightly around him, the corporal hero lay dead. The moonlight hitting his clean forehead was announcing news of a happy tomorrow.²⁴

The drawing that accompanies the text makes the image visually clear: a soldier lies dead with the flag covering his chest. Both text and artwork render the flag a metonym of the nation that is intended to induce children's patriotic sentiments and loyalty to the state. The curriculum situates the flag's colors in a symbolic field of associations. Its crimson red color is meant to evoke the blood shed by the schoolchildren's warrior ancestors. The author of the third-grade life studies reader indeed stresses this dimension of the flag: "The color of our flag comes from the blood of martyrs. For this reason our flag is holy. We have never allowed anyone to trample it; we will never allow this to happen. We will defend the flag even at the cost of our lives. This is a national duty. . . . We will willingly give our lives for our flag."[25] As is evident in the passage, children are expected to picture the banner as the life-giving arteries of the national body.

The schoolchildren, thus, are expected to believe in the same reasons for which the soldiers died an exemplary death. That is to say, they must feel indebted to the blood their ancestors sacrificed on the battlefield. The textual accounts in their primers serve to bind the present schoolchildren to earlier generations of Turkish warriors, from the medieval epic heroes in the Book of Dede Korkut to the more recent soldiers at Çanakkale (Gallipoli) and the War of Liberation. School primers exhibit a naïve realism in which "textual" war veterans are bestowed with an authoritative voice to fashion the children's collective memory. These veterans, most often portrayed as grandfatherly figures, become spokesmen in whom children must place their faith. In class the children read out loud the narratives about Turkey's military past and, in particular, how war veterans offered their lives for the future of the Turkish nation. Second graders, for example, are (silent) interlocutors to the fictional amputee's patriotism in the story "My Grandfather's Arm." The grandfather explains to his grandson how he lost his arm during the War of Liberation: "We died, we sacrificed our arms, we got wounded but we did not give up the hill to the enemy. We entered the war dedicating ourselves for this fatherland."[26] By mimicking the family gathering where elders transmit their memories to the younger generations, these generic grandfathers textualize and thus impart an authoritative voice to otherwise fictional testimonies of the national past. Raised on these wartime narratives, every schoolchild is enjoined to model himself after the earlier exploits of his textbook elders.

The schoolchildren's kinship with the personal life of the self-sacrificing Turkish soldier, and their fictive genealogical connection with the textbook war veteran, provides a way for children to imagine and identify with a primordial military ethos common to all Turks. Here, the association sought is that the Turkish people's willingness to sacrifice itself can be attributed to the military origins of the Turkish nation. The minister of Education, Avni Akyol, reaffirmed this position in his Directive on Social Sciences in the fourth and fifth grades for the 1990–1991 school year. According to the directive, elementary students must learn in their social science lessons that "they are children of a great nation with a glorious past and will increase their confidence in the nation's future and acquire enough [knowledge] to risk their lives in order to realize the ideals of the Turkish nation. . . . They will willingly . . . see themselves as self-sacrificing Turkish youth."[27] That is, pupils should draw from their lessons that the Turks are born to serve in the military and die for their nation.

This point is reiterated throughout their school years. Third graders, for example, read that "We Turks give importance to military service. We are even known by the world nations as a nation of soldiers (*asker bir millet*). Military service is a holy duty to the country, ensuring protection of fatherland and nation. Every Turkish youth lovingly does this duty. The Glorious Turkish Army results from heroic soldiers. When we grow up we will become soldiers and take the duty of protecting our country."[28] This passage, like many others children encounter in their school years, assumes the interchangeability of race, ethnicity, nation, and culture—a thesis that harks back to the first decades of the republic. More importantly, it socializes children for military service and allegiance to the state.

Integral to the cultivated ideal of the soldier nation is the Turkish people's battle record of no defeats. If textbooks eulogize the bravery and victory of the Turkish forces at Çanakkale, a battle in which Mustafa Kemal Atatürk played a major commanding role, they never explicitly admit to the ultimate defeat of the Ottoman armies in World War I. Rather, second graders will have read that "our armies won victories on many fronts. At the end of the [world] war Germany was defeated and surrendered. Upon Germany's surrender, we wanted peace too."[29] Collective remembrance of victorious battles are intended to connect with the commemoration of soldiers who had fallen in war; in turn, it obligates those men who continue to live to make further sacrifices in memory of the fallen. Moreover, victories validate the eternal strength of the Turks' warrior state, the present Turkish nation. As one of the school teachers proudly told me, "We are 'the Turks who make the whole world tremble'; we're the best in bed and at war." To suggest otherwise is to undermine the emotional bond between virility and personhood, between heroic performance and national identity.

Clearly, the curriculum reinforces a hegemonic masculinity, in which the image of the male warrior is an object of identification and emulation. Manhood is associated with displaying bravery in the face of danger and unflinchingly facing death for the nation. Military service reproduces a patriarchal hierarchy of both national and local society. Soldiering, the ultimate civic duty, is an all-male exclusive domain that qualifies men as fully integrated citizens of the nation. It also signifies the final transition from childhood to adulthood; upon discharge at age twenty-two, men are considered ready to take on adult responsibilities, which include establishing a family and participating in discussions and decisions of the community.

It would, however, be amiss to assume that the military discourse in the curriculum is directed only at the boys, who are the future conscripts of the Turkish armed forces. If men are expected to protect the nation against potential enemies, women are also held responsible for upholding national honor. While girls are not taught to kill, they must nevertheless be prepared to die for the country. Any school references to women in military encounters are organized around the discourse of sexual virtue, which puts forward a different course of action for girls. A major theme in school readers centers on the girl whose chastity is threatened in wartime. Her duty is to avoid physical contact with the enemy, even under duress. Third graders, for example, are taught that death is preferable to loss of virginity. In the story "Huriye's Spring," pupils read that immediately after World War I, French soldiers invaded a small town in Anatolia and were intent on kidnapping the beautiful young protagonist Huriye. At the moment of abduction, it began to rain and the heroine beseeched Allah to "make me into water; let me disappear with the rain."[30] Allah complied, and Huriye died a virgin and was thus spared shaming the Turkish nation. Here, the girl, and by association all women, embody the fear of penetration and violation of the national geobody. The crime of rape acquires meaning only because foreign interlopers put the reputation of the nation at stake.

Intricately linked to military forms of female subjectivity are different representations of women over the course of their lives. No less important a role for national survival is motherhood. At school, boys and girls learn to link men's military deeds to female nurture. This lesson was impressed on fourth graders in one of their readings, "Anatolia" (*Anadolu*). The author of the passage traces the etymology of the word Anatolia to a legend about a virtuous old woman who served buttermilk to mobilized Ottoman soldiers. Every time she tells the soldiers, "Fill up my brave men" (*doldurun yiğitlerim*), they would answer, "Mother, it is full" (*Ana, dolu*).[31] What is relevant here is not the legendary etymology of the Anatolian peninsula, but the links between milk and womanhood, on the one hand, and nationhood, on the other. In fact, in a class I attended, seventh graders observed that mother's milk gives strength to Turkish soldiers. Nurturing soldiers for the war effort resonates with how many local townswomen linked breast-feeding with gender. Most women claimed to nurse sons longer than daughters; often well past age three. A few women justified the gendered difference in breast-feeding on infant boys' higher mortality rate. More often, they claimed that because mother's milk is sinless, pure and clean, it contributed to their son's virility and, hence, military heroism. Behind this claim is the popular belief in the close relationship between blood, semen, and milk. Townspeople of Yayla believe that the opaque white semen flows in a man's veins and originates in the mother's breast milk, which is assumed to derive from the menstrual blood not shed during pregnancy.[32] The potent male is said to be full of health, to have much "blood and soul" (*kanlı canlı*), desirous and able to serve nation and family.[33] As the youth boarded a bus that took them to the induction center, townswomen shouted out to their departing sons, "My lion, my child, may the milk and goodness I have given you bring you good luck." And just as the new recruits are expected to defend the homeland, upon their return from military service they are expected to fend for their self-sacrificing mothers.

Maternal devotion to the nation is closely associated with women's roles as nurturers of boys, future soldiers of the state. This is most evident on Mother's Day. Then, the hallways and classrooms in elementary schools are decorated with quotes honoring motherhood. For this commemorative day, third graders at the Dilek Gunay elementary school had placed two posters in front of the perennial Atatürk Corner: "Above all other duties, the most important, useful, and virtuous duty to fall on our women is to be a 'good mother'—[signed] Atatürk" and "It was a Turkish mother who gave birth to Atatürk." After the father of the country, the person most mentioned in the curriculum is his mother, Zubeyde Hanım. Rarely does the curriculum refer to either Atatürk's father or sister; his brief marriage to Lâtife Hanım (1923–1925) is never mentioned. Textbooks limit the graphic representations of the statesman's family life to one motif—Atatürk, as school child or adult statesman, kissing his mother's hand. Most often she is depicted as a smiling elderly woman wearing metal-rimmed oval glasses and a large headscarf.

School programs expect children to identify with this paradigmatic woman. During Family Day, fifth graders are required to study the unit "Turkish Women's Place in History" in their social sciences class; almost the entire unit is dedicated to how Zubeyde devoted her life to raising her son.[34] All the same, the mother-son relationship serves as a pretext to express national gratitude for all that the soldier-statesman had done for his country. Thus, in the third-grade natural sciences primer, children read that "Atatürk, the country's greatest person, was surprised that his mother wanted to kiss his hand. Zubeyde Hanım answered with great pride: 'I'm your mother. You kissed my hand because I'm your mother. But you saved this nation. Because you are the nation's greatest person, I kiss your hand.'" This and similar reading passages, which prescribe and celebrate motherly devotion, reinforce widely held ideas about sons protecting and supporting their mothers through old age. This lesson is not lost on local middle school girls, many of whom were already preparing their trousseaux. Hatice, then in eighth grade, stated, "'Houses without sons don't give out smoke'. Who will take care of me when I get old and my husband has passed away?"[35] It is not coincidental that the birth of a son is marked by much celebration. The mother wears a headband whose color is exactly the same as the one for the national flag. "To wear red" (*allar giymek*) literally means to rejoice. The son is the future soldier of household and nation.

The military themes taught at school, thus, often complement local perceptions of the relationship between gender, nature, and nurture. Children at Yayla readily identify with military service and the Turkish people's martial values. An apt example comes from a middle school child's essay on "Our People"; it allows one to gauge the children's enthusiasm for their fellow countrymen's heroism.

> Our people, the people of Turkey, are great. The Turkish people's holy symbol is our flag. The Turkish people's anthem is the Independence An-

them. . . . The Turkish people are brave. They are also courageous. They do not even flinch at the greatest dangers. No matter how powerful the enemies are they never shirk from fighting. What comes to our mind at the mention of the "Turkish people" is courageous people.

Such a positive response to military service resonates with those stories about soldiers and women who in the distant and recent past fought for flag and country. Understood is that these textbook heroes and heroines who defended national honor fell for the future welfare of schoolchildren. Understandably, boys and girls overwhelmingly embrace military service as both an honor and a duty, as "a debt to the nation" (*vatan borcu*).

Defenders of the Faith

The master narrative of "a nation of soldiers" has been a consistent feature of the curriculum since the founding of the republic. What is radically new since the military's direct intervention in the educational system in 1980 is how the country's military leaders have disseminated, through reworked textbooks and pedagogical directives, earlier myths and images to articulate a new collective representation—the Turkish soldier as pious defender of the nation. In turn, the civilian governments led by the right-of-center ANAP pursued this policy further and recycled it as if it were the prerepublican concept of statecraft, the duality of state and religion (*din-u devlet*). This change in pedagogy has not been haphazard. Rather, it reflects the shift toward allying military and religious heritage of the country, beginning with Turkey's participation in the bipolar Cold War on the side of the Western allies.[36] Support of a more Islamic political culture has only intensified since the 1980 coup as the military blamed atheistic communists for much of the civic unrest in the country.

It is against this background that the junta leaders found the Turkish Islamic Synthesis to hold strategic value. To achieve national unity, the military endorsed faith as the weapon that could reunite the country. In a directive on psychological warfare, the military adviser to the Ministry of Education ended his list of effective "weapons" against outside provocation with the tenets of Islam: "Believe in the existence of Allah. Avoid the things forbidden in our religion and conform to its dictates."[37] And as if to buttress his argument, the same adviser quoted the few instances in which Atatürk had publicly tempered his antireligious policies: "Atatürk, speaking in 1930 on Islam, said that religion is a necessary institution. A nation without religion has no chance to survive. Only that religion [Islam] is a personal relation between Allah and the believer. The Turkish nation must be with all simplicity a religious nation. However much we place faith in the truth, so must we believe in our religion."[38] In this way, the founding statesman's words came to sanction the military leadership's novel syncretism of religion and nationalism.

Not surprisingly, military traditions and service in the armed forces are similarly portrayed as compatible, if not congruent, with Islam. This fit with the historical and social views of the Turkish Islamic Synthesis, which both the military junta and subsequent civilian governments openly endorsed. Central to this ideology is the notion that before the introduction of Western institutions in the first half of the nineteenth century, the religious scholars and the Ottoman Janissaries (the "ancestors" of the modern Turkish army) had supported one another.[39] Indeed, the post-1980 curriculum reflects this link between the Turkish people's martial spirit and their Islamic heritage. This was even more apparent with the educational reforms instituted by the ruling ANAP. In 1986, the minister of Education Vehbi Dinçerler had all textbooks completely revised to conform to the tenets of the Turkish Islamic Synthesis. The new texts extol the alliance between the military and religion as native to the Turks' cultural essence. And it is to this essential alliance that the author of the eighth-grade religion textbook wants to draw the attention of young readers.

> The Turks are from birth a nation of soldiers. Islam also commands one to fight for the fatherland all the time. . . . Among the [pre-Islamic] settled Turks there were those adepts of the Zoroastrian, Buddhist, Manichaean, Jewish, and Christian religions. Yet it is seen that these religions did not conform to the Turks' spirit of warfare.[40]

Both the military ethos and the Muslim faith become timeless attributes of the Turkish people. Understood is that all the wars that the Turks have ever waged were fought in the name of Islam.

Current textbooks graphically and textually immerse this ideal of the Muslim warrior into the moral universe of the modern Turkish child. The primers constantly appeal to narratives about the military exploits of the Anatolian Seljuks and Ottoman Turks. In this endeavor, textbook writers have reasserted the tradition of the *gazi* and *şehit*, respectively, the warrior fighting and the martyr dying, both on behalf of Islam. The martyr's immediate reward is entry to *Cennet*, the Muslims' Paradise. Fourth graders, for example, vicariously relive the Seljuk Turks' defeat of the Byzantine army at the battle of Manzikert/Malazgirt in 1071.[41] In the passage "Forever Anatolia," the children in the classroom are expected to take on the role of the Turkish warriors listening to their commanding sultan on the eve of battle.

> My lions! No matter how few we are and how many the enemy are we will attack. Do not forget that right now all the Muslims are praying for us. Either we are gazi heroes or we are martyrs. If there is someone who wants to separate from us let him leave immediately. I am hence wearing the burial shroud of a martyr. I am no longer a sultan, just one of you. I pray to God that the victory is ours.[42]

In reinstating the prerepublican ideal of holy warfare (the *gaza*) in the curriculum, state educators are portraying commitment to the military heritage as a religious duty that extends into the present era.

In this narrative mode, the devout Turkish mother is co-opted to the religious formulation of military service. Third graders begin their reader with the text "Hennaed Mehmet."[43] As described in the text, a village mother smeared henna on her son's hands before his induction into military service. Henna is often applied on auspicious occasions, most notably on the eve of the wedding when the hands of groom and bride are smeared with it. Many townspeople in Yayla do likewise and believe that henna symbolizes the sacred soil of Paradise. The henna on the recruits' hands visually marks him as one willing to sacrifice himself for the Muslim faith. He shares the lot of the religious gazi warriors and martyrs. The presumably urban/e officer in the third-grade text is ignorant of the custom, and the twenty-year-old recruit too cannot explain his painted hands. The commander asks the son's mother to explain. She dutifully writes the officer,

> We stain the sheep for sacrifice with henna so that they are a sacrifice to Allah. Also, my son, we put henna on the young men who go to the army. We smear henna on them so that they may be a sacrifice to the fatherland. We

sacrificed your grandfather in the Balkan Wars [in 1913] and your uncle at
Çanakkale. If it need be, my child, you will be a sacrifice for this fatherland.[44]

The text relates that the reply so moved the officer that his eyes welled with
tears. Here, the traditional Turkish mother is the pedagogue of her son's
commander: she teaches him the religious foundations of military service,
the relation between Islam and self-sacrifice for the nation.

The moral of such textbook passages for the pupils is obvious: they must
be prepared to sacrifice themselves for their Muslim nation and state. This
point is continuously harped on in civics education. Thus, in their civics lessons, eighth graders are taught not only that national identity subsumes
identification with Islam but also that the state is a religiously sanctioned institution: "the state from the religious point of view is an institution that Allah created for mankind's benefit."[45] The secular polity becomes as inviolable as the sacred realm. It goes without saying that faith in the state
includes total submission and obedience to the authorities, which in the context of post-1980 Turkey means the representatives of the armed forces and
the civilian governments they subsequently approved. In the curriculum,
state and statesmen metonymically represent one another, and both are religiously sanctioned. As is written in the eighth-grade reader on religion and
morals, all children who consider themselves to be Muslims are expected to
accept as truth that "we, the Turkish nation, love our state and our national
existence in the person of the statesman. People who sacrifice their own existence for that of the nation and state are worthy to be loved and respected.
They shoulder an important responsibility towards God in their duties."[46]
The text ends with a personal plea to the male students: "My son, let him
grow up and become a soldier. If he dies he will be a martyr for the faith; if
he lives, a holy warrior." Here, the textbook's author explicitly makes the
connection between patriotism and the future recruits' religious identity.

According to this religious interpretation of military service, school-
children are expected to take pride in how their ancestors militarily spread
Islam all over the Old World. In a worldview pitting nation against nation,
Turkey emerges as the leading nation in the Muslim world. Such is the tenor
of "Directives on Basic Instruction of Atatürk's Reforms and Principles for
Primary and Secondary Schools": both teachers and textbooks must stress
"how the Turks have rendered [military] services throughout the history of
Islam [and] how the Turkish War of Liberation was a victory for Islam."[47]

The eighth-grade history book makes explicit this point. "Since the day the Turkish nation accepted Islam it has sacrificed itself for this religion. It had taken upon itself to promote and defend Islam; it had established this religion in all parts of the old world and gave millions of martyrs to this religion."[48] Emphasis on how Turks contributed to world and Islam civilization has been standard practice since the beginning of the republic. What is novel here is bringing up Turkish martyrdom for Islam without consideration of the historical context.

Clearly, the Turkish Islamists have inserted their religious agenda into a curriculum that places heavy emphasis on the concepts of military pride and self-sacrifice to the nation. It is equally evident that the leaders of the armed forces have been a willing party in this new orientation in national education. Islam once more had become a foundation of the state; the state army, its defenders. Such a reconfiguration of the tropes of religious-inspired military and martial religion has become central in the cultural politics of the current school system in Turkey. And many pupils at Yayla readily identify themselves as Muslims and Turkey as a nation of warriors. These two identities are evident in an essay on "My People," which Orhan, then thirteen years old, wrote: "My people are a very good people. They came from Central Asia and began to settle in Anatolia after the victory at Malazgirt. My people's religion is Islam. . . . My people are very much devoted to the fatherland. At war, women, children and men fight together."

The religious and martial values Orhan and many other students juxtaposed in their essays cannot be understood as simply perpetuating centuries-old ideals. The relationship between secularist and religious visions of the military and their dissemination through the national educational system, which I have traced in this chapter, changes according to new political contingencies. What is clear is that, since the 1980 coup, the curriculum has not only sought to homogenize the concept of Islam for Turkish schoolchildren but, no less important, militarize it.

Despite the symbiosis between religious policy makers and the military, their relations have remained ambiguous, if not tense. The present consensus over the religious orientation of the country's schools did not mean sharing the political space on an equal footing. The military remained wary of the religious infringing upon their turf. In 1990, the struggle between the two camps revolved around admission to military academies. Staunch defenders of what they consider to be Atatürk's secular policies, the military regents did not welcome religious students in their academic institutions. (The selective admission policy was made possible because the academies remain under the jurisdiction of the armed forces, instead of the Ministry of Education.)

Military academies provide one of the finest academic programs available in the country. One cadet on leave proudly showed me his annual yearbook. It was an exact replica of a glossy-paged, American preparatory school yearbook, including photos of modern computer and language laboratories. He boasted of his school's television and film programs. Its Olympic-caliber sports facilities are unmatched in the nation's universities. Moreover, a close-knit social network exists among graduates of the different military academies, many of whom have become leaders in the country's military, financial, and political domains. Until Turgut Özal, an electrical engineer by training, acceded to the presidency in 1990, all the presidents of the Turkish Republic had graduated from the military academies and pursued careers in the armed forces. Among the graduates are the military commanders who staged the 1980 coup. It was thus all the more disconcerting to the devout public that these elite institutions have consistently refused to admit graduates of religious-track schools. Since 1983, graduates of İmam-Hatip high schools are eligible to enroll in all higher-education institutions, except for military academies. A commander's speech at an academy justified the exclusion of religious-minded youth from obtaining positions of power in the armed forces: "A great deal of harm has been done by persons who . . . exploited religion and traditions of the past for political purposes. . . . On no account should such people be allowed to assume authority or responsibility."[49] In 1990, only graduates of the secular-track teachers' colleges, high schools, and magnet Anatolian High Schools were permitted to apply.[50]

Religious parliamentarians have been trying to legally fudge the entrance requirements so that graduates of the religious-track İmam-Hatip high schools can enroll in these prestigious and powerful academies. In the fifth five-year government plan (1985–1989), these parliamentarians established the magnet Anatolian İmam-Hatip high schools. Their graduates could theoretically enroll in military academies, like their counterparts from the secular-track Anatolian High Schools.[51] The military has successfully countered this move by periodically identifying and expelling students with religious beliefs.

So religious statesmen and intellectuals have taken the issue directly to the public. One widely publicized example of such criticism appeared in the religious newspaper *Zaman*. Ömer Okçu, better known as Hekimoğlu İsmail, journalist and author of the religious best-selling *Abdullah of Miniye*, criticized the entrance requirements of military academies and suggested that the military establishment pursued a life of loose morals. The journalist, who had served as a tank officer, implied the armed forces were religion's enemy. "Take, take my son to the Military Academy. Take just a few who don't drink alcohol, don't gamble; take just a few who pray and fast."[52] Given the military's attempts to disseminate a more religious cultural agenda in national education, Hekimoğlu's accusations were not taken lightly. The best-selling author and his newspaper editor were fined for defamation of the state.

Journalists are not alone in questioning the military academies' entrance policies. At the youth coffeehouse in Yayla, a local graduate of an İmam-Hatip high school, who had applied to the academies, bitterly vented the rejection of his candidacy. As he put it: "Aren't we, the graduates of the İmam-Hatip high schools, children of this country? Didn't God create us too? If there's a topic that warrants debate, it's that we graduates of İmam-Hatip high schools are not admitted into military academies. All those leftists who cry out for more freedoms keep mum on this topic. They don't believe in equal opportunities in education." To this embittered youth, the military not only fails at redressing social wrongs, but also upholds the country's inequalities.

Equally problematic for the religiously observant public was what they perceived to be the military's pro-Western, secular stance in the national culture. Ironically, the generals' self-professed progressive identity was perceived as a case of senility. The same youth showed me a cartoon that appeared in the militant religious satirical journal *Cıngar* (28 December 1990) and illustrated the religious sector's perceptions of the military.[53] The visual puns play on multiple verbal references that validate subaltern readings of society. In the cartoon, a tottering general bedecked with medals and a young soldier are strolling in an apple orchard as the former says, "Soldier, come with me. Let's walk a bit in the garden. . . . Look at those pear trees. Who knows what they would say if they had tongues." The soldier thinks to himself, "Most likely they would say we're not pear trees; we're apple trees." The cartoonist plays on the popular Turkish expression "a pear tree does not bear apples" (*armut ağacı elma vermez*), which means that one cannot expect a person to do what is not natural to him. Drawing upon the cartoon, the youth suggested that the military is out of touch with the public's religious values and compared the generals with bears, popularly understood as slow-witted creatures who cannot distinguish between right and wrong.[54] Rather, as he put it, they constantly push secular modernization at the expense of the country's Islamic heritage. Lest I failed to get his point, he quoted the proverb about the bear "who knows forty stories—all about wild pears." The youth was allying the military with secular leftists, both repeatedly flouting as it were national interest. Not surprisingly, the admissions criteria of military academies fueled acrimonious debates about secularism and the role of the military in fashioning the country's political culture and educational policies.

The Fortress State

The outstanding differences between the military and religious public figures notwithstanding, both shared an anxiety about Turkey's geopolitical position in the world. Transnational flows of ideas, media, culture, and capital appeared to unravel the seams binding the country. The issue was how to cope with the overlap in the global circulation of cultural and economic forms within a national context. Neoliberal industrialists and business would argue that the educational system should focus on better training a workforce capable of participating in the "global village," including mastery of rapidly developing technologies. Neither the military nor religious nationalists would disagree with these objectives. What both parties feared, however, was that the increasing cultural porosity of external borders was alienating the youth from national values and creating anarchy in the country.

To reestablish ideologically more impenetrable internal borders within the citizenry, the generals took the lead in defining which communities of interest were allowed to work out their differences in the national culture. Two days after the coup, the generals announced that "in education . . . measures will be taken to prevent our children . . . from being trained in foreign ideologies rather than in Atatürkism. Otherwise, they will end up as anarchists."[55] Henceforth, all textbooks, including mathematics, were legally required to include at least one passage warning against domestic subversion.

The military-endorsed curriculum sought to prevent at all costs the consolidation of identities that threatened to fragment the nation into a politics of differences—whether rooted in socioeconomic status, ethnicity, or sectarianism. Setting up the terms for participation in and exclusion from the national culture meant first of all building consensus around categories of enmity. In 1990, the nation's enemies were any social and political group that denied the ascendancy of Turkish nationalism. As I will show later, particular emphasis was on the constant danger that foreign ideologies and nations pose to the Turkish nation. Thus, school children were taught to be wary of internal and external threats (*tehdit*) to Turkish unity and to take preventive measures (*tedbir*) to stifle these threats.

In the imagined polity of the military, there was no room for non-nationalist ideologies like Marxism-Leninism. Ever since Turkey joined NATO in 1952, Cold War politics has generated foes out of domestic critics. The left became an elastic moral category in which all the features of anarchy the military shunned could be dumped. Leftists with their emphasis on international union of oppressed peoples represented the antithesis of the disciplined and orderly citizen-soldiers loyal to the nation-state. In fact, the military held communists responsible for the political violence that plagued the country throughout the 1970s, that is, for purposely weakening Turkish society by undermining its nationalist foundations. A year and a half after the 1980 coup, the defense secretary attached to the Ministry of Education accused communists of accentuating identity differences among the people and thereby imploding national unity. To him, communists were agents provocateurs who fomented conflicts among the different Muslim sects and between the "so-called 'Kurdish' citizens" and the rest of the population. Thus, he boldly asserted,

> In infusing "minority racialism," communists try to call some of our citizens who are spotlessly clean and completely Turkish "Kurds" and thus instigate them against Turkishness and the Turkish state. They also foster "majority racialism": they instigate some of our citizens against the so-called "Kurdish" citizens. . . . Also, communists have convinced some of our [nonorthodox] Alevi citizens that our Sunni citizens are "right-wing backward fascists"; they do the same with our Sunni citizens claiming that the Alevi citizens "are leftist communists." Thus, they are trying to foment an ideological "struggle between the left and the right," between the two religious sects.[56]

The overall aim of the report was threefold: one, to assimilate different ethnic or linguistic communities, such as the Kurds, into a single, unqualified Turkish "nation"; two, to co-opt the different factions of Islam into a singular, nationalist version of Islam; and three, to withdraw citizenship to any individual who denies the centrality of nationalism.

My aim here is not to question the historicity of the defense secretary's assertions. Rather, I draw attention to how he invoked the rhetoric of state security to create mutually exclusive political categories and thus delineate clear, punishable categories of people. In orienting the school system to those political and ethnic distinctions the army supported, the school system de-legitimated and silenced any interest group that advocated alternative collective identities and thereby justified their exclusion from participating in the public sphere.

The military's fear of a fifth column in the country has found expression in the curriculum. The last chapter in the eighth-grade geography textbook began with a lengthy discussion on the "internal threats" aimed at weakening the country.

> Since ancient times, foreigners have coveted our Fatherland. We know that nations can only exist if there is, first of all, unity of culture, language, religion, country, history, and ideals. Attempts at weakening these features of the nation or encouraging divisions will eventually destroy a country. This is called *Internal Threat*.
>
> Foreigners who covet our country do their utmost to sever our ties to the nation and destroy us from within. One of the most important internal threats is the destruction of national values. We must defend and look after our national culture, which we inherited from our forefathers centuries ago. Those coveting our Fatherland expend enormous efforts to break our cultural unity and thereby keep us in a state of animosity among ourselves. . . . Several foreign ideologies which oppose the principles and reforms of Atatürk seek to divide Turkish society. These ideologies want to destroy our Republic; they have set about to shatter our material and spiritual values. . . .
>
> Our forefathers watered this heavenly Fatherland with their blood. . . . To protect our fatherland against all types of internal threats is to attain national unity and cooperation.[57]

Nowhere did the text explicitly define which ideologies threatened the country. The task of elaborating on the text fell upon the geography teacher, whom I shall call here Ibrahim, who hailed from the eastern province of Yozgat.

But before I address in more detail the teacher's elaboration of the text and the pupils' responses therewith, it is crucial to attend to the prevalent relationship between knowledge, speech, and performances of hierarchy in the classroom. Often, I heard instructors matter of factly say, "God gave children two ears and only one mouth." The idea is that only instructors have acquired sufficient reason (*akıl*) to speak in class. In their capacity as arbiters of knowledge, only their words pass (*sözü geçer*) unchallenged. Pupils, on the other hand, remain silent until called upon to read a text, summarize a reading passage, or answer a specific question. Whenever pupils did speak out of turn, teachers reminded pupils that they "did not know their limits" (*haddinizi bilmezsiniz*). According to many teachers I came to know in the course of my research, familiarity breeds contempt for authority and prevents pupils from learning from their elders. To speak is to command, and children learn early on that it is incumbent upon them to listen to their elders. It is common for the teacher to stand in front of the class, his lectures closely following the textbook, and dictate them to the students, who copy them word for word into their notebooks. In the classroom, it is clear who is the master and who is the student, who has knowledge and who is receiving it. The upshot is that the teacher's voice dominates classroom instruction, and rote learning is the norm. There is little space for pupils to question the teacher's in-class representations and explanations. Instructors do not simply transmit facts, however. Instructors often take on the role of a surrogate author of a textbook as they have the privilege of interpolating their personal experiences and political views in the lessons.[58] Within certain parameters, they can choose what to emphasize or deemphasize, what to exclude from a text or to include in it. But as I will show, no individual can deliver complete order to a concept or discourse because both the language of politics and the politics of language are deeply entrenched in contingent power relations at *all* levels of society.

In the lesson on Turkey's geopolitical situation, which I attended, the instructor wove his religious nationalist views into the reading passages. Through his performance of the text in class, the instructor not only articulated the reasons for his political beliefs but also actualized them. An outspoken supporter of the Turkish Islamic Synthesis, he took advantage of his role as teacher to explicitly link foreign ideologies to Marxism-Leninism. In class, he asserted that the internal threat was none other than those atheistic leftists who served the interests of Moscow and were intent on "weakening the Turkish people's religious unity" and "creating divisions among the people with their materialist ideologies." He concluded the lesson by reminding the pupils that they were "permanent soldiers on duty" who must keep alert to dangerous, subversive atheists. Later, after class, in the teachers' room, he extended his criticism of Marxists to cover all Western critics of the country's human rights record. "For centuries we have defended Islam against the West. We're a fortress constantly being bombarded with Western propaganda. Now they criticize us about how we treat the [Kurdish] refugees out east.[59] Turks don't have any friends (*Türkün Türkten başka dostu yoktur*). . . . You must know that only faith will protect us against the incursion of foreign ideologies and their Jewish and Christian backers in the West."

The following lesson, Ibrahim covered the section on external threats. The textbook censured the expansionist politics of the Greek and Israeli nation-states. The Armenian people fared worse. The geography textbook not only stated that "claims to an Armenian State on our soil have no basis," but condemned Armenian "assassins . . . [for] striking our representatives abroad from the back."[60] There is a widespread fear among officials and policy makers that Armenians covet Turkey's southern and eastern provinces. Moreover, as a result of the assassinations of Turkish diplomatic personnel abroad in the 1970s and 1980s, allegations of what officials called "the so-called Armenian genocide" before and during World War I became a public issue. The national educational system responded in kind. A government circular instructed teachers to "point out that we [Turks] had no problems with *Armenians*, who had earlier lived under the Byzantine yoke in Anatolia. It must be explained that in recent times they have been supported by foreign powers and that bloody crimes have been perpetrated on our diplomatic representatives abroad. It must be made clear that the Turkish Nation has been trapped into political intrigues with terrorist aims and that, as always, it patiently waits for the justice of its case to be accepted."[61] History textbooks followed closely the official position on Armenians. They countered allegations of Turkish brutality with numerous narratives about atrocities Armenians committed against Muslims. In these narratives, the Turkish people are portrayed as unsuspecting, innocent victims; the Armenians as brutal, cowardly, and dishonest terrorists. Thus, the third-grade life sciences reader simply states that "the Armenians who for years had lived with Turks began to oppress and torture the Turks."[62] In eighth grade, pupils read graphic accounts of Armenian atrocities in their history textbook. They study, for example, the report a Turkish general submitted to his British colleague after World War I: "The massacre at Erzincan was horrible. . . . They burned Muslim people inside buildings they set on fire; they filled the wells with corpses. . . . All the children were bayoneted, the elderly and the women stuffed with hay and burned, the youth chopped up with axes. Livers and hearts were seen hung on nails."[63] Commemoration of the intercommunity conflict is not limited to the classroom. Periodically, the political regime and national press commemorate those Turkish victims who had suffered from Armenian violence. Thus, President Evren unveiled a monument at a village near Erzurum (eastern Turkey); there, he stated that "278 innocent children, women, and aged men were indiscriminately butchered and it has gone down in history books."[64] Testimony by historical eyewitnesses and records establish as it were the factual evidence to counter any charges of Turkish wrongdoing in the past.

Neither the eighth-grade geography nor history textbook elaborated on the historical reasons for the violence between the two communities or, for that matter, the reasons for believing that Israel, which has no common border with Turkey, poses a physical threat to the country. Once more, Ibrahim interpolated his religious and nationalist views to portray the three major non-Muslim communities (Greeks, Armenians, and, Jews), who together make up less than 1 percent of the total population, as well-organized internal enemies who had since the late Ottoman Empire actively cooperated with their national representatives (Greece, Armenia, and, since its establishment, Israel) outside the country's borders. Moreover, he questioned these communities' allegiance to the Turkish Republic; he was of the opinion that the minorities served the interests of a West intent on keeping Muslims and Turks politically weak.[65] He concluded the lesson by juxtaposing his religious views with a widely circulated martial slogan: "Without our Islamic beliefs, these nations would succeed in dispossessing us of our Fatherland. 'Duty to the fatherland is a duty of honor; martyrs do not die; the homeland will not be divided.'"

Figuring the country's non-Muslim religious communities in Turkey as representatives of foreign, belligerent nations works into the official political culture that makes a clear distinction between citizenship and national descent. A year before, the same eighth graders had read in their seventh-grade geography textbook that the religious "minorities are under the protection of the Turkish state. . . . These citizens of ours (*vatandaşlarımız*) co-exist peacefully with the Turkish people (*Türk halkı*)."[66] In effect, the passage reinforces conflation of the modern, secular notion of citizen (*vatandaş*) with the prerepublican notion of subject belonging to a religious community (*tebaa*).[67] The townspeople of Yayla, young and old, make similar distinctions between citizenship and collective national identity. Irrespective of their level of religiousness, children and their parents identify with their Muslim faith. To the question, "Are you a Turk?" invariably the person answered, "Of course. . . . I'm a Muslim." When I specifically asked whether Jews or Armenians are Turks, most would answer, without any hesitation, that they are Turkish citizens but not Turks.

To townspeople, nominal adherence to Islam and the Islamic community suffice to index a citizen's Turkishness. The geography teacher went further, however. He not only rendered non-Muslim citizens into foreign nationals but also questioned the racial origins of Turkish-speaking, nonbelieving Muslims. Thus, he contrasted the classroom of "pure and innocent true Turks" (*saf ve temiz öz Türk*) with cosmopolitan (*kosmopolit*) and half-breed (*melez*) communists and religious minorities; the latter's alien origins explaining their lack of national sentiments. Here, exclusive political categories of people, both descriptive and moral, served to figure the country's population into native citizens and foreign interlopers. In making a clear-cut distinction between place of birth as religious descent and place of birth as geographical place, he suggested that a Turkish child could neither develop relations of trust with nor count on the loyalty of these non-Turks because they denied the ascendancy of Islam. Thus, all the while excluding individuals and social groups whose political and religious identities he opposed, he had no qualms about assimilating different ethnic and regional communities (e.g., Kurds and Black Sea Laz) into the Islamic national community he held dear.

The eighth graders, who identified themselves as Muslims and Turks, did not feel threatened by the geography teacher's comments. Only leftists and non-Muslims remained outside the borders of his imagined besieged state. In any case, in the context of the geography lessons I attended, there was little exchange of ideas between instructor and pupils. Ibrahim made it clear that he alone had the authority to state his views as unquestionable facts and definitions; his voice monopolized the lessons. Yet deference to hierarchical relations in the classroom should not be construed as pupils' acceptance of their teacher's interpretation of national enemies. The lessons on Turkey's geopolitical situation provided an opportunity to witness how children, dialogically engaging with school knowledge and its representations, transformed a didactic lesson into an integral part of their community's particular historical consciousness. In a question-and-answer session that followed the two lessons, the middle school students responded quite differently from what either the teacher Ibrahim or I had expected. The few pupils who spoke up figured the lessons in terms of widely held stereotypes about the immediate region's ethnic groups: they identified the internal threat with the heterodox Tahtacıs, an Alevi Muslim community of nomadic woodcutters who reside in two nearby villages, and the external threat with the descendants of Armenians, who left Yayla after 1920.

In Yayla, it is common knowledge that the two neighboring Alevi villages support left-of-center political parties.[68] While I never heard any townsperson mention the fact that Alevis vote against parties that support Sunni Islam platforms, many were convinced that the Alevis were committed communists. In class, one of the students suggested as much. He repeated the conceit that leftists want everybody to share all property (*mal*), which in local parlance includes wives. The rumor was that Alevis held their *cem* assembly meetings in total darkness and indiscriminately shared women among themselves in adulterous orgies.[69] The popular explanation for the indiscriminate promiscuity is that Alevis lack a sacred book of their own, such as the Qur'an or the Christians' New Testament.[70] As with the Gypsies, whom I discussed in the previous chapter, any religious community deemed to be "without a [holy] book" (*kitapsız*) is accused of idolatry, which, moreover, implies a lack of code of ethics that separates human beings from other animals. Alevis do not perform ritual ablution (*gusül abdesti*) after engaging in sexual intercourse, which it is assumed characterizes their animal-like way of life. (A complete ablution entails cleaning all orifices, including mouth and ears.) Indeed, many a townsperson in Yayla would recount, with disgust, the parable on cucumbers that they attributed to Alevis: "A person drops a cucumber on the ground from his bag of cucumbers. Does he wash all the cucumbers or just the one that got dirty? We wash only the dirty one, not the clean ones." Recounting the parable was self-serving: townspeople of Yayla come off as spiritually clean and respectable; their Alevi neighbors, spiritually tainted and smelling dirty. The collective pollution assumed of Alevis has prevented much physical contact between the two communities, let alone intermarriage.[71] It has also perpetuated the idea that Alevis transgress communal norms of private property and moral propriety and, thereby, pose a threat to the Sunni community's cosmology.

While schoolchildren are well aware of the Alevi presence in the immediate area, none had any contact with either Jewish or Christian citizens of Turkey. Armenians remained ever present in their community's collective memory, however. Up until 1920, the town had a significant Armenian population, who according to both official sources and popular memory, enjoyed cordial relations with their Muslim neighbors.[72] Uzun Mehmet, an eighty-two-year-old man, for example, recalled that "there were eight to ten Armenian houses, with names like Bedon, Tikran, Nazar, Melkon—all infidels. . . . They worked as coffeehouse owners, makers of vinegar, and water peddlers. . . . Melkon had a large gramophone; the large speaker could be seen in the window of the coffeehouse. . . . There was a Bedon, an Armenian who was the head of the subdistrict whom the *çete* [irregular soldiers during the War of Liberation] killed. . . . Upon hearing about his death, the rest of the Armenians left Yayla." Then, all the tradesmen were Armenians, and to this day, townspeople refer to good workmanship as "Armenian-ness" (*Ermenilik*); it is the local seal of approval.[73]

Appreciation for Armenian craftsmanship aside, a visceral fear of Armenians returning to Yayla and reclaiming their lands still gripped local imagination. To prevent such a possibility, townspeople had leveled Armenian homes to their foundations and uprooted the orchards. Locals still referred to a totally denuded hill to the south of the present town as the "market" (*çarşı*), a reference to the many shops that once lined the thoroughfare leading to the castle and that made Yayla an important summer resort a century ago.[74] Fear of the Armenians' imminent return was equally present in the geography lesson I attended. At some point in the discussion about external enemies, some pupils wondered out loud whether I had come to spy on behalf of Armenian descendants or to unearth hidden treasures they may have left behind. Schoolchildren were not alone in conflating past events with present anxieties. Older members of the community often attributed Armenian origins to those European or American non-Muslims with whose politics they strongly disagreed. At the time of my research, television news covered extensively the American senator Bob Dole's unsuccessful attempts to pass a congressional bill that would observe a day of commemoration for Armenians. During the month-long news coverage, coffeehouse patrons explained American politics in terms of Turkish-Armenian rivalry. Irrespective of partisan politics, they all agreed that President John F. Kennedy had been a friend (*dost*) of the Turkish people, whereas his successor, Lyndon B. Johnson, an enemy. President Johnson had sent what many Turks perceived as a humiliating letter during a crisis over Cyprus in 1964. A generation later, these patrons still talked of the humiliation and pegged it to the national origins of the two American presidents: many believed that Kennedy's mother was a Turk and pinned Kennedy's assassination on Armenians.

The local townsmen's ethnic interpretation of world affairs resonated with the government policy of eliminating heterogeneity from the Turkish geo-body. During the nationwide municipality elections in February 1989, the then ruling ANAP took out a full-page advertisement in all the major newspapers. In appealing to voters "who are neither divisive nor racist nor separatist," the ad suggested that a vote to alternative parties would once more bring about anarchy. Yet the political unity as advanced in the curriculum reinforced political and social divisions in the country. Leftists and non-Muslims remained outside the geopolitical borders of the generals' imagined besieged state. According to this militarized security discourse, there is no neutral space or no-man's land: Turkish children had to either accept the curricular definitions of state enemies or risk being considered a national threat themselves.

Discipline and Punish

Not all accept the curricular definitions of state enemies, a stance that can draw a sharp reaction from the school system. Some teachers and pupils mobilize the political categories to fit their own particular understandings of modernity, social identities, political regime, and way of life. Should the state consider these individuals to have transgressed what it understands to be the social and ideological bases of the Turkish state, then in its capacity as guardian of the public order it will intervene. To stem any dissension, the national educational system has made a special effort to discipline pupils and teachers into obedient citizens. Emphasis is on both discipline (*disiplin*) and total allegiance to the state and prescribed social norms.

At face value, the curriculum focused on norms usually associated with the liberal, bourgeois public sphere—freedom of expression and tolerance of differences. Thus, passages from civics textbooks make frequent reference to the prerepublican sultans' abuse of their authority, in particular, their draconian censorship of ideas. But in practice, the school system emphasizes obedience to "law and commanders" over freedom of speech and action. An obedient, compliant student body takes precedence over subject matter covered in class. Or as the program of social studies for fourth- and fifth-grade pupils states, "Pupils must develop an understanding of law, acquire feelings, and exercise habits that demonstrate compliance with laws and state authorities. . . . Teachers must teach students to have self-discipline (*disiplinli*)." [75]

Ideally, children willingly consent to (and adopt as their own) school rules and regulations. To ensure such compliance, the school system subjects children to a comprehensive social etiquette that emphasizes self-control and, above all, active obedience. From the very first day of school, they are required to master the school codes of conduct (*Okul Yasası*), hung right outside the principal's office. All fifteen of the injunctions are concerned with maintaining order and discipline. An abridged version appears in the third-grade natural sciences textbook. Thus, in their first lesson of the year, aptly called "Let's get to know our surroundings," third graders are expected to do the following:

1. Prepare lessons and complete homework assignments in a timely manner.
2. Arrive at school on time.
3. Not make noise in classrooms, corridors, and playground.
4. Show respect to elders and cherish the young.
5. Use school equipment and class materials in an orderly and clean manner.
6. Put pens, erasers, kerchiefs, and money found in the lost-and-found box.
7. Wait your turn to buy.
8. Not buy food sold in public. [76]

The logic of the lesson is not simply submission to school regulations. The injunctions articulate those spatializing practices that organize the school grounds into a stable architecture of spaces, rules, and behaviors that form a coherent system among themselves and whose coherence is owing to a unity designed to bring forth stability.[77] Already in their second year of schooling, elementary pupils learn how an orderly pupil must behave. In their life science primer, they read that

> one waits quietly for your teacher in the classroom. Then, one does the necessary preparations. When the teacher enters the classroom, one gets up on one's feet. One doesn't bother with anything else while doing one's lesson. One doesn't talk without getting permission. One listens quietly to the classmates who are talking. . . .
>
> CHILDREN WHO ADJUST THEIR BEHAVIOR TO THESE RULES ARE CONSIDERED ORDERLY. THESE CHILDREN ARE ALWAYS SUCCESSFUL AND LOVED BY THEIR ELDERS. LET US BE LIKE THEM.[78]

Year after year, the curriculum repeats the same injunctions. Not surprisingly, schoolchildren often measured a school's success by its attention to order. Thus, Meryem, who was attending the Adana Girls High School, proudly stated that her "school was not only the best one in [the city of] Adana but also very disciplined." Conversely, schoolchildren who exhibit a too-cavalier attitude toward regulations are scolded for their total disregard for social harmony. This was the gist of the elementary school principal's remarks to me on discipline. "Disorganization at school brings about unhappiness. Disorganized pupils are never calm and happy. Nor do they bring peace and happiness to those around them. Without discipline, no school, no society can survive. First, one has to secure obedience and order; otherwise, there is no disciplined school, no disciplined society."

Worse still is to question the authority binding pupils to rules and regulations. At the very bottom of the social hierarchy, schoolchildren are expected to respect and obey their teachers. To challenge the hierarchical relations between school personnel and pupils means not only disturbing the collectivist rationale that is promoted by Turkish state and society, but also disrupting the social order. An outspoken pupil is then labeled a rebellious (*isyankâr*) person who "does not take anyone's words" (*kimsenin sözünü tutmaz*). As a sixth-grade reader states, "Mutual support is 'everybody for everybody' not 'everybody for himself'; this is both social, national, and in the widest sense, humane thought."[79] To think otherwise means that one is selfish and antisocial, and this kind of behavior borders on the rebellious, if not the treasonous.

Connecting social and political stability with continual vigilance of schoolchildren, including their extracurricular activities, has long dominated educational policies in Turkey. This connection took on greater impetus immediately following the 1980 coup, when the army legitimated its monopoly of the means of violence upon the supervisory control of deviance. In his keynote speech to open the school year in 1981, Hasan Sağlam, the military-appointed minister of Education, exhorted parents "to closely follow your children, to protect them from harmful habits, and to keep them away from activities that have no relation to their studies."[80] To the minister, only morals and discipline could ensure the existence of law-abiding citizens and the inviolability of the state. These objectives tapped into the ideological platform of the subsequent civilian governments led by the right-of-center ANAP.

Thus, both the military and state officials considered their task to consist of turning children into law-abiding citizens. To this end, parents, teachers, and officials were mobilized to manage, supervise, and control children. Thus, the family unit, the school, and the state were all depicted in the curriculum as responsible for fostering the same rules, regulations, order, and above all, obedience. In constituting this obedient citizenry, parents were positioned by the curriculum as surrogate pedagogues. School primers often exhibited a naïve realism in which generic fathers and mothers are endowed with an authoritative voice to impart those civic norms state educators endorsed. Fifth-grade children, for example, became silent interlocutors to the moral citizen-father in the story "The Constitution and the Duties of Citizens."

> The child Aysel was thinking about the policeman taking away a man in handcuffs. His father said, "My son, we all live in a large society. Above all there has to be order in society. Laws and some social regulations constitute social order. All of us must abide by the laws and social regulations and uphold them. This is the most important duty of a citizen. The State apprehends and punishes those people who do not carry out this duty. When citizens cooperate with the state all of us are happy."[81]

Parents were expected to fully cooperate with the state and prevent their children from running afoul of the authorities.

Should pupils, however, refuse to cooperate with teachers, or should they persist in expressing ideas that diverged considerably from the intentions of the curriculum, they were assumed to pose a danger to state and society. The school system justified punishment of divisive behavior as maintaining order. Periodically, schoolchildren were reminded what offenders of law and order could expect from school (and state) authorities. Less than a year after the 1980 coup, the ministry published a detailed list of offenses, ranging from disrespect of persons of authority to politically objectionable activities. Until recently, punishment has ranged from temporary withdrawal to permanent ban from the school system.[82]

Teachers were not exempt from the military's disciplinary gaze. In post-1980-coup Turkey, teachers were expected to behave as a disciplined, orderly corps that unconditionally served under Atatürk and his present-day spokesmen, the generals. The homology between teachers and officers was equally evident in the concluding remarks the minister of Education, Hasan Sağlam, gave for the opening of the 1981–1982 school year: "I deeply believe that you carry in your hands the torch of national education that our Atatürk ignited. This torch will certainly succeed in enlightening the Turkey of the future." The minister played up three tropes that continue to define the teaching profession in Turkey: Atatürk as the eternal head teacher (*başöğretmen*) of the country,[83] the teachers as the army of knowledge (*irfan ordusu*), and the torch as the symbol of knowledge. This triad is graphically represented on the front cover of the seventh-grade religion textbook—a photograph of the Head Teacher Atatürk monument that stands before the National Teachers Association in the capital city of Ankara. Offset by an opened, flattened-out book, Atatürk, hovering over teachers, is holding the torch of enlightenment, which keeps the book open. On the left page of the monument, right above a group of young, confident-looking male and female schoolchildren, is a quote from Atatürk, "Teachers! You, the Republic's self-sacrificing teachers and educators, will raise the new generation. The new generation will be your work." Outside the main elementary school building at Yayla appears the same quote.

The visual and textual references to the head teacher puts school instructors in the position of incontestable spokespersons, whose duty is to pass on the torch of knowledge to the rest of the country. This is most evident on Teachers' Day, celebrated on 24 November. As on all official occasions, school staff and pupils congregate in front of Atatürk's bust in the courtyard.

There, teachers vow to follow the statesman's example and wage "a war against ignorance." The oath not only celebrates the pedagogical mission of teachers but also underscores their subservient relationship to the state. In the highly centralized school system, instructors who taught or behaved independently of ministerial directives was liable to be accused of lacking discipline (*disiplinsizlik*), creating divisiveness (*bölücülük*), and displaying anarchy in their duties (*görev anarşisi*). All three accusations were sufficient grounds for charging a teacher with being a threat to national interests and security.[84]

Indeed, the junta held instructors responsible in large part for the politicization in the schools before 1980. Rather than being role models for national unity, teachers had been positioned as wayward orderlies who had led their wards astray. Abdullah Nişancı, the military-appointed counselor to the Ministry of Education, accused "some teachers, even if only a few, to have separated themselves from the principles of Atatürkism and pursued deviant ideologies."[85] As a result of these accusations, all teachers found objectionable were immediately relieved from their duties. Then, to prevent any further subversion, the military reactivated the 1945 laws forbidding teachers, as state officials, from participating in political activities. Teachers represent the state but have no representation themselves: they could neither negotiate their salaries nor discuss the pros and cons of the curriculum. (In 1990, Turkey was one of six countries in the world without a teachers' union.) Finally, the junta went as far as using slightly modified military laws and regulations for teachers. In 1982, all forty clauses of the Turkish Armed Forces' Home Service Regulations (*Türk Silah Kuvvetleri İç Hizmet Yönetmenliği*) were applied in writing up the Ministry of Education's Personnel Regulations (*Millî Eğitim Bakanlığı Yönetmenliği*).[86] In short, the very state powers that supplied teachers with training, diplomas, salaries, and institutional support could choose, if need be, to fine or fire teachers or, worse, imprison them.

Teachers at Yayla took pride in their pedagogical duties. They were also well aware of the institutional constraints in their profession. Only in the most intimate quarters of their homes would they voice controversial opinions. Except for the few teachers who were native sons and daughters of the town, most looked forward to the prospect of being relocated to a more urban environment. Consequently, they did their utmost to not jeopardize their relocation.

Envoi

Following the 1980 coup, the military had definite ideas about how a civilian educational system should function and how an ideal citizenry should participate in their pedagogical mission. From their perspective, schoolchildren ought to fuse as much as possible their private selves to state interests, to become obedient and disciplined citizens who completely identify with the armed forces. Thus, the generals set about structuring their conception of the ideal school system—a civilian version of the armed forces in which school children and personnel would behave like their military counterparts, the soldiers and their officers. To a large extent, they have succeeded. The national educational system forged powerful emotional bonds between the military institution and the civilian population: the curriculum simultaneously instilled the idea that law-abiding citizens should dedicate their lives to army and nation, that strong-armed solutions to social conflict and political differences seemed logical and necessary, and that military service was a positive part of male citizenship. Moreover, identification with Atatürk and martial figures, as well as emphasis on military episodes of Turkish history and self-sacrifice, resonate with commonsense notions of gender and adulthood in Yayla. Townspeople, both men and women, repeatedly told me that the army teaches a youth to be a man (*erkek*), and thus they considered military service to be a crucial rite of passage. Conversely, motherhood was viewed as crucial for the survival of Turkish state and society, since it provides the means for the biological reproduction of soldiers.

What sociologist Sarit Helman described about the prevailing militarism in Israeli political culture could easily be applied in the context of Turkey: "indicative of the strength of educational practices . . . [is that] the readiness and motivation to join the army are turned into an emotional, cognitive, and interpretative disposition."[87] Children and adults readily identified with the military institution and the virile, martial ideals taught at school. Representing stability and continuity, the army enjoyed high credibility among citizens. Yet not everybody identified with the military leaders of the country and their political ideals.

Generals may have proclaimed themselves to be power-neutral champions of Atatürk's secular republicanism, but their ambiguous flirtation with adherents of the Turkish Islamic Synthesis not only has resulted in Islamizing the curriculum but also has ironically helped politicize their own corporate identity and ideals. The military politics of no politics notwithstanding, the particular syncretism of military nationalism and religious-inspired militancy has spawned unanticipated tensions between the military and major politically motivated groups in the public sphere. Given that the military is a critical sign of the nation, and that the sign of nation should include both devout and less devout citizens in uniform as its signifiers, then the exclusion of the devout from the military academies is an exclusion from full citizenship. Demand for equality exposes the contradiction that lay at the heart of any vision of the nation as signified and embodied in its armed services. What was unclear in 1990 was how the military would work out their differences with politically dominant associations. In this ongoing war of positions, the Turkish people's military heritage was presented as a source of unity. Nevertheless, this heritage remained hotly contested.

Notes

1. Aware of the potential of mass media to disseminate desired values, the generals issued a secret report in which it was decided to broadcast more religious programs; see Yelda Arslan, Sefa Kaplan, and Erdal Kılıçoğlu, "Din eğitimi, laiklik ve ötesi," *Nokta* (26 March 1989), pp. 16–25.

2. George S. Harris, "The Role of the Military in Turkey in the 1980s: Guardians or Decision-Makers?" in *State, Democracy and the Military: Turkey in the 1980s*, ed. Metin Heper and Ahmet Evin (New York: Walter de Gruyter, 1988), pp. 182–83; Paul Magnarella, "State Politics: Desecularization, State Corporatism, and Elite Behavior in Turkey," in *Human Materialism: A Model of Sociocultural Systems and a Strategy for Analysis* (Gainesville: University Press of Florida, 1993), pp. 87–113.

3. Alan Mitchell, *Victors and Vanquished: The German Influence on Army and Church in France after 1870* (Chapel Hill: University of North Carolina Press, 1984), pp. 151–52. Gesturing back to the previous chapter, I note that contemporary observers also credited the Prussians' victory over the French in 1870 to their successful use of industrial time; namely, the ability to effectively use the railroads to mobilize and transport troops to the front in as short a time as possible; see Stephen Kern, *The Culture of Time and Space 1880–1918.* (Cambridge, MA: Harvard University Press, 1983), p. 269. Others attributed France's defeat to its declining birth rate; Germany's rapid population growth became a yardstick for military strength; see Martine Segalen, *Historical Anthropology of the Family* (Cambridge, UK: Cambridge University Press, 1986), p. 289.

4. Yahya Akyüz, "Atatürk ve 1921 Eğitim Kongresi," in *Cumhuriyet döneminde eğitim* (İstanbul: Millî Eğitim Basımevi, 1983), p. 90.

5. Charles Tilly, "War Making and State Making as Organized Crime," in *Bringing the State Back In*, ed. Peter B. Evans, Dietrich Reuschemeyer, and Theda Skocpol (Cambridge, UK: Cambridge University Press, 1985), pp. 169–87.

6. Ayse Gul Altinay, *The Myth of the Military Nation: Militarism, Gender, and Education in Turkey* (New York: Palgrave Macmillan, 2004).

7. E.g., George Helling and Barbara Helling, "Values Implicit in Turkish Images of Human Types: An Empirical Approach," *Turkish Studies Association Bulletin* 10 (1986), pp. 87–97.

8. E.g., Daniel Lerner and Richard D. Robinson, "Swords and Ploughshares: The Turkish Army as a Modernizing Force," *World Politics* 13 (1960), pp. 19–44. At one time, illiterate villagers learned to read and write in special literacy courses, popularly known as "Ali schools" (*Ali okulu*). Although the army abolished these courses in 1972, every year some twenty thousand conscripts are taught to read and write and the basic notions of hygiene and diet. See Mehmet Ali Birand, *Shirts of Steel: An Anatomy of the Turkish Armed Forces*, trans. Saliha Paker and Ruth Christie (London; New York: Tauris, 1991), pp. 122–23.

9. At the time of my research, several Marxist and neofascist men were still serving sentences. See Chapter 2, note 26.

10. Karayiğit and Karayiğit, *Çukurova için hayat bilgisi*, pp. 44, 49.

11. The Turkish parliament bestowed on him while still living the last name Atatürk, which means "Father of the Turks."

12. This apolitical self-image has been cultivated since the 1924 demotion of the General Staff from an autonomous ministry to a body dependent on the president and minister of Defense. William Hale, *Turkish Politics and the Military* (London: Routledge, 1994), p. 92. In the military academies, Turkish cadets are taught that the military is responsible for the permanent existence of the republic: "The overall task of the Turkish Armed Forces is to ensure a strong structure for the Turkish state.... The Turkish Armed Forces constitute the unshakable foundation of the state" (quoted in Birand, *Shirts of Steel*, p. 84).

13. "Atatürk inkılap ve ilkelerinin öğretim esasları yönergesi," *TD* 45 (18 January 1982), p. 36.

14. An earlier generation of school children knew him as the "eternal chief" (*Ebedî Şef*), as opposed to his immediate successor, İsmet İnönü, who took the title national chief (*Millî Şef*).

15. "Atatürk inkılap ve ilkelerinin öğretim esasları yönergesi," *TD* 45 (18 January 1982), pp. 36–38.

16. "Altı yaş grubu programı," *TD* 48 (9 September 1985), p. 346.

17. Karayiğit and Karayiğit, *Çukurova için hayat bilgisi*, pp. 50–51; emphasis in original.

18. "Psikolojik savaş ve psikolojik savunma," *TD* 45 (1 February 1982), p. 76.

19. *İlkokul Türkçe ders kitabı 1* (İstanbul: Karacan Yayınları, 1989) p. 22.

20. *İlkokul Türkçe ders kitabı 5*, p. 59; capital letters in original.

21. For example, in the fourth-grade reader (*İlkokul Türkçe ders kitabı 4*), eight texts out of a total of fifty-one refer to soldiers' exploits and self-sacrificing deeds.

22. "1940–1941, 1941–1942, 1942–1943 ders yıllarında ilkokullarında okutulmak üzere yazdırılacak okuma kitapları şartnamesi," *TD* 1 (13 February 1939), p. 19.

23. "Millî eğitim bakanlığı 1981–1982 öğretim yılı direktifi," *TD* 44 (17 August 1981), p. 293.

24. Aydoğdu, *Türkçe ilkokul 3*, pp. 106–07.

25. *İlkokul hayat bilgisi 3*, p. 68.

26. Aydoğdu, *Türkçe ilkokul 2*, p. 23.

27. "İlkokul 4 ve 5'inci sınıf 'sosyal bilgiler' dersi öğretim programı'nın kabulü," *TD* 53 (25 June 1990), pp. 457–58.

28. *İlkokul hayat bilgisi 3*, p. 63.

29. Vedat Öğün, *Özetli-testli ilkokul hayat bilgisi sınıf 2*, p. 52.

30. *İlkokul Türkçe ders kitabı 3*, p. 44.

31. *İlkokul Türkçe ders kitabı 4*, p. 12.

32. The close relation between blood and milk works into townspeople's ideas about incest. Before the availability of formula milks, some thirty years ago, women who could not lactate hired a wet-nurse. The latter remained a second mother for the child's life. Given the belief that the husband's semen of the wet-nurse came through her breast, the nursing child was in part a descendant of her husband. Accordingly, her children and the nursing child could not marry one another.

33. An impotent person is said to suffer from anemia, to be literally without blood (*kansız*). Fear of impotence haunts seriously wounded men. A doctor at the state hospital in Tarsus explained to me that many village men refused to accept blood transfusions, lest the anonymous donor irreversibly affect the patient's virility.

34. "İlkokul 4 ve 5'inci sınıf 'sosyal bilgiler' dersi," *TD* 53 (25 June 1990), p. 471.

35. Virilocality is the norm in most households in Turkey; a patrilineal household is popularly associated with the hearth (*ocak*) and its smoke.

36. This was evident when Turkey participated in the Korean conflict. This was the first time that the Turkish army had fought outside the country's borders. The government publicly represented the conflict as one between one between holy warriors and atheist infidels. As John Patrick Kinross, who resided in Turkey at the time, stated, "the Turkish troops in Korea fought in the name of Islam, attended religious services before going into battle, and were led (at least in the war posters) by officers carrying the Koran." See his *Within the Taurus* (London: John Murray, 1954), p. 21.

37. "Psikolojik savaş ve psikolojik savunma," *TD* 45 (1 February 1982), p. 77.

38. "Psikolojik savaş ve psikolojik savunma," *TD* 45 (1 February 1982), p. 76.

39. Güvenç et al., *Türk-İslam sentezi dosyası* p. 210.

40. Cihad Tunç, *Ortaokullar için din kültürü ve ahlâk bilgisi 3* (İstanbul: Millî Eğitim Basımevi, 1987), p. 115. Already in the 1950s, religious-minded intellectuals advanced the thesis of an organic continuity between pre-Islamic Turks and holy warfare. The historian Osman Turan, a DP deputy in the 1954 parliament and editor in chief of the neo-Ottomanist newspaper *Yeni İstanbul* and monthly *Türk Yurdu*,

applied the notion of cultural survival to argue that the Turks had from time immemorial had a martial ethos: "The shamanist creed which, contrary to the religions originating among the un-warlike races of India yet in line with the Islamic conception of Holy War, promises a reward in proportion to the number of foes killed in action, cannot be explained fully without considering the war-like life and spirit of the Turks." See his "The Ideal of World Domination among the Medieval Turks," *Studia Islamica* 4 (1955), p. 77.

41. The Seljuks' victory at Malazgirt heralded the Turkish tribesmen's settlement of Anatolia.

42. *İlkokul Türkçe ders kitabı 4*, p. 132.

43. The generic name for soldier in Turkey is *Mehmetçik*, which derives from Mehmet. Mehmet here metonymically refers to all soldiers.

44. *İlkokul Türkçe ders kitabı 3*, p. 15; the text uses the term *kurban verdik*, which literally means "we gave as sacrifice [the male family members]." On the Feast of Sacrifice, an animal (usually a sheep) is sacrificed in commemoration of the prophet Ibrahim who had been ready to sacrifice his son Ishmail for Allah.

45. Vatandaşlık bilgisi orta 3 (İstanbul: Millî Eğitim Basımevi, 1987), p. 72.

46. Tunç, Ortaokullar için din kültürü ve ahlâk bilgisi 3; p. 89.

47. "Atatürk inkılap ve ilkelerinin öğretim esasları yönergesi," *TD* 45 (18 January 1982), p. 38.

48. Parmaksızoğlu, *Ortaokullar için Türkiye Cumhuriyeti İnkılâp Tarihi ve Atatürkçülük*, p. 145.

49. Birand, *Shirts of Steel*, p. 74.

50. Despite the high command's refusal to admit İmam-Hatip graduates, military academies have embraced many of the ideals of the Turkish Islamic Synthesis in their curricula. Since the 1980 coup, cadets are required to take a course on religion. The textbook *Askerin Din Bilgisi (Religious Knowledge for Soldiers)*, which the Armed Forces Command published, aimed at demonstrating the close connection between Sunni Islam and Turkish nationalism. To make salient this demonstration, the curriculum draws the cadet students' attention to the parallel salvationist roles of the prophet Muhammad and Atatürk to produce an overarching narrative of collective suffering and national redemption. Both men are credited with having militarily redeemed their respective community from persecution: Muhammad's sojourn (the Hegira) to Medina initiated the period of Muslim expansion; Atatürk's journey from the Black Sea city of Samsun initiated the expulsion of foreign armies from the country in 1923. The close links between religion and military campaigns were evident during the War of Independence; Atatürk was popularly known as "Warrior of the Faith" (*Gazi*), a title many Ottoman sultans had taken. Later, during his presidency when he set about instituting a secular polity, he often signed his name with this holy title. Metin Heper, "Islam, Polity and Society in Turkey: A Middle Eastern Perspective," *Middle East Journal* 35 (1981), p. 352.

51. "İmam-hatipliye harp okulu yolu açılıyor," *Güneş* (21 November 1990), p. 2.

52. "Hekimoğlu İsmail'e 1 yıl hapis," *Güneş* (15 December 1990), p. 1.

53. In 1990, the religious press came out with several militant satirical journals to compete with the long-established *Gırgır*, which often attacked the growing influence of the religious public in education and national politics. The name *Cıngar*, which means "a noisy dispute," suggests its polemical stance.

54. A tottering fool is popularly known as the "master of the wild pear" (*ahlat ağa*).

55. *Pulse* (15 September 1980).

56. "T.C. milli eğitim bakanlığı savunma sekreterliğinden: kamu kuruluşları ve milli beraberlik," *TD* 45 (1 February 1982), pp. 68–69. At the time of my research, Kurds were banned from forming any ethnic or regional association that might be taken to impair national unity. Newspapers and television news programs regularly carried pictures of stockpiles of weapons and seditious literature, which the army allegedly collected from Kurdish or leftist hideouts. These pictures, I believe, were intended to justify the military's heavy-handed actions against political dissidents.

57. M. Ayçin Ergintürk and İhsan Esatoğlu, *Ortaokullar için millî coğrafya ana ders kitabı 2* (İstanbul: Millî Eğitim Basımevi, 1987), p. 135; emphasis in original.

58. On the notion of teacher as a surrogate author, see Carmen Luke, Suzanne DeCastell, and Alan Luke, "Beyond Criticism: The Authority of the School Text," *Curriculum Inquiry* 13 (1983), p. 124.

59. Ibrahim was referring to the international outcry over the sanitary conditions of some seventy thousand Kurdish refugees from northern Iraq who received sanctuary in Turkey. Danielle Mitterand, then the French president's wife, took up the cause of the Kurds in Turkey and demanded greater cultural and political rights for them.

60. Ergintürk and Esatoğlu, *Ortaokullar için millî coğrafya ana ders kitabı 2*, p. 135.

61. "Atatürk inkılap ve ilkelerinin öğretim esasları yönergesi," *TD* 45 (18 January 1982), p. 38.

62. Tekışık, *Hayat bilgisi ünitelerine kaynak kitap 3*, p. 55.

63. İsmet Parmaksızoğlu, *İnkılâp tarihi ve Atatürkçülük* (İstanbul: Millî Eğitim Basımevi, 1988), p. 96.

64. *Güneş* (10 July 1986).

65. This resonates with my discussion on certain religious nationalists' views on birth control as a Judeo-Christian conspiracy; see previous chapter.

66. Oğuz Ünal, and Cafer Tayyar Karaoğuz, *Ortaokullar için, millî coğrafya ana ders kitabı 1* (İstanbul: Millî Eğitim Basımevi, 1987), p. 77.

67. Before the secularizing reforms in the second half of the nineteenth century, Muslim rulers extended protection to non-Muslims in exchange for their legal subordination to Muslims.

68. At Yayla, the left-of-center parties have never succeeded in capturing a majority in free elections. In the municipality elections of 1989, the two main right-of-center parties—ANAP and DYP—together captured 69 percent of the votes. Support for left-of-center parties often results from rivalries among important patrilineages. The electoral results in Yayla are consistent with other Sunni commu-

nities in the district. As for the Alevi electorate, it has overwhelmingly voted for left-of-center parties that support secular platforms. Official censuses do not differentiate between Sunnis and Alevis; the latter make up between one sixth to one third of the total population of the country.

69. Sunni detractors of Alevis frequently refer to the latter's rituals as *mum söndü* (literally, "the candle went out").

70. Because the Directorate of Religious Affairs recognizes neither the Alevis as a religious school of legal thought (*mezhep*) nor its spiritual leaders, the state appoints Sunni imams to their communities. Nor can they be officially considered a religious brotherhood (*tarikat*); the constitution bans any Muslim brotherhood.

71. Despite these prejudices, several townspeople maintained good working relations with their Tahtacı neighbors. In 1988, an enterprising shepherd, Hasan, built a cement sheepfold. As his brothers refused to help him out, he borrowed money from an Alevi friend. Later, they cemented their partnership by becoming spiritual godfathers (*kirvelik*) to each other's sons. Hasan discounted the rumors on the Alevis' lack of cleanliness.

72. At the turn of the last century, Léonce Alishan, an ardent supporter for an Armenian state in the region, stated that "from what the travelers say, they [Muslims and Armenians] live together in pretty good harmony"; see his *Sissouan, ou l'Arméno-Cilicie* (Venice: St. Lazare, 1899), p. 131. The French, who occupied the region after World War I, were equally surprised at the exceptionally good relations between the two communities in the immediate area (e.g., Ministère des Affaires Etrangères, Nantes 311-1, no. 1816; 22 August 1919).

73. Appositely, a flimsily made article is deprecated as "Turkish work" (*Türk işi*). To note, a few middle-age craftsmen in Yayla learned their trade from those descendants of Armenians who took up residence in Istanbul.

74. Only the names of the two major neighborhoods, Panzin Çukuru and Tekfur Kozu, recall the Armenian presence in the past. According to the townspeople, Panzin was an Armenian originally from the "market" area outside the medieval castle. "Tekfur" derives from the word *tekûr* or *tekvur*, which means the local Christian lord who controlled fortified settlements. On the Armenian community in the nineteenth century, see Theodor Kotschy, *Reise in den Cilicischen Taurus über Tarsus* (Gotha: Verlag von Fustus Berthes, 1858), p. 74; Victor Langlois, *Voyage dans la Cilicie et les montagnes du Taurus: éxécuté pendant les années 1852–53* (Paris: Benjamin Duprat, 1861), p. 361.

75. "İlkokul 4 ve 5'inci sınıf 'sosyal bilgiler' dersi," *TD* 53 (25 June 1990), pp. 458, 460.

76. *İlkokul hayat bilgisi 3*, p. 14.

77. See de Certeau, *The Practice of Everyday Life*, p. 120.

78. Karayiğit and Karayiğit, *Çukurova için hayat bilgisi*, p. 20; capital letters in original.

79. Abdullah Birkan et al., *Ortaokullarda Türkçe dersleri 1* (İstanbul: Ders Kitapları Anonim Şirketi, 1987), p. 144.

80. "İlk ve orta dereceli okulların 1981–1982 öğretim yılına başlaması nedeniyle milli eğitim bakanı Hasan Sağlam'ın açış konuşması," *TD* (28 September 1981), p. 310.

81. *İsmail Aydoğdu, Türkçe ilkokul 5*, Ankara: Türk Tarih Kurumu Basımevi, 1988, p. 63. Likewise, in the seventh-grade religion textbook, pupils read that "laws are . . . for preventing confusion. We must always abide by them. When we don't, we will be punished"; Tunç, *Ortaokullar için din kültürü ve ahlâk bilgisi 2*, p. 68.

82. "Milli eğitim bakanlığına bağlı temel eğitim II. kademe (ortaokul) ile ortaöğretim kurumları disiplin yönetmenliğinin 5., 11., 15., 18., 22., 27., 29., 38., 55., 56. ve 59. maddelerinin değiştirilmesi hackında yönetmelik," *TD* 44 (8 June 1981), pp. 233–34. Of course, how school administrators and state prosecutors follow these guidelines is subject to interpretation. In 1989, a 16-year-old student, M. Ç., served four months at a maximum-security prison for writing "leftist" ideas in his notebook. On M. Ç.'s release, the state prosecutor wanted to incarcerate the youth for another fifteen years. "M.Ç. yeniden gözetim altına alınıyor," *Cumhuriyet* (29 April 1989), p. 1.

83. In addition to the title of commander in chief (*Başkumandan*), which Atatürk received during the War of Liberation, the 1924 decree on "The Organization of the National School" declared him the nation's headmaster. The two titles cement the homology between army and school.

84. Before the republic, state officials were already concerned about what worldviews teachers transmitted in class. In 1904, for example, the Ottoman government set up a commission that investigated those teachers lacking a "healthy conscience." Faik Reşit Unat, *Türkiye eğitim sisteminin gelişmesine tarihî bir bakış* (Ankara: Millî Eğitim Basımevi, 1964), p. 33.

85. "Millî eğitim bakanlığı müsteşarı Abdullah Nişancı'nın 1980–1981 öğretim yılı ilköğretim haftasını açış konuşması," *TD* 43 (29 September 1980), p. 202.

86. While the order of regulations differ in these two sets of instructions, their language and content are almost identical. They differ in two respects: one, the military regulations refer to soldiers and officers, while the educational regulations refer to civilian teachers and supervisors; and two, some of the vocabulary had been updated. Thus, for example, the twenty-eighth clause in the educational regulation emphatically states, "All National Education personnel must know that behaviors which contravene the spirit of discipline of the Turkish National Education shall never remain unpunished." The seventh clause of the military regulation states: "All personnel of the Armed Forces must know that behaviors which contravene the spirit of discipline of the Turkish Armed Forces shall never remain unpunished." See Mete Çubukçu, "Emret Hocam!" *Nokta* (30 July 1989), p. 61.

87. Sarit Helman, "Militarism and the Construction of the Life-World of Israeli Males: The Case of the Reserves System," in *The Military and Militarism in Israeli Society*, ed. Edna Lomsky-Feder and Eyal Ben-Ari (Albany: State University of New York Press, 1999), p. 201.

CHAPTER SIX

Educational Postfoundations

We don't need no education
We don't need no thought control
No dark sarcasm in the classroom
Teacher, leave the kids alone
Hey!, Teacher, leave us kids alone
All in all you're just another brick in the wall
All in all you're just another brick in the wall

—PINK FLOYD   "Another Brick in the Wall Part 2" (1979)

Facts of the past become historical phenomena only when they become significant for a subject which itself stands in history and is involved in it.

—RUDOLPH BULTMANN   *Essays Philosophical and Theological*

The story of education in Yayla did not finish with my fieldwork.[1] I left shortly after the outbreak of the first Gulf War in 1991. Townspeople, young and old, continued with their lives. Almost all the schoolchildren whom I got to know have started their own families, and within a few years, they will be sending their children to schools. And since my two-year stint at Yayla, I have become a proud parent of two boys; one recently finished elementary school, the other junior high.

From the beginning, my research on a local school system in Turkey was (and remains) incomplete and inconclusive—partial, transient, and above all, dated. I had begun my project based on a literature that described a secular state at loggerheads with a tradition-bound, religious society. Thus, in his study of a Turkish rural community, Joe Pierce stated that "Islam is a way of life and is the dominant factor in the making of any decision, no matter how slight, in the mind of the villager."[2] Along similar lines, other ethnographers argued that religious cosmologies patterned the social practices of most Turkish citizens.[3] Drawing on functionalist or structuralist paradigms, these scholars perceived continuity and change as a feature of an integrated culture and a bounded system of social relations. Because they privileged stability and coherence, they assumed that fixed, nonnegotiable cultural forms structured social life. Accordingly, tradition is a perpetual baseline, until a secular modernity kicks in: any significant changes in a society result when an alternative, external cultural system successfully infiltrates and implodes a supposedly cohesive cosmology. To be fair, all these studies have provided a wealth of insights for my own research. They also reveal how dated theoretical paradigms become.

In the past twenty years, research interests have changed. On the one hand, scholars are more interested in transformation, rather than reproduction, of society. On the other, they have been attending to the links between state institutions, multiple systems of signification, human agency, and power relations. Of particular importance has been highlighting the mutability, contingency, and heterogeneity of social practices in a locality to draw out the specific ways people come to live in the subjectivities offered by institutional sites. Squarely situated in this approach is my study of Turkish education. Thus, unlike earlier ethnographic studies on Turkey, my research of a local school system led me to explore the unstable and volatile cultural politics operating at all levels of society, from the corridors of the Ministry of Education in the capital city of Ankara to local homes and classrooms.

Very quickly, I had to considerably revise the initial premises of my project. I had expected to find religion dominating social life. Instead, I discovered that influential officials, opinion and policy makers were intent to save the citizens from atheistic individualism, to re-Islamize the ostensibly Muslim population. I also came to realize that other politically motivated associations, most notably neoliberal industrialists and the military, had a stake in the state and its pedagogical mission and, thus, struggled for control of the country's student body, the next generation of adult citizens. Thus, the idea of a monolithic state pitted against society did not reflect the different ways these associations compete in constituting collective boundaries and differences and, thereby, producing particular kinds of citizens through the educational system. All these associations attempted to implement authoritative meanings of language and thereby mold schoolboys and schoolgirls according to their political canons. Likewise, I discovered that cosmologies, however constituted, played a far less significant role among the townspeople in Yayla. More often, ostensibly religious topics became platforms from which men and women discussed secular issues in civil society and, above all, the role of the state in education. Thus, in my fieldwork, I ended up exploring how the curricula were both a vehicle for personal and collective notions of citizenship and a prompt to the reconfiguration of these notions. The tensions between attempts at homogenizing a citizenry through the curriculum and the multiple social contexts that make up the day-to-day lives of citizens have rendered education arguably the most politically volatile issue in Turkey.

Emergent Individualities

Despite the political volatility of education, a strong state tradition persists in the national school system in Turkey. Educators, officials, businesspeople, and the military all tap into a paternalistic understanding of the relation between the state and citizenry and thus expect citizens, beginning with schoolchildren, to fuse as much as possible their private selves to state dictates. The systematic intervention into children's subjectivities is primarily keyed to foster allegiance to the nation and obedience to state institutions and officials. Thus, the curriculum has consciously worked at inculcating authoritative interpretations of society and polity. These pedagogical intentions have come to inhabit the political consciousness of pupils—but in ways the curriculum never intended. Quite a few observers of Turkish society maintain that home and school succeed in socializing children into "core authoritarianism."[4] The government directives, curriculum, and pedagogical practices, which I explored in the previous chapter, would warrant such an opinion. The entire school system links didactic methods with monologic themes to demarcate clear-cut definitions of citizenship and classificatory boundaries between state and society with which each child will identify during and after her formal schooling. Yet many of the schoolchildren thought and acted otherwise. Far from wholeheartedly accepting authoritarian social norms, they aspired to more egalitarian social relations—and in large part, this was a result of their school knowledge.

The multiple discourses of citizenship to which young men and women have been exposed throughout their years at school make possible comparative assessments of different ways of thinking about one's life in terms of both immediate *and* potentially very different social practices. Ironically, the curricula through which the national educational system tries to fashion a homogeneous collectivity have become the means for negatively evaluating the prevalent authority relations in the classroom and society at large. What I am suggesting is that the norms and values pupils acquire at school instill a selfhood that subverts and (partially) unhinges the moral links between collective identity and unwavering obedience to either state or adult figures of authority. Because the educational sphere disseminates ambivalent and vacillating representations about modernity, state, and society, the curricula become a forum for reflecting on power and social relations, narrating more emancipating life courses and life strategies, and most importantly, imagining alternative ways of thinking about self, other, and world. Specifically, schoolchildren encode their interests in the language of individual rights and thus reconceptualize their political selves. Individualism, as in relying upon one's own insight, has become both a desirable means and an end for those young men and women trying to exert some degree of autonomy in otherwise constraining social and political relations.[5] That is to say, children cum adults can come to understand themselves as part of a larger public sphere; they are able to articulate their autonomy in the very terms that their schooling provides and, thus, imagine themselves as part of a Turkish collective.

In the following I present the case of physical punishment to show how the curriculum has unwittingly provided the means with which schoolchildren reflect on and react to the discrepancy between the rhetoric of enlightened education and their experiences of authoritarian power relations in the classroom. This discrepancy emerged in essays in which schoolchildren establish discursive autonomy vis-à-vis state institutions; namely, they appropriate the discourse of democracy to indict undemocratic teaching methods.

One means used to instill knowledge and respect for authority is physical discipline. Beating reason into a recalcitrant child is accepted practice.[6] Many a father hands over the child to his teacher with the popular saying "His flesh is yours, his bones are mine" (*eti senin kemiği benim*).[7] With this formulaic phrase, which translates as "be as rough as you want with him/her," the parent acknowledges the teacher's right to discipline his child.

This is despite ministerial directives that, since 1847, have forbidden teachers from hitting children, and where the punishment to teachers includes fines and removal from the profession.[8] In 1990, in a directive that received wide coverage in the press, Avni Akyol, then minister of Education, declared that corporal punishment was contrary to "scientific and modern" pedagogical methods of "developed countries," such as Turkey. He also made it clear that hitting pupils was counterproductive and led to rebellious behavior— an allusion to the violence leading to the 1980 coup.[9]

The school system sometimes acknowledges the violence that children might receive from their parents after submitting a poor report card, but nowhere does it suggest that teachers themselves hit pupils.[10] This is despite numerous examples from the press and schoolchildren's own testimonies. Fatime, an eleven-year-old pupil who had recently transferred to a private school, recalled how her elementary school instructor on religious culture "was a very tense and irritable person. If he saw a pupil talking in class while he was teaching, he would get angry and hit the pupil. This didn't suffice for him. He would then throw the student out of the class. Because of what he did, the pupils . . . called him the beater (*dayakçı*)." Nevertheless, the textual accounts taught in class have given the pupils the means to criticize ongoing pedagogical practices. Today children compose their (national) identities through the ideological prism of incremental progress and have come to associate physical punishment with the devalued prerepublican school system. Before the republic, when the only form of instruction most children received was catechism, instructors were known to use the rod to ensure accurate recitation of the Qu'ran.[11] In the currently used readers, drawings unfavorably comparing the stick and bastinado to modern pedagogical practices complement the potted histories of the reforms instituted under the republic. Progressive history offers a transformed mode of action and expression. To wit, in an essay on "Modern and Cultured People," one of my middle school students, Burak, wrote that

> as time advances, people are on the way to becoming more sophisticated and modern. For example after the sultanate period in Turkey, many things were replaced with something new, thanks to the people and Atatürk. For example, in the past backward *hodjas* [religious teachers] . . . taught children the old Ottoman language in Arabic characters unlike those we use today.

And for every error the children made, the *hodjas* would badly beat them with the rod. We now read many stories about the education in those times.

These stories have become part of the school lore from which children draw their collective memory. They also implicitly indict present abusers of authority as living signs of the backward and despotic past. Abusers may include the pupils' current teachers, whom students (privately) accuse of not living up to the enlightened norms of the state. This was first brought to my attention in an essay Bayram, then twelve years old, wrote about his education. Awarded a scholarship for needy, bright children, Bayram was attending a prestigious magnet school, where much of the teaching staff comes from Germany. In the essay, he drew out the differences in pedagogical approaches between the Turkish instructors and their German colleagues.

> What a shame that . . . some teachers think that they can educate by hitting the students. This is a deficiency in our education. The level of education in my school is above Turkish standards but I can't say it is excellent since there are still . . . teachers who hit pupils in our school. According to Turkish law, hitting is the last punishment to be given. That is, according to Turkish laws, hitting has still not been abolished. . . . In my school there are German teachers. Not one of these teachers even slaps a student. Because hitting has definitely been abolished in these teachers' country. And a teacher who hits a pupil [there] even has to go to court. This is the case for almost all Western countries. When these [German] teachers heard about hitting from the students at first they were surprised and then they laughed a lot. What a shame that . . . some teachers think that they can educate by hitting the students. My school is one of . . . Turkey's most important schools. In comparing this school with other schools one accepts that my school is better. For example, I hear about hitting in my neighborhood school every day. In my school there are cases of hitting, but very little. And the teachers who hit are certain people. I have dwelled on this topic [hitting] because it is widespread in Turkey and negatively affects students. The main negative influences are truancy, lack of interest in the lesson, and dislike of teachers.

Impressed with how well he articulated his frustration with the current pedagogical practices, I later asked Bayram how he coped with the simultaneously different teaching methods. He associated the German and Turk-ish teachers with two incommensurable mentalities (*zihniyet*), separated from each other by an unbridgeable chronological gap. Until the Turkish teachers caught up with their German colleagues, Bayram would learn to maneuver between what he called "democratic" and "despotic" pedagogical systems.

Through the rhetoric of progress, this bright youth evaluated contempo-rary relations of power in the school system. Likewise, in the same written assignment, eleven-year-old Ali associated corporal punishment with "prim-itive" (*ilkel*) people whose "behavior dates from olden times." Thus, he de-scribed his physical education teacher as "merciless" and "always hitting the older students." Democracy and modernity here are, as it were, an after-the-fact appeal to reconsider the pedagogical practices and a prompt to recon-figure the hierarchical relations at school. It is but one of many discursive means with which Bayram and Ali expressed personal angst and reformist longings—in short, a poignant restatement of school-based discourses that reaffirms a narrative of emancipation, all the while challenging teachers' violence.

Despite their criticisms of physical discipline, schoolchildren continued to suffer corporal punishment, which remains a prerogative of adult author-ity figures. But my point is not about the incongruity between pedagogical ideas and their physical manifestations in the classroom. Rather, my point is to show how a perceptive youth like Bayram actively engaged with multiple discourses emanating to some extent from within the educational system to criticize the prevalent violence at school—even if only in fragmented, writ-ten and oral comments. This was possible because of the structural contra-diction inherent in the Turkish school system: Pupils are simultaneously represented as the temporal culmination of the national narrative and re-peatedly reconstituted as the unfulfilled ideals of the valorized future. Si-multaneously taught "who we ideally are" and "what we ought to be," boys and girls deflected this dilemma to their superiors; in the case of Bayram, to his Turkish teachers. Thus, self-conscious youth like Bayram were able to reconfigure and inflect the political terms of progress to challenge the lack of modernity among some of their teachers and, by implication that of the school system and its state sponsors.

It is evident that schooling has contributed to generating new modes of thinking about social identities and relations. An earlier emphasis on conformity is giving way to epistemological individualism. The curricula have equipped children with the intellectual skills to evaluate ways of life different from their parents and unwittingly have made individual autonomy and reflexivity a desired way of being. Very much like George Herbert Mead's notion of "I" emerging in contradistinction from "me," schoolchildren are collectively achieving individuality through a self-conscious, critical appraisal of their experiences at school.[12]

Notions of individual choice and responsibility are not limited to reactions to children's responses to corporal punishment. Thanks to legal constructs of citizenship, which the educational system disseminates, what were once deemed to be under the purview of communitarian and familial control are increasingly understood as the responsibility of the individual. I recall here that the young female graduates of the Qur'an course argued that, out of personal piety, a prospective groom must override his parents' choice of bride; conversely, that the pious bride-to-be should impose conditions on her matchmaking parents and future groom. Likewise, some children expected their parents to take responsibility for their fertility and limit the number of children in response to an increasingly commodified society. Still others questioned the reasoning the military has used to dismiss the individual merits of devout students.

All these cases exemplify what Foucault defines as a "critical ontology of self." Pupils critically reflect on their education and thus partially succeed in resisting the more totalizing tendencies of state schools. This is not to deny the fact that pedagogical practices and discourses considerably restrict children's reflexivity, comportment, and identity. But no school system can deliver complete order. As a result of the contradictions and tensions within the curriculum, pupils are able to imagine what changes are possible and desirable and determine the form these changes should take. The very norms, models, and subject positions—to which children are subjected at school—present multiple strategies to historicize their experience of the present historical moment and, thus, realize alternative forms of experience. That is to say, their education has provided the means to interrogate existing configurations of power and knowledge and, more importantly, to "experiment with the possibility of going beyond them."[13] The implications are far-reaching, if not counterintuitive. Schoolchildren, and not their adult peers, are the ones most able to release themselves from the systematic discourses of modern governance and, thereby, accede to a state of maturity.[14] If this insight is correct, then both childhood and children's education must not be treated as simply derivative of the majority adult culture; rather, children actively contribute to the shaping and transfiguring of that culture.

Renvoi

Educational policies are intended to forge a consensual understanding of state and society, to homogenize the citizenry, and to define national experience for children. Despite the claims to the contrary, the Turkish national school system foments as much division as it fosters unity in society. While statesmen and educators of all political persuasions desire Turkey to be an economically, morally, and militarily strong country, they do not hold a monolithic understanding of education. The school system is shot through with contested moral imaginaries as different politically motivated associations have divergent understandings about the relationship between citizenship and education, between state and society. In the context of post-1980 Turkey, all three major associations—the religious nationalists, the neoliberal industrialists, and the military—respectively tried to impose their specific interpretations on key social issues through the curricula. Thus, discourses and concepts about citizenship with which school knowledge were framed were often at variance with one another.

This is not to suggest that there were incommensurable differences among the different associations. On the contrary, each association dialectically engaged its ideas about society and polity with and against those of their ideological opponents. All shared fundamental assumptions about the role of education and associated educational practices. They invariably linked pedagogy and school knowledge with the moral and social imaginary they believed best epitomized the national values of the citizenry. It was the particular interpretation of these representations that fueled debates about the relation between faith and collective national identity, the viability and justice of laissez-faire capitalism, and the nation's military role in the world. Thus, however much these groups differed in social and political agendas, their faith in the national educational system reinforced the epistemic superiority of the state vis-à-vis the citizenry. No association questioned the ability of schools to effect positive transformations on the essential character of children. Implicit in all the (often contentious) debates over education was an assimilationist rhetoric whereby a child's potential to become an enlightened citizen is predicated upon total acceptance of the curricula. Thus, in jockeying for the authority to determine the roles schoolchildren should inhabit in their lives, the different associations affirmed the pedagogical role of the state in creating citizenship.

It is with this political axiom that different ideological associations operating under the sign of the state have assumed the right to articulate not only the essential differences between the Turkish citizenry and the rest of the world but also to impose a historical framework with which all schoolchildren are expected to identify. In determining the moral traits of citizens, opinion and policy makers—all of whom act as pedagogues of the nation—define what change is and what kinds of change are important. Their pedagogical ideas and ideals have served to evaluate the integration of different citizens into the desired national order; a child's education comes to define his or her ability to ensure the survival of the state. It is against this background of competing social and political imaginaries that schooled children and their adult guardians try to make sense of their day-to-day lives. Turkish schoolchildren are far from being passive social actors. Nor does the school system mold a coherent or cohesive student body. Children within a society are positioned differently in terms of life history, gender, age, socioeconomics, and consciousness and, thus, differently experience schooling.

This brings me to my final point. The book starts with a story about the educational foundations of a community and then goes on to elaborate on a series of pedagogical ideals, some of which are difficult if not impossible to untangle from one another. Moreover, certain outstanding questions resist definite answers. Who is ultimately represented in the national educational system: Is it the nation or the state? Who formulates the educational needs of the country: the body of elected representatives of the nation, civilian, and military functionaries; independent think tanks that operate in conjunction with state organs; or all of them together? What can be definitely answered is that the overwhelming majority of citizens, whether policy makers or townspeople, believe that school knowledge eclipses all other forms of intergenerational transmission of a society's norms and values. And because of the belief in the instrumental value of education, the attempts to define collective identities will always involve political struggles. Educational policies are inherently arbitrary given that any consensus presupposes different perspectives within a society.

Today, all countries are pedagogical states, or at least endeavor to be. The educational issues with which I have dealt throughout the book find expression in one way or another all over the world. Non-Turkish readers will find many of the issues both familiar and controversial: the place of religious instruction in public schools; the representation of ethnic, racial, gender, and cultural differences in the curriculum; changing family roles and demographics; allegiance to civilian and military institutions; the separation of professional and technical training from a shared liberal education; and educational policies catering to local needs as opposed to national goals. Implicit in these often contentious debates over educational goals and curricula is a global understanding of political socialization. Schools are believed to be the most influential institutional site in establishing the political consciousness with which children will identify during and after their formal schooling, in fashioning an individual's identification with nation and state.

Even though no one school system can bind all persons to a single civic pedagogy, all of them together have succeeded in "pedagogizing" our thinking of self, other, and world. Today, we conceive of schooling mainly as preparation for citizenship but rarely as a set of distinctively organized processes with which children reproduce and transform the signs defining polity and society. The very modes of representation and discourses, which schools use to consolidate a citizenry, spur novel forms of desire, action, and purpose. Thanks to the pedagogical culture of modern states, children and adults insert their intimate selves in educational discourses and, in the process, reconceptualize their political and social selves.

Notes

1. Because this study is inherently historical, this is not the place for a full review of educational developments since I left Yayla in 1991. Very briefly, the religious nationalists, neoliberal industrialists, and the military have yet to work out many of their differences, but all have had to adapt to new political contingencies, including the end of the Cold War, continual privatization of the economy and educational system, candidacy into the EU, and considerable restrictions on religious-track education following military intervention in 1997.

2. Joe Pierce, *Life in a Turkish Village* (New York: Holt, Rinehart, & Winston, 1964), p. 87.

3. E.g., Delaney, *The Seed and the Soil*; and Julie Marcus, *A World of Difference: Islam and Gender Hierarchy in Turkey* (London: Allen & Unwin, 1992).

4. Cigdem Kagitçibasi, "Social Norms and Authoritarianism: A Turkish-American Comparison," *Journal of Personality and Social Psychology* 16 (1970), p. 444; Serif Mardin, "Youth and Violence in Turkey," p. 242; and David Shankland, *Islam and Society in Turkey* (Huntingdon, UK: Eothen, 1999).

5. Too often, social scientists have blindly accepted the binary sociocentric versus individualistic cultures argument, the latter cultures being characterized by the self-conscious, rational, and pragmatic individual who operates on his own. The atomistic and disengaged Cartesian subject is an ideological fiction to which many scholars ascribe. Upper-middle-class Anglo Americans, for instance, are no less socially embedded and interdependent as individuals from other societies. In other words, conceptions of the (Western) self must be considerably complexified. See Melford E. Spiro, "Is the Western Conception of the Self 'Peculiar' within the Context of the World Cultures?" *Ethos* 21 (1993), pp. 107–53; and Adrie Suzanne Kusserow, "Crossing the Great Divide: Anthropological Theories of the Western Self," *Journal of Anthropological Research* 55 (1999), pp. 541–62.

6. Parents frequently invoke popular sayings or traditions attributed to the prophet Muhammad to justify using physical discipline: "Keep your son and daughter in line or you will regret it later," "Hang the whip in a place visible to all the members of the household," and "Beat children older than ten years of age who abandon their prayers."

7. The expression resonates with the opposition of flesh and bones, integral to the Turco-Mongolian kinship system. The bone represents the patrilineal descent, the flesh matrimonial alliance. See Claude Lévi-Strauss, *Les structures élémentaires de la parenté* (Paris: Mouton, 1967), p. 454ff; and Roberte Hamayon, "L'os distinctif et la chair indifférente," *Etudes mongoles et sibériennes* 6 (1975), pp. 99–122. In this virilocal patrilineal kinship system, each side of the matrimonial alliance contributes to the education of the offspring: for the son, the maternal uncle (*dayı*); for the daughter who most often moves into her husband's paternal household upon marriage, the pa-

ternal sister (*hala*). The folk maxim "The son takes after the *dayı*, the daughter after the *hala*" underscores the mentoring role of the child's affinal relatives. In this regard, teachers take on the avuncular role of mentor. No townsperson, however, ascribed a child's biological genesis with the father providing the bone, the mother the flesh. Only in the death of an individual does the Turco-Mongolian kinship system find popular expression in Yayla. According to the older townsmen, death breaks down first the alliance between the patrilineal bones and the matrimonial flesh and then the patrilineal essence itself. It is common practice to commemorate twice the breaking down of the dead person's physical constitution: forty days after the burial when "the bones separate from the flesh"; and twelve days later, when "the bones of the dead separate from one another." Many liken these commemorative occasions as good works (*hayır hasenât*). Officials in the Directorate of Religious Affairs disagree and have labeled them as a heretical innovation.

8. Hasan Ali Koçer, *Türkiye'de modern eğitimin doğuşu ve gelişimi (1773–1923)* (İstanbul: Millî Eğitim Basımevi, 1970), p. 58.

9. "Ceza yoluyla öğrenci davranışlarının değiştirilip yönlendirilemeyeceği," *TD* 53 (23 July 1990), pp. 554–55. Newspapers (e.g., "Öğrencilere dayak yasak," *Hürriyet*, 22 August 1990, pp. 3, 14) printed summaries of the directive. To note, only in 1986 was corporal punishment formally abolished in state schools in England and Wales.

10. A poem, "The Report Card," which appeared in a second-grade life science textbook, ends with the following verses: "A report card full of F's / We will get if we don't work / Father and mother will get angry / Maybe we'll get a thrashing" (in Öğün, *Özetli-testli ilkokul hayat bilgisi sınıf 2* [Ankara: Öğün Yayınları, 1982], p. 174).

11. The close links between religious salvation, education, and punishment are captured in two widely used expressions, "Roses sprout from where a teacher has struck" and "Thrashing is a heavenly means of education." Both sayings suggest that those parts of body struck will become roses and not burn in hell. As roses blossom eternally in Paradise, the punished child will be spared harsher treatment in afterlife. In the Judeo-Christian tradition, there exists a similar justification for corporal punishment; see Proverbs 23:14.

12. See George Herbert Mead, *Mind, Self, and Society* (Chicago: University of Chicago Press, 1934), pp. 6, 140.

13. Michel Foucault, "What Is Enlightenment?" in *The Foucault Reader*, ed. Paul Rabinow (New York: Pantheon, 1984), p. 50.

14. Immanuel Kant, "What Is Enlightenment?" in *On History*, ed. Lewis White Beck (Indianapolis: Bobbs-Merril, 1963), p. 3.

Selected Bibliography

TEXTBOOKS

Aydoğdu, İsmail. *Türkçe ilkokul 2.* Ankara: Öğün Yayınları, 1986.
———, *Türkçe ilkokul 3.* Ankara: Öğ ün Yayınları, 1986.
———, *Türkçe ilkokul 5,* Ankara: Türk Tarih Kurumu Basımevi, 1988.
Birkan, Abdullah, et al. *Ortaokullarda Türkçe dersleri 1.* İstanbul: Ders Kitapları Anonim Şirketi, 1987.
Ergintürk, M. Ayçin, and İhsan Esatoğlu, *Ortaokullar için millî coğrafya ana ders kitabı 2.* İstanbul: Millî Eğitim Basımevi, 1987.
İlkokul hayat bilgisi 3. İstanbul: Millî Eğitim Basım, 1990.
İlkokul Türkçe ders kitabı 1. Istanbul: Karacan Yayınları, 1989.
İlkokul Türkçe ders kitabı 3. Ankara: Türk Tarih Kurumu Basımevi, 1990.
İlkokul Türkçe ders kitabı 4. İstanbul: Media Print, 1990.
İlkokul Türkçe ders kitabı 5. İstanbul: Hurriyet Ofset, 1990.
Karayiğit, Mehmet, and Birgül Karayiğit. *Çukurova için hayat bilgisi—Türkçe kaynak kitabı sınıf 2.* Adana: Güney Matbaası, 1986.
Necmeddin Sadık. *Sosyoloji, liseler için yeni programa göre.* Ankara: Devlet Matbaası, 1936.
Öğün, Vedat. *Özetli-testli ilkokul hayat bilgisi sınıf 2.* Ankara: Öğün Yayınları, 1982.
Parmaksızoğlu, İsmet. *Ortaokullar için Türkiye cumhuriyeti inkılâp tarihi ve Atatürkçülük.* İstanbul: Millî Eğitim Basımevi, 1988.
Resimli yeni aile bilgisi sınıf 4. İstanbul: Biryayınevi, 1959.
Tekışık, Hüseyin Hüsnü. *Hayat bilgisi ünitelerine kaynak kitap 3.* Ankara: Tekışı k Matbaası ve Rehber Yayınevi, 1983.
Tunç, Cihad. *Ortaokullar için din kültürü ve ahlâk bilgisi 2.* İstanbul: Millî Eğitim Basımevi, 1987.
Tunç, Cihad. *Ortaokullar için din kültürü ve ahlâk bilgisi 3.* İstanbul: Millî Eğitim Basımevi, 1986.
Ünal, Oğuz, and Cafer Tayyar Karaoğuz. *Ortaokullar için, millî coğrafya ana ders kitabı 1.* İstanbul: Millî Eğitim Basımevi, 1987.

Vatandaşlık bilgisi orta 3. İstanbul: Millî Eğitim Basımevi, 1987.

BOOKS AND ARTICLES

Abrams, Philip. "Notes on the Difficulty of Studying the State." *Journal of Historical Sociology* 1 (1988), pp. 58–89.

Abu-Lughod, Lila. "Do Muslim Women Really Need Saving? Anthropological Reflections on Cultural Relativism and Its Others." *American Anthropologist* 104 (2002), pp. 783–90.

Agha, Asif. "Register." *Journal of Linguistic Anthropology* 9 (2000), pp. 216–19.

Ahmad, Feroz. *The Turkish Experiment in Democracy, 1950–1975.* Boulder, CO: Westview, 1977.

——. "Politics and Islam in Modern Turkey." *Middle Eastern Studies* 27 (1991), pp. 3–21.

Ahmed Emin, *Turkey in the War.* New Haven, CT: Yale University Press, 1930.

Aksoy, Mustafa. "Akif'e göre aile, eğitim ve aydınlar." *Millî Eğitim* 95 (1990), pp. 39–42.

Akyol, Avni. "TÜSİAD ın hazırlattığı 'Türkiye'de eğitim' raporu üzerine." *Millî Eğitim* 102 (1990), pp. 4–12.

Akyüz, Yahya. "Atatürk ve 1921 Eğitim Kongresi." In *Cumhuriyet döneminde eğitim,* pp. 87–104. İstanbul: Millî Eğitim Basımevi, 1983.

Ali, Kamran Asdar. *Planning the Family in Egypt: New Bodies, New Selves.* Austin: University of Texas Press, 2002.

Alishan, Léonce. *Sissouan, ou l'Arméno-Cilicie.* Venice: St. Lazare, 1899.

Altinay. Ayse Gul. *The Myth of the Military Nation: Militarism, Gender, and Education in Turkey.* New York: Palgrave Macmillan, 2004.

Anagnost, Ann. *National Pastimes: Narrative, Representation, and Power in Modern China (Body, Commodity, Text).* Durham, NC: Duke University Press, 1997.

Apaydın, Talip. *Karanlığın kuvveti: Köy Enstitüsü yılları.* İstanbul: Ararat Yayınevi, 1967.

Appadurai, Arjun. "Global Ethnoscapes: Notes and Queries for a Transnational Anthropology." In *Recapturing Anthropology: Working in the Present,* ed. Richard Fox, pp. 191–210. Santa Fe, NM: School of American Research Press, 1991.

Arat, Yesim. "The Project of Modernity and Women in Turkey." In *Rethinking Modernity and National Identity in Turkey,* ed. Sibel Bozdoğan and Reşat Kasaba, pp. 95–112. Seattle: University of Washington Press, 1997.

Arendt, Hannah. *The Life of the Mind,* vol. 1. London: Secker & Warburg, 1978.

Aretxaga, Begoña. "Terror as Thrill: First Thoughts on the 'War on Terrorism.'" *Anthropological Quarterly* 75 (2002), pp. 39–150.

Aries, Philippe. *Centuries of Childhood: A Social History of Family Life.* New York: Vintage, 1962.

Arkın, Ramazan Gökalp. *İlkokul öğretmenine temel kitap: köy ve şehir öğretmenlerinin, öğretmen olacakların ve ilköğretimle ilgililerin kitabı.* İstanbul: Türkiye Yayınevi, 1966.

Arrighi, Giovanni. *The Long Twentieth Century: Money, Power, and the Origins of Our Times.* London: Verso, 1994.

Asad, Talal. *Formations of the Secular: Christianity, Islam, Modernity.* Stanford, CA: Stanford University Press, 2003.

Atatürk, Mustafa Kemal. *Atatürk'ün Söylev ve Demeçleri II.* Ankara: Maarif Matbaası, 1952.

Bakhtin, M. M. "Discourse in the Novel." In *The Dialogic Imagination: Four Essays by M. M. Bakhtin,* ed. Michael Holquist, trans. Caryl Emerson and Michael Holquist, pp. 259–422. Austin: University of Texas Press, 1981.

Baloğlu, Zekâi. "Atatürk et l'enseignement religieux en Turquie." In *La Turquie et la France à l'époque d'Atatürk,* ed. Paul Dumont and Jean Louis Braqué-Grammont (Paris: Association pour le développement des études turques, 1981), pp. 215–28.

———. *Türkiye'de eğitim, sorunlar ve değişime yapısal uyum önerileri.* İstanbul: TÜSİAD Yayınları, 1990.

Başgöz, Ilhan, and Howard E. Wilson. *Educational Problems in Turkey 1920–1940.* Bloomington: Indiana University Publications, 1968.

Bashford, Alison. *Imperial Hygiene: A Critical History of Colonialism, Nationalism and Public Health.* Basingstoke, UK: Palgrave Macmillan, 2004.

Baudrillard, Jean. "Consumer Society." In *Jean Baudrillard: Selected Writings,* ed. Mark Poster, pp. 29–56. Cambridge, UK: Polity Press, 1988.

Bauman, Richard, and Charles L. Briggs. "Poetics and Performance as Critical Perspectives on Language and Social Life." *Annual Review of Anthropology* 19 (1990), pp. 59–88.

Benjamin, Walter. "The Storyteller." In *Illuminations,* ed. Hannah Arendt, pp. 83–109. New York: Shocken, 1985.

Ben-Rafael, Eliezer. *Language, Identity and Social Division.* Oxford: Clarendon, 1994.

Berkes, Niyazi. *The Development of Secularism in Turkey.* Montreal: McGill University Press, 1964.

Bernstein, Basil. "A Sociolinguistic Approach to Socialization, with Some Reference to Educability." In *Directions in Social Linguistics: The Ethnography of Communication,* ed. J. G. Gumpertz and D. Hymes, pp. 465–97. New York: Holt, Rinehart, & Winston, 1972.

Bhabha, Homi K. "DissemiNation: Time, Narrative, and the Margins of the Modern Nation," pp. 291–322. In *Nation and Narration.* London: Routledge, 1990.

Bhargava, Rajeev. *Individualism in Social Science: Forms and Limits of a Methodology.* Oxford: Clarendon, 1992.

Bianchi, Robert. *Interest Groups and Political Development in Turkey.* Princeton, NJ: Princeton University Press, 1984.

Bilgegil, M. Kaya. *Ziyâ Paşa üzerinde bir araştırma*. Erzurum: Atatürk Üniversitesi Basımevi, 1970.

Bilgiseven, Amiran Kurtkan. *Millî eğitim sistemimiz nasıl olmalıdır?* İstanbul: Türk Dünyası Araştırmaları Vakfı, 1986.

Birand, Mehmet Ali. *Shirts of Steel: An Anatomy of the Turkish Armed Forces*, trans. Saliha Paker and Ruth Christie. London: Tauris, 1991.

Bourdieu, Pierre. "The School as a Conservative Force: Scholastic and Cultural Inequalities." In *Contemporary Research in the Sociology of Education*, ed. John Eggleston, pp. 32–46. London: Methuen, 1974.

———. *Outline of a Theory of Practice*, trans. Richard Nice. Cambridge, UK: Cambridge University Press, 1977.

———. "Rethinking the State: Genesis and Structure of the Bureaucratic Field." In *State/Culture: The Study of State Formation after the Cultural Turn*, ed. George Steinmetz, pp. 53–75. Ithaca, NY: Cornell University Press, 1999.

Brown, Richard Harvey. "The Position of the Narrative in Contemporary Society." *New Literary History* 11(1979–80), pp. 545–50.

Brubaker, Roger. *Citizenship and Nationhood in France and Germany*. Cambridge, MA: Harvard University Press, 1992.

Brysk, Alison. *From Tribal Village to Global Village: Indian Rights and International Relations in Latin America*. Stanford, CA: Stanford University Press, 2000.

Bugra, Ayse. "The Place of the Economy in Turkish Society." *South Atlantic Quarterly* 102 (2003), pp. 453–70.

Butler, Judith. "Contingent Foundations: Feminism and the Question of 'Postmodernism.'" In *Feminists Theorize the Political*, ed. Judith Butler and Joan Scott, pp. 3–22. New York: Routledge, 1992.

Chakrabarty, Dipesh. "Postcoloniality and the Artifice of History: Who Speaks for 'Indian' Pasts." *Representations* 37 (1992), pp. 1–26.

Chatterjee, Partha. "History and the Nationalization of Hinduism." *Social Research* 59 (1992), pp. 111–49.

Cinar, Alev. "National History as a Contested Site: The Conquest of Istanbul and Islamist Negotiations of the Nation." *Comparative Studies in Society and History* 43 (2001), pp. 364–91.

Cohn, Bernard S. "The Census, Social Structure and Objectification in South Asia." In *An Anthropologist among the Historians and Other Essays*, pp. 224–54. New Delhi: Oxford University Press, 1990.

Collins, James. "Our Ideologies and Theirs." In *Language Ideologies: Practice and Theory*, ed. Bambi Schieffelin, Kathryn Woolard, and Paul Kroskrity, pp. 256–70. Oxford, UK: Oxford University Press, 1998.

Corrigan, Philip, and Derek Sayer. *The Great Arch: English State Formation as Cultural Revolution*. Oxford: Basil Blackwell, 1985.

Cunningham, Hugh. "Histories of Childhood." *American Historical Review* 103 (1998), pp. 1195–1208.

da Cunha, Manuela Carneiro. "Children, Politics and Culture: The Case of Brazilian Indians." In *Children and the Politics of Culture*, ed. Sharon Stephens, pp. 282–91. Princeton, NJ: Princeton University Press, 1995.

Das, Veena, and Deborah Poole, eds. *Anthropology in the Margins of the State*. Santa Fe, NM: School of American Research Press, 2004.

de Certeau, Michel. *The Practice of Everyday Life*, trans. Steven F. Rendall. Berkeley: University of California Press, 1984.

Değerler ve Yaşam Biçimleri Araştırması. *Values and Lifestyles Research. Part II: Quantitative*. İstanbul: Doğrudan Pazarlama A. Ş., 1989.

Delaney, Carol. *The Seed and the Soil: Gender and Cosmology in Turkish Village Society*. Berkeley: University of California Press, 1991.

———. 1994. "Untangling the Meanings of Hair in Turkish Society." *Anthropological Quarterly* 67 (4), pp. 159–72.

Deringil, Selim. "The Ottoman Origins of Kemalist Nationalism: Namik Kemal to Mustafa Kemal." *European History Quarterly* 23 (1993), pp. 165–92.

———. *The Well-Protected Domains: Ideology and the Legitimation of Power in the Ottoman Empire, 1876–1909*. London: I. B. Tauris, 1998.

Derrida, Jacques. "Structure, Sign and Play in the Discourse of the Human Sciences." In *Writing and Difference*, trans. Alan Bass, pp. 278–93. London: Routledge, 1978.

de Rudder, Véronique. "L'obstacle culturel: la différence et la distance." *L'homme et la société* 77–78 (1985), pp. 23–48.

Desrosières, Alain. *The Politics of Large Numbers: A History of Statistical Reasoning*, trans. Camille Naish. Cambridge, MA: Harvard University Press, 1998.

Dilipak, Abdurrahman. *Bu din benim dinim değil: "resmi din" öğretisine eleştirel bir yaklaşım*. İstanbul: İşaret-Ferşat Ortak Yayınları, 1990.

Dinçer, Nahid. *1913'ten günümüze imam-hatip okulları meselesi*. İstanbul: Şule Yayınları, 1998.

Duben, Alan, and Cem Behar. *Istanbul Households: Marriage, Family and Fertility, 1880–1940*. Cambridge, UK: Cambridge University Press, 1991.

Eickelman, Dale F. "Mass Higher Education and the Religious Imagination in Contemporary Arab Societies." *American Ethnologist* 19 (1992), pp. 643–55.

Erdentuğ, Nermin. *Hal köyü'nün etnolojik tetkiki*. Ankara: Türk Tarih Kurumu Basımevi, 1954.

Euben, Roxanne L. *Enemy in the Mirror: Islamic Fundamentalism and the Limits of Modern Rationalism, a Work of Comparative Political Theory*. Princeton, NJ: Princeton University Press, 1999.

Faroqhi, Suraiya. "Rural Society in Anatolia and the Balkans in the Sixteenth Century, I." *Turcica* 9 (1977), pp. 161–95.

Ferguson, Ann Arnett. 2000. *Bad Boys: Public Schools in the Making of Black Masculinity*. Ann Arbor: University of Michigan Press, 2000.

Fleischer, Cornell. "Royal Authority, Dynastic Cyclism, and 'Ibn Khaldūnism' in

Sixteenth-Century Ottoman Letters." *Journal of Asian and African Studies* 18 (1983), pp. 198–220.

Fortna, Benjamin C. *Imperial Classroom: Islam, the State and Education in the Late Ottoman Empire*. Oxford, UK: Oxford University Press, 2002.

Foucault, Michel. *Language, Counter-Memory, Practice*. Trans. Donald Bouchard. Ithaca, NY: Cornell University Press, 1977.

———. "Truth and Power." In *Power/Knowledge: Selected Writings 1972–1977*, ed. Colin Gordon. New York: Pantheon, 1980, pp. 109–33.

———. *The History of Sexuality, Volume 1: An Introduction*. Harmondsworth, Middlesex, UK: Penguin, 1981.

———. "What Is Enlightenment?" In *The Foucault Reader*, ed. Paul Rabinow, pp. 32–50. New York: Pantheon, 1984.

———. "Governmentality." In *The Foucault Effect: Studies in Governmentality*, ed. Graham Bruchell et al., pp. 87–104. Chicago: University of Chicago Press, 1991.

Frazer, Elizabeth, and Nicola Lacey. 2003. "Public-Private Distinctions." In *Contemporary Political Thought*, ed. Alan Finlayson. Edinburg: Edinburgh University Press, pp. 328–32.

Friedl, Erika. "Why Are Children Missing from Textbooks." *Anthropology News* 43 (2002), p. 19.

Gal, Susan, and Judith Irvine. "The Boundaries of Languages and Disciplines: How Ideologies Construct Difference." *Social Research* 62 (1995), pp. 966–1001.

Gal, Susan, and Gail Kligman. *The Politics of Gender after Socialism: A Comparative-Historical Essay*. Princeton, NJ: Princeton University Press, 2000.

Gani, Veysel. "Osmanlı eğitim sistemi, *Millî Eğitim* 85 (1989), pp. 49–55.

Geertz, Clifford. "Concepts of Culture." In *The Interpretation of Cultures: Selected Essays*, pp. 249–54. New York: Basic Books, 1973.

———. *Negara: The Theatre State in 19th Century Bali*. Princeton, NJ: Princeton University Press, 1981.

Gil'adi, Avner. *Children of Islam: Concepts of Childhood in Medieval Muslim Society*. New York: St. Martin's, 1992.

Gill, Stephen. "Globalisation, Market Civilisation and Disciplinary Neoliberalism." *Millennium* 24 (1995), pp. 399–423.

Goffman, Erving. *The Presentation of Self in Everyday Life*. New York: Doubleday, 1959.

Gökalp, Ziya. *Turkish Nationalism and Western Civilization*, ed. and trans. Niyazi Berkes. London: Allen & Unwin, 1959.

Goldberg, H. I., and A. Toros. "The Use of Traditional Methods of Contraception among Turkish Couples." *Studies in Family Planning* 25 (1994), pp. 122–28.

Göle, Nilufer. *The Forbidden Modern: Civilization and Veiling*. Ann Arbor: University of Michigan Press, 1996.

Gould, Andrew Gordon. "Lords or Bandits? The Derebeys of Cilicia." *International*

Journal of Middle Eastern Studies 7 (1976), pp. 485–506.

Gramsci, Antonio. *Selections from the Prison Notebooks*, trans. Quintin Hoare and Geoffrey N. Smith. New York: International Publishers, 1971.

Grosz, Elizabeth. *Becomings: Explorations in Time, Memory and Futures*. Ithaca, NY: Cornell University Press, 1999.

Guha, Ranajit. "The Small Voice of History." In *Subaltern Studies IX*, ed. Shahid Amin and Dipesh Chakrabarty, pp. 1–42. New Delhi: Oxford University Press, 1996.

Güvenç, Bozkurt, et al. *Türk-İslam sentezi dosyası*. İstanbul: Sarmal Yayınevi, 1991.

Haarman, Ulrich W. "Ideology and History, Identity and Alterity: The Arab Image of the Turk from the Àbassids to Modern Egypt." *International Journal of Middle Eastern Studies* 20 (1988), pp. 175–96.

Hacettepe Institute for Population Studies. *The 1988 Turkish Population and Health Survey*. Ankara: HIPS, 1989.

Hacking, Ian. "How Should We Do the History of Statistics?" In *The Foucault Effect: Studies in Governmentality*, ed. Graham Burchell, Colin Gordon, and Peter Miller, pp. 181–96. Chicago: University of Chicago Press, 1991.

Hale, William. *Turkish Politics and the Military*. London: Routledge, 1994.

Hamayon, Roberte. "L'os distinctif et la chair indifférente." *Etudes mongoles et sibériennes* 6 (1975), pp. 99–122.

Handler, Richard. *Nationalism and the Politics of Culture in Quebec*. Madison: University of Wisconsin Press, 1988.

Handwerker, W. Penn. "The Modern Demographic Transition: An Analysis of Subsistence Choices and Reproductive Consequences." *American Anthropologist* 88 (1986), pp. 400–417.

Hansen, Thomas Blom, and Finn Stepputat, ed. *States of Imagination: Ethnographic Explorations of the Postcolonial State*. Durham, NC: Duke University Press, 2001.

Harris, George S. "The Role of the Military in Turkey in the 1980s: Guardians or Decision-Makers?" In *State, Democracy and the Military: Turkey in the 1980s*, ed. Metin Heper and Ahmet Evin, pp. 177–200. New York: Walter de Gruyter, 1988.

Harvey, David. *The Condition of Postmodernity: An Enquiry into the Origins of Cultural Change*, Oxford: Basil Blackwell, 1989.

Heath, Shirley Brice. *Ways with Words: Language, Life, and Work in Communities and Classrooms*. Cambridge, UK: Cambridge University Press, 1983.

Helling, George, and Barbara Helling. "Values Implicit in Turkish Images of Human Types: An Empirical Approach." *Turkish Studies Association Bulletin* 10 (1986), pp. 87–97.

Helman, Sarit. "Militarism and the Construction of the Life-World of Israeli Males: The Case of the Reserves System." In *The Military and Militarism in Israeli Society*, ed. Edna Lomsky-Feder and Eyal Ben-Ari, pp. 191–221. Albany: State University of New York Press, 1999.

Heper, Metin. "Islam, Polity and Society in Turkey: A Middle Eastern Perspective." *Middle East Journal* 35 (1981), pp. 345–63.

Herzfeld, Michael. *The Social Production of Indifference: Exploring the Symbolic Roots of Western Bureaucracy.* Chicago: University of Chicago Press, 1992.

Heywood, Colin. *A History of Childhood: Children and Childhood in the West from Medieval to Modern Times,* Malden, MA: Blackwell, 2001.

Hiner, N. Ray, and Joseph M. Hawes, ed. *Growing up in America: Children in Historical Perspective.* Urbana: University of Illinois Press, 1985.

Hirschfeld, Lawrence. *Race in the Making: Cognition, Culture, and the Child's Construction of Human Kinds.* Cambridge, MA: MIT Press, 1996.

———. "The Inside Story." *American Anthropologist* 102 (2000), pp. 620–29.

Holzhausen, Walter. "The Population Problem in Turkey (as Seen from the Perspective of a Foreign Donor)." *Nufusbilim Dergisi/Turkish Journal of Population Studies* 9 (1987), pp. 63–73.

Hunt, Lynn Avery. *The Family Romance of the French Revolution.* Berkeley: University of California Press, 1992.

Huntington, Samuel P. *The Clash of Civilizations and the Remaking of World Order.* New York: Simon & Schuster, 1996.

Inalcik, Halil. "State, Sovereignty and Law during the Reign of Süleyman." In *Süleymân the Second and His Time,* ed. Halil Inalcik and Cemal Kafadar, pp. 59–92. Istanbul: Isis Press, 1993.

İnan, M. Rauf. "Anaysalarımızda ve anayasalarda eğitim." In *VIII. Türk tarih kongresi: kongreye sunulan bildiriler: Ankara, 12–15 ekim 1976,* 3:2117–185. Ankara: Türk Tarih Kurumu Basımevi, 1983.

Işık, Emin. "Geleneksel aile yapımızı neye borçluyuz." *Türk Edebiyatı* 202 (1990), pp. 35–36.

Jacob, P. Xavier. *L'enseignement religieux dans la Turquie moderne.* Berlin: Klaus Schwarz Verlag, 1982.

Jahoda, Gustav, and I. M. Lewis. *Acquiring Culture: Cross Cultural Studies in Child Development.* London: Routledge, 1988.

Jameson, Frederic. "Postmodernism, or, the Cultural Logic of Late Capitalism." *New Left Review* 146 (1984), pp. 59–92.

Joseph, Suad. "The Public/Private—The Imagined Boundary in the Imagined Nation/State/Community: The Lebanese Case." *Feminist Review* 57 (1997), pp. 73–92.

Kagitçibasi, Cigdem. "Social Norms and Authoritarianism: A Turkish-American Comparison." *Journal of Personality and Social Psychology* 16 (1970), pp. 444–51.

Kanad, Halil Fikret. *Ailede çocuk terbiyesi.* İstanbul: Millî Eğitim Basımevi, 1969.

Kandiyoti, Deniz. "Women's Place in Turkish Society: A Comparative Approach." *Current Turkish Thought* 30 (1977), pp. 1–21.

———. "Women and Household Production: The Impact of Rural Transformation in Turkey." In *The Rural Middle East: Peasant Lives and Modes of Production,* ed. Kathy Glavanis and Pandeli Glavanis, pp. 183–95. London: Zed, 1989.

———. "The Politics of Gender and the Conundrums of Citizenship." In *Women and Power in the Middle East*, ed. Suad Joseph and Susan Slyomovics, pp. 52–58. Philadelphia: University of Pennsylvania Press, 2001.

Kant, Immanuel. "What Is Enlightenment?" In *On History*, ed. Lewis White Beck, pp. 3–10. Indianapolis: Bobbs-Merril, 1963.

Kaplan, İsmail. *Türkiye'de Millî Eğitim ideolojisi ve siyasal toplumsallaşma üzerindeki etkisi*. İstanbul: İletişim, 1999.

Kaplan, Sam. "Education and the Politics of National Culture in a Turkish Community, ca. 1990." PhD diss., Department of Anthropology, University of Chicago, 1996.

———. "Documenting History, Historicizing Documentation: French Military Officials' Ethnological Reports on Cilicia." *Comparative Studies in Society and History* 42 (2002), pp. 344–69.

———. "Nuriye's Dilemma: Turkish Lessons of Democracy and the Gendered State." *American Ethnologist* 30 (2003), pp. 401–17.

———. "Territorializing Armenians: Geo-texts, and Political Imaginaries in French-occupied Cilicia, 1919–1922." *History and Anthropology* 15 (2004), pp. 399–423.

Karpat, Kemal H. "The People's House in Turkey." *Middle East Journal* (1963), pp. 55–67.

Karslı, Ferid. *Bir köy öğretmeninin anıları*. Ankara: Köyhocası Basımevi, 1935.

Kasaba, Resat. "Migrant Labor in Western Anatolia, 1750–1850." In *Landholding and Commercial Agriculture in the Middle East*, ed. Çaglar Keyder and Faruk Tabak, pp. 113–21. Albany: State University of New York Press, 1991.

Keane, Webb. *Signs of Recognition: Powers and Hazards of Representation in an Indonesian Society*. Berkeley: University of California Press, 1997.

Kern, Stephen. *The Culture of Time and Space 1880–1918*. Cambridge, MA: Harvard University Press, 1983.

Keyder, Çağlar. *State and Society in Turkey: A Study in Capitalist Development*. London: Verso, 1987.

Keyes, Charles F. "The Proposed World of the School: Thai Villagers' Entry into a Bureaucratic State System." In *Reshaping Local Worlds: Rural Education and Cultural Change in Southeast Asia*, ed. Charles F. Keyes, pp. 87–138. New Haven, CT: Yale Center for International and Area Studies, 1991.

Kinross, John Patrick. *Within the Taurus*. London: John Murray, 1954.

Koçer, Hasan Ali. *Türkiye'de modern eğitimin doğuşu ve gelişimi (1773–1923)*. İstanbul: Millî Eğitim Basımevi, 1970.

Koselleck, Reinhart. "'Progress' and 'Decline': An Appendix to the History of Two Concepts." In *The Practice of Conceptual History: Timing History, Spacing Concepts*, trans. Todd Samuel Presner et al., pp. 218–35. Stanford, CA: Stanford University Press, 2002.

Kotschy, Theodor. *Reise in den Cilicischen Taurus über Tarsus.* Gotha: Verlag von Fustus Berthes, 1858.

"Köy öğretmen ve eğitmeni yetiştirme işi," *Ülkü* 8 (1936), pp. 259–67.

Kur, İsmet. *Turkiye'de süreli çocuk yayınları.* Ankara: Atatürk Kültür Merkezi, 1991.

Kusserow, Adrie Suzanne. "Crossing the Great Divide: Anthropological Theories of the Western Self." *Journal of Anthropological Research* 55 (1999), pp. 541–62.

Lacan, Jacques. "Of the Gaze as *Objet Petit a.*" In *The Four Fundamental Concepts of Psycho-Analysis,* ed. Jacques-Alain Miller, trans. Alan Sheridan, pp. 67–119. New York: Norton, 1978.

Landau, Jacob M. *Politics and Islam: The National Salvation Party in Turkey.* Salt Lake City: Middle East Center, University of Utah, 1976.

Langlois, Victor. *Voyage dans la Cilicie et les montagnes du Taurus: éxécuté pendant les années 1852–53.* Paris: Benjamin Duprat, 1861.

Lave, Jean, Paul Duguid, Nancy Fernandez, and Eric Axel. "Coming of Age in Birmingham: Cultural Studies and Conceptions of Subjectivity." *Annual Review of Anthropology* 21 (1992), pp. 257–82.

Lave, Jean, and Etienne Wenger. *Situated Learning: Legitimate Peripheral Participation* Cambridge, UK: Cambridge University Press, 1991.

Leder, Arnold. *Catalysts of Change: Marxist versus Muslim in a Turkish Community.* Austin: University of Texas Press, 1976.

Lerner, Daniel. *The Passing of Traditional Society: Modernizing the Middle East.* New York: Free Press, 1958.

Lerner, Daniel, and Richard D. Robinson. "Swords and Ploughshares: The Turkish Army as a Modernizing Force." *World Politics* 13 (1960), pp. 19–44.

Lévi-Strauss, Claude. *Les structures élémentaires de la parenté.* Paris: Mouton, 1967.

Levinson, Bradley A., Douglas Foley, and Dorothy Holland, eds. *The Cultural Production of the Educated Person: Critical Ethnographies of Schooling and Local Practice.* Albany: State University of New York Press, 1996.

Lewis, Bernard. "Islamic Revival in Turkey." *International Affairs* 28 (1952), pp. 38–48.

———. *The Emergence of Modern Turkey.* Oxford, UK: Oxford University Press, 1968.

Lomnitz, Claudio. *Deep Mexico, Silent Mexico: An Anthropology of Nationalism.* Minneapolis: University of Minnesota Press, 2001.

Luke, Carmen, Suzanne DeCastell, and Alan Luke. "Beyond Criticism: The Authority of the School Text." *Curriculum Inquiry* 13 (1983), pp. 111–27.

Magnarella, Paul. "Turkish Townsmen View Apollo." *The Middle East Journal* 26 (1972), pp. 181–83.

———. "Civil Violence in Turkey: Its Infrastructural, Social and Cultural Foundations." In *Sex Roles, Family and Community in Turkey,* ed. Çiğdem Kâğıtçıbaşı, pp. 383–401. Bloomington: Indiana University Turkish Studies, 1982.

———. "State Politics: Desecularization, State Corporatism, and Elite Behavior in

Turkey." In *Human Materialism: A Model of Sociocultural Systems and a Strategy for Analysis*, pp. 87–113. Gainesville: University Press of Florida, 1993.

Mahmood, Saba. "Feminist Theory, Embodiment, and the Docile Agent: Some Reflections on the Egyptian Islamic Revival." *Cultural Anthropology* 16 (2001), pp. 202–36.

Makal, Mahmut. *A Village in Anatolia*, trans. Wyndham Deedes. London: Valentine, Mitchell, 1954.

Mandel, Ruth. "Turkish Headscarves and the 'Foreigner Problem': Constructing Difference through Emblems of Identity." *New German Critique* 46 (1989), pp. 27–46.

Marcus, Julie. *A World of Difference: Islam and Gender Hierarchy in Turkey*. London: Allen & Unwin, 1992.

Mardin, Serif. *The Genesis of Young Ottoman Thought: A Study in the Modernization of Turkish Political Ideas*, Princeton, NJ: Princeton University Press, 1962.

———. "Youth and Violence in Turkey." *Archives européennes de sociologie* 19 (1978), pp. 229–54.

———. "The Just and the Unjust." *Daedalus* 120 (1991), pp. 113–29.

———. "Projects as Methodology: Some Thoughts on Modern Turkish Social Science." In *Rethinking Modernity and National Identity in Turkey*, ed. Sibel Bozdoğan and Reşat Kasaba, pp. 64–80. Seattle: University of Washington Press, 1997.

Marshall, Judith. *Literacy, Power, and Democracy in Mozambique: The Governance of Learning from Colonization to the Present*. Boulder, CO: Westview, 1993.

McClintock, Anne. *Imperial Leather: Race, Gender, and Sexuality in the Colonial Contest*. New York: Routledge, 1995.

Mead, George Herbert. *Mind, Self, and Society*. Chicago: University of Chicago Press, 1934.

Meeker, Michael. "The New Muslim Intellectuals in the Republic of Turkey." In *Islam in Modern Turkey: Religion, Politics and Literature in a Secular State*, ed. Richard Tapper, pp. 189–219. London: I. B. Tauris, 1991.

Mehmet Saffet, "Köycülük nedir?" *Ülkü* 6 (1933), pp. 422–30.

Menemencioğlu, Nermin. *The Penguin Book of Turkish Verse*, collab. Fahir Iz. Harmondsworth, Middlesex, UK: Penguin, 1978.

Merleau-Ponty, Maurice. *Phenomenology of Perception*, trans. Colin Smith. New York: Humanities Press, 1962.

Millî Eğitim Bakanlığı. *İlkokul programı*. İstanbul: Millî Eğitim Basımevi, 1968.

Mitchell, Allan. *Victors and Vanquished: The German Influence on Army and Church in France after 1870*. Chapel Hill: University of North Carolina Press, 1984.

Mitchell, Timothy. *Colonising Egypt*. Cambridge, UK: Cambridge University Press, 1988.

Moore, Barrington, Jr. *The Social Origins of Dictatorship and Democracy*. New York: Beacon, 1966.

Moore, Sally Falk. "Explaining the Present: Theoretical Dilemmas in Processual Ethnography." *American Ethnologist* 14 (1987), pp. 727–36.

Navaro-Yashin, Yael. *Faces of the State: Secularism and Public Life in Turkey.* Princeton, NJ: Princeton University Press, 2002.

Nettle, David. "On the Status of Methodological Individualism." *Current Anthropology* 38 (1997), pp. 283–86.

Neumann, Iver B., and Jennifer M. Welsh. "The Other in European Self-definition: An Addendum to the Literature on International Relations." *Review of International Studies* 17 (1991), pp. 327–48.

Nietzsche, Friedrich. *On the Genealogy of Morals.* New York: Vintage, 1967.

Olson, Emilie. "Muslim Identity and Secularism in Contemporary Turkey: 'The Headscarf Dispute.'" *Anthropological Quarterly* 58 (1985), pp. 161–71.

Organisation for Economic Co-operation and Development (OECD). *Turkey.* Washington, DC: OECD Publications and Information Center, 1989.

Ong, Aihwa. *Flexible Citizenship: The Cultural Logics of Transnationality.* Durham, NC: Duke University Press, 1999.

Onuncu Millî Eğitim Şûrâsı. *Onuncu Millî Eğitim Şûrâsı: 23–26 Haziran 1981.* Ankara: Millî Eğitim Basımevi, 1981.

Ortaylı, İlber. *İmparatorluğun en uzun yüzyılı.* İstanbul: Hil Yayın, 1983.

Özgönenç, Fikret. *Ailenin eğitim görevleri.* İstanbul: Remzi Kitabevi, 1972.

Page, Kirby. "Nationalism Interprets Islam." *Christian Century* 47 (1930), pp. 113–14.

Parla, Taha. *The Social and Political Thought of Ziya Gökalp 1876–1924.* Leiden, Netherlands: E. J. Brill, 1985.

Petryna, Adriana. *Life Exposed: Biological Citizenship After Chernobyl.* Princeton, NJ: Princeton University Press, 2002.

Pierce, Joe. *Life in a Turkish Village.* New York: Holt, Rinehart, & Winston, 1964.

Prakash, Gyan, "Can the 'Subaltern' Ride? A Reply to O'Hanlon and Washbrook." *Comparative Studies in Society and History* 34 (1992), pp. 168–84.

Pratt, Mary Louise. "Scratches on the Face of the Country; or, What Mr. Barrow Saw in the Land of the Bushmen." *Critical Inquiry* 12 (1986), pp. 119–43.

Proctor, Robert. *Racial Hygiene: Medicine under the Nazis.* Cambridge, MA: Harvard University Press, 1988.

Psacharopoulos, George, and Maureen Woodhall. *Education for Development: An Analysis of Investment Choice.* New York: Oxford University Press, 1985.

Ram, Kalpana, and Margaret Jolly. *Borders of Being: Citizenship, Sexuality and Reproduction in Asia and the Pacific.* Ann Arbor: University of Michigan Press, 2001.

Reed, Howard. "Turkey's New Imam-Hatip Schools." *Welt des Islam* 4 (1956), pp. 150–63.

———. "Secularism and Islam in Turkish Politics." *Current History* 32 (1957), pp. 333–38.

Reed-Danahay, Deborah. *Education and Identity in Rural France: The Politics of*

Schooling. Cambridge, UK: Cambridge University Press, 1996.

Rosaldo, Renato, ed. *Cultural Citizenship in Island Southeast Asia: Nation and Belonging in the Hinterlands*. Berkeley: University of California Press, 2003.

Sahin, Abdullah. "Critical/dialogic Islamic Education: Modes of Religious Subjectivity towards Islam among British Muslim Youth." PhD diss., Department of Education, University of Birmingham, 2003.

Saktanber, Ayse-Nur. *Living Islam: Women, Religion and the Politicization of Culture in Turkey*. London: I. B. Tauris, 2002.

Salnâme-i Vilâyet-i Adana. Adana: Vilayeti Matbaası, [1312] 1894.

Sartre, Jean-Paul. *Being and Nothingness*, trans. Hazel E. Barnes, New York: Philosophical Library, 1956.

Sassen, Saskia. "Economic Globalization and the Redrawing of Citizenship." In *Moral Imperialism: A Critical Anthology*, ed. Berta Esperanza Hernanez-Truyol, pp. 135–50. New York: New York University Press, 2002.

Scognamillo, Giovanni. *Türk sinema tarihi: ikinci cilt 1960–1986*. İstanbul: Metis Yayıncılık, 1987.

Segalen, Martine. *Historical Anthropology of the Family*. Cambridge, UK: Cambridge University Press, 1986.

Shankland, David. *Islam and Society in Turkey*. Huntingdon, UK: Eothen Press, 1999.

Silverstein, Michael. "The Uses and Utility of Ideology: A Commentary." In *Language Ideologies: Practice and Theory*, ed. Bambi Schieffelin, Kathryn Woolard, and Paul Kroskrity, pp. 123–45. New York: Oxford University Press, 1998.

———. 2003. "The Whens and Wheres—As well as Hows—of Ethnolinguistic Recognition." *Public Culture* 15 (2003), pp. 531–57.

Silverstein, Michael, and Greg Urban. "The Natural History of Discourse." In *Natural Histories of Discourse*, ed. M. Silverstein and G. Urban, pp. 1–17. Chicago: University of Chicago Press, 1996.

Sirman, Nükhet. 1990. "State, Village, and Gender in Western Turkey." In *Turkish State, Turkish Society*, ed. Andrew Finkel and Nükhet Sirman, pp. 21–51. London: Routledge, 1990.

———. "Friend or Foe? Forging Alliances with Other Women in a Village of Western Turkey." In *Women in Modern Turkish Society: A Reader*, ed. Sirin Tekeli, pp. 199–218. London: Zed, 1995.

Solberg, Ann. "Negotiating Childhood: Changing Constructions of Age for Norwegian Children." In *Constructing and Reconstructing Childhood: Contemporary Issues in the Sociological Study of Childhood*, ed. Allison James and Alan Prout, pp. 126–44. London: Falmer, 1997.

Soysal, Yasemin Nuhoglu. *Limits of Citizenship: Migrants and Postnational Membership in Europe*. Chicago: University of Chicago Press, 1994.

Spiro, Melford E. "Is the Western Conception of the Self 'Peculiar' within the Context of the World Cultures?" *Ethos* 21 (1993), pp. 107–53.

Sparke, Matthew, "Passports into Credit Cards: On the Borders and Spaces of Neoliberal Citizenship." In *Boundaries and Belonging: States and Societies in the Struggle to Shape Identities and Local Practices*, ed. Joel S. Migdal, pp. 251–83. Cambridge, MA: Cambridge University Press, 2004.

Spivak, Gayatri Chakravorty, "Can the Subaltern Speak?" In *Marxism and the Interpretation of Culture*, ed. Cary Nelson and Lawrence Grossberg, pp. 271–313. Urbana: University of Illinois Press, 1988.

Stambach, Amy. *Lessons from Mount Kilimanjaro: Schooling, Community, and Gender in East Africa*. New York: Routledge, 2000.

Starrett, Gregory. "Margins of Print: Children's Religious Literature in Egypt." *Journal of the Royal Anthropological Institute* 2 (1996), pp. 117–39.

————. *Putting Islam to Work: Education, Politics and Religious Transformation in Egypt*. Berkeley: University of California Press, 1998.

State Institute of Statistics. *Statistical Year Book of Turkey, 1993*. Ankara: Devlet İstatistik Enstitüsü Matbaası, 1993.

Stocking, George W., Jr. "Bones, Bodies, Behavior." In *Bones, Bodies, Behavior: Essays on Biological Anthropology*, ed. George W. Stocking, pp. 3–17. Madison: University of Wisconsin Press, 1988.

Stolcke, Verena. "Talking Culture: New Boundaries, New Rhetorics of Exclusion in Europe." *Current Anthropology* 36 (1995), pp. 1–24.

Szyliowicz, Joseph S. *A Political Analysis of Student Activism: The Turkish Case*. London: Sage, 1972.

Tanyu, Hikmet. *İslâm dininin düşmanları ve Allah'a inananlar*. İstanbul: Burak Yayınevi, 1989.

Tapper, Nancy, and Richard Tapper. "The Birth of the Prophet: Ritual and Gender in Turkish Islam." *Man* 22 (1987), pp. 69–92.

Tekeli, İlhan. "Türk-İslam Sentezi üzerine." *Bilim ve Sanat* 77 (1987), pp. 5–8.

Teoman, Zeki. "Tarih boyunca Mersin." *Tarih ve edebiyat mecmuası* 14 (1978), pp. 83–91.

Thompson, E. P. "History from Below." In *The Essential E. P. Thompson*, ed. Dorothy Thompson, pp. 481–89. New York: New Press, 2001.

Thorne, Barrie. *Gender Play: Girls and Boys in School*. New Brunswick, NJ: Rutgers University Press, 1993.

Tilly, Charles. "War Making and State Making as Organized Crime." In *Bringing the State Back In*, ed. Peter B. Evans, Dietrich Reuschemeyer, and Theda Skocpol, pp. 169–87. Cambridge, UK: Cambridge University Press, 1985.

Toprak, Binnaz. "Politicization of Islam in a Secular State: The National Salvation Party in Turkey." In *From Nationalism to Revolutionary Islam*, ed. Said Amir Arjomand, pp. 119–33. Oxford, UK: Macmillan, 1984.

————. "The State, Politics and Religion in Turkey." In *State, Democracy and the Military: Turkey in the 1980s*, ed. Metin Heper and Ahmet Evin, pp. 119–36. Berlin: Walter de Gruyter, 1988.

————. "Religion as State Ideology in a Secular Setting: The Turkish-Islamic Synthesis." In *Aspects of Religion in Secular Turkey*, ed. Malcolm Wagstaff, pp. 10–15. Durham, NC: Center for Middle Eastern and Islamic Studies, University of Durham, 1990.

Toprak, Zafer. "II. Meşrutiyet döneminde devlet, aile ve feminizm." In *Sosyokültürel değişme sürecinde Türk ailesi*, ed. Ezel Erverdi, pp. 228–37. Ankara: T. C. Başbakanlık Aile Araştırma Kurumu, 1992.

Toros, Taha. *Şair Ziya Paşa'nın Adana valiliği*. Adana: Yeni Adana Basımevi, 1940.

Trouillot, Michel-Rolph. *Haiti, State against Nation: The Origins and Legacy of Duvalierism*. New York: Monthly Review Press, 1990.

Tüccarzâde İbrahim Hilmi, "Aile hayatımızda Avrupalılaşmanın tesiri." In *Avrupalılaşmak, felaketlerimiz esbâbı*. İstanbul: Matbaa-ı Hayriye ve Sürekâsı, [1332] 1916.

Turan, Osman. "The Ideal of World Domination among the Medieval Turks." *Studia Islamica* 4 (1955), pp. 77–90.

Türkdoğan, Orhan. "Yaile yapıları." *Türk Edebiyatı* 202 (1990), pp. 41–42.

Turner, Graeme. *British Cultural Studies: An Introduction*. Boston, MA: Unwin Hyman, 1990.

Turner, Victor. "Dewey, Dilthey, and Drama: An Essay in the Anthropology of Experience." In *The Anthropology of Experience*, ed. Victor W. Turner and Edward M. Bruner, pp. 33–44. Urbana: University of Illinois Press, 1986.

Unat, Faik Reşit. *Türkiye eğitim sisteminin gelişmesine tarihî bir bakış*. Ankara: Millî Eğitim Basımevi, 1964.

Vogel, Ursula. "Is Citizenship Gender-Specific?" In *The Frontiers of Citizenship*, ed. Ursula Vogel and Michael Moran, pp. 58–85. London: Macmillan, 1991.

Vološinov, V. N. *Marxism and the Philosophy of Language*. Cambridge, MA: Harvard University Press, 1973.

Vygotsky, L. *Mind in Society: The Development of Higher Psychological Processes*. Cambridge, MA: Harvard University Press, 1978.

Weber, Max. *Economy and Society, II*. Berkeley: University of California Press, 1968.

Wedeen, Lisa. *Ambiguities of Domination: Politics, Rhetoric, and Symbols in Contemporary Syria*. Chicago: University of Chicago Press, 1999.

Weiker, Walter F. *The Turkish Revolution, 1960–1961: Aspects of Military Politics*. Washington, DC: Brookings Institution, 1963.

Wertsch, James V. *Voices of the Mind: A Sociocultural Approach to Mediated Action*. Cambridge, MA: Harvard University Press, 1991.

White, Jenny B. *Islamist Mobilization in Turkey: A Study in Vernacular Politics*. Seattle: University of Washington Press, 2002.

Wilk, Richard. "Learning to Be Local in Belize: Global Systems of Common Difference." In *Worlds Apart: Modernity through the Prism of the Local*, ed. Daniel Miller, pp. 110–33. London: Routledge, 1995.

Willis, Paul. *Learning to Labour: How Working Class Kids Get Working Class Jobs*.

New York: Columbia University Press, 1977.

Wilson, Fiona. "In the Name of the State: Schools and Teachers in an Andean Province." In *States of Imagination*, ed. Thomas Blom Hansen and Finn Stepputat, pp. 313–44. Durham, NC: Duke University Press, 2001.

Winegar, Lucien T., and Jaan Valsiner, eds. *Children's Development Within Social Context: Metatheory and Theory*. Hillsdale, NJ: Erlbaum, 1992.

Wittgenstein, Ludwig. *Philosophical Investigations*. New York: Macmillan, 1953.

XX. "L'Islam et son avenir." *Revue des deux mondes* 64 (1921), pp. 655–82.

Yalçin-Heckmann, Lale. "Anthropological Studies on Turks in Turkey and in European Migration: Recent Works in German Language." *New Perspectives on Turkey* 16 (1987), pp. 105–14.

Yalman, Ahmet. "The Struggle for Multi-party Government in Turkey." *Middle East Journal* 1 (1947), pp. 46–58.

Yalman, Nur. "Islamic Reform and the Mystic Tradition in Eastern Anatolia." *Archives européennes de sociologie* 10 (1969), pp. 41–60.

Yashar, Deborah. 1998. "Indigenous Movements and Democracy: Contesting Citizenship in Latin America." *Comparative Politics* 31 (1998), pp. 23–42.

Yingling, Thomas. *AIDS and the National Body*, Durham, NC: Duke University Press, 1997.

Young, Iris Marion. *Intersecting Voices: Dilemmas of Gender, Political Philosophy and Policy*. Princeton, NJ: Princeton University Press, 1997.

Žižek, Slavoj. *The Sublime Object of Ideology*. London: Verso, 1989.

Index

abortion, 133, 135, 137, 140, 167*n*24
Abrams, Philip, 13
acculturation: Islamist censure of, 54–55, 70*n*67, 78. *See also* cultural authenticity
Adana, 3, 4, 130, 144, 166*n*14; schools in, 205
advertisements, 111, 142, 143, 153, 162, 203
agency, 22, 128; female, 96, 113
Ahmed Vefik Pasha, 28*n*5
Akbulut, Yıldırım, 141
Akyol, Avni, 50, 51–52, 53, 69*n*58, 108, 118*n*14, 141, 183, 221
Alevi, 195, 201–2, 215*nn*68–71
Alishan, Léonce, 215*n*72
Altınay, Ayşe Gül, 174
anarchy: discourse on, 163, 175, 194, 208
Anatolia, 79, 185, 213*n*41; and backwardness, 146, 152, 169*n*47; in pupil essays, 191; in school texts, 185, 189, 198; and Turkishness, 77, 166*n*17
ancestors: military, 182, 189, 190; and national identity, 82, 119*n*22, 200; patrilineal, 123*n*83, 212*n*35, 228*n*7
anthropology: political use of, 91–92; structural-functionalist, 218
Apaydın, Talip, 152
Appadurai, Arjun, 17
Arabic alphabet, 50, 69*n*48, 110
Arendt, Hannah, 56
Aretxaga, Begoña, 62
Armenians, 198–99, 202–3, 215*nn*72–74; in directive, 198; in school texts, 198, 199
Arrighi, Giovanni, 165*n*3

Aryan race, 80, 118*n*15
Asad, Talal, 49
associations, politically motivated: definition of, 14
Atatürk, Mustafa Kemal, 183; in cartoon, 50; as commander-in-chief, 216*n*83; in curricula, 176–79, 185, 207, 213*n*50; in directives, 178, 179, 181, 188, 207; and education, 9, 41, 50, 68*n*32, 69*n*48, 207; as headmaster, 50, 69*n*48, 207, 216*n*83; in pledge of allegiance, 178; in pupil essays, 180, 221; quotes from, 87, 155, 185, 188, 207; and religion, 89, 188; religious critics of, 120*n*41; in school texts, 84, 85, 87, 141–42, 155, 177, 178, 179, 180, 186, 196; in sculpture, 207
Atatürkism, 178, 179–80; in directives, 120*n*36, 194. *See also* Kemalism
authority: challenges to, 77, 114, 130, 205, 208, 216*n*82, 222; in directives, 204; epistemic, 51–52, 129, 166*n*12, 218; figures, 85, 114, 160, 190, 223; obedience to, 86, 190, 200–201, 204–5, 216*n*81; patriarchal, 92, 113, 114, 123*n*83, 175–76; in pupil essays, 222; religious, 5, 42, 114; reversal of, 114, 146; in school texts, 206; social, 197, 220; state, 8, 14, 29*n*14, 126; textual, 23, 58, 79, 182
autonomy: bodily, 135; children's, 22, 220, 224; cultural, 17; discursive, 221; female, 96
Aykan, Cevdet, 134

247